Human Dignity, Religion and the Law

The concept of human dignity is already embedded in the constitutional architecture of the European Union and throughout the world, but it remains a slippery and elusive concept. In this volume, leading commentators from across the globe address the shift from the monolithic influence of major world religions in the past towards religious pluralism coupled with the increased secularism of civil society. The contributors, drawn from different backgrounds and traditions, explore how the deployment of a nuanced understanding of human dignity can provide a way to maximise religious liberty for all within liberal democracies. Specific consideration is given to the reasonable accommodation of religious practices through exemptions to generally applicable laws, conscientious objection on the grounds of religious beliefs, the interplay between religious pluralism and legal pluralism, balancing religious sensibilities with same-sex marriage, exercising the right to change one's religion, both generally and with a particular focus on data protection, protecting the right to asylum in the light of recent changes in migratory flows and exploring its impact on those enjoying non-theistic beliefs, as well as the complex relationship between the Ukrainian and Russian Orthodox Churches in these febrile times. Through the prism of informed investigation of these matters of specificity, the volume offers readers fresh insights and analysis which collectively contribute to an overall picture of governments in liberal democracies being encouraged and enabled to foster laws and practices whereby pluralism can be encouraged, and human dignity can flourish. The book will be of interest to academics, researchers and policy-makers working in the areas of Law and Religion, Human Rights Law, Constitutional Law and International Relations.

Mark Hill KC practises at the Bar in London and is Global Professor of Law and Distinguished Fellow at the University of Notre Dame London Law Programme.

María-José Valero-Estarellas is Vice-Chancellor of Research and Innovation and Associate Professor of Law at Universidad Internacional Villanueva in Madrid.

ICLARS Series on Law and Religion

Series Editors:
Silvio Ferrari
University of Milan, Italy
Russell Sandberg
Cardiff University, UK
Pieter Coertzen
University of Stellenbosch, South Africa
W. Cole Durham, Jr.
Brigham Young University, USA
Tahir Mahmood
Amity International University, India

The *ICLARS Series on Law and Religion* is a new series designed to provide a forum for the rapidly expanding field of research in law and religion. The series is published in association with the International Consortium for Law and Religion Studies, an international network of scholars and experts of law and religion founded in 2007 with the aim of providing a place where information, data and opinions can easily be exchanged among members and made available to the broader scientific community. The series aims to become a primary source for students and scholars while presenting authors with a valuable means to reach a wide and growing readership.

Other titles in this series:

Religion and Contract Law in Islam
From Medieval Trade to Global Finance
Valentino Cattelan

Culture, Secularization and Democracy
Lessons from Alexis de Tocqueville
Edited by Sophie van Bijsterveld and Hans-Martien ten Napel

Religious Freedom and COVID-19: A European Perspective
A European Perspective
Edited by Jelle Creemers and Tatiana Kopaleishvili

Human Dignity, Religion and the Law
Pluralism and Reasonable Accommodation of Religious Practices
Edited by Mark Hill KC and María-José Valero-Estarellas

For more information about this series, please visit: www.routledge.com/ICLARS-Series-on-Law-and-Religion/book-series/ICLARS

Human Dignity, Religion and the Law

Pluralism and Reasonable Accommodation of Religious Practices

Edited by Mark Hill KC and María-José Valero-Estarellas

Routledge
Taylor & Francis Group
LONDON AND NEW YORK

First published 2025
by Routledge
4 Park Square, Milton Park, Abingdon, Oxon OX14 4RN

and by Routledge
605 Third Avenue, New York, NY 10158

Routledge is an imprint of the Taylor & Francis Group, an informa business

British Library Cataloguing-in-Publication Data
A catalogue record for this book is available from the British Library

ISBN: 978-1-032-82076-7 (hbk)
ISBN: 978-1-032-82077-4 (pbk)
ISBN: 978-1-003-50284-5 (ebk)

DOI: 10.4324/9781003502845

Typeset in Galliard
by Apex CoVantage, LLC

Contents

Contributors

Silvia Baldassarre (Università degli Studi di Firenze, Italy) is a researcher in law and religion. She has a PhD in law from the University of Padua. Her interests concern the legal status of minorities of religion and belief, comparative law and religion, law-religion-human rights and their interaction in time and space. She is the author of numerous scientific publications and lectures at many national and international conferences on these topics.

Fabio Balsamo (Università degli Studi di Napoli Federico II, Italy) is a researcher in ecclesiastical and canon law. He has focused his scientific interests on the relations between state and religious denominations, on the ecclesiastical entities and on the legal issues relating to the exercise of the right to religious freedom. His monographic works ('La protezione dei dati personali di natura religiosa', 2021; 'Le normative canoniche antimafia', 2019) deal respectively with the impact of religious laws in the protection of personal data and the role of Canon law as a tool for preventing and countering crime in the life of the Catholic Church.

Stefano Testa Bappenheim (Università di Camarino, Italy) is graduate cum laude in law, PhD cum laude in Droit Ecclésiastique de l'État at the Université Paris XI, Marie Curie Fellow at the University of Tübingen and professor of ecclesiastical law at the School of Law of the University of Camerino. He has participated in numerous national and international conferences and is regularly published in prestigious books and specialised journals. He is the author of over 100 publications, some of which have been translated and published in several European countries.

Burkhard J. Berkmann (Ludwig-Maximilian-University Munich, Germany) has been a professor of canon law since 2016. He has a doctorate in both law and theology as well as a license degree in canon law. His main fields of research include the theological principles of canon law and comparative law of religions, as well as the relationship between the European Union and religious communities. Religious pluralism, fundamental rights and their implications on Canon Law are among his primary research interests.

Frank Cranmer (Cardiff University, United Kingdom) is an honorary Research Fellow at the Centre for Law and Religion at Cardiff University, of which he is a graduate, and a Fellow of St Chad's College, Durham. His recent research has focused on religion and human rights, weddings law and charity law as it affects religion. With David Pocklington, he co-writes the Law and Religion UK blog: https://lawandreligionuk.com. He was formerly Clerk of Bills in the House of Commons.

Jasper Doomen (Open University, The Netherlands) is an assistant professor of constitutional law and legal theory. He has previously worked in the same capacity at Utrecht University. He holds a Ph.D. (Leiden University), a B.A and an M.A. in philosophy (Leiden University), a B.A. in Philosophy of a Specific Discipline (Leiden University) and an LL.B. (Utrecht University). Doomen has published books and articles in national and international peer-reviewed journals on various topics in the fields of law, philosophy and linguistics.

Mark Hill KC (Inner Temple, London, United Kingdom) is Global Professor of Law and Distinguished Fellow at the University of Notre Dame London Law Programme, Extraordinary Professor at the University of Pretoria, South Africa, Adjunct Professor at Notre Dame University, Sydney and Visiting Professor at the Dickson Poon School of Law, King's College, London. His recent publications include: *Islam, Religious Liberty and Constitutionalism in Europe* (2024); *Religious Confession and Evidential Privilege in the Twenty-first Century* (2022); *Religion and Law in the United Kingdom* (3rd edn, 2021); *The Routledge Handbook on Freedom of Religion or Belief* (2020); *Christianity and Criminal Law* (2020); *Religion, Law and Security in Africa* (2018); *Ecclesiastical Law* (4th edn, 2018); *Great Christian Jurists in English History* (2017); *Magna Carta, Religion and the Rule of Law* (2015); *Religion and Discrimination Law in the European Union* (2012). He is Vice-President of the International Consortium for Law and Religion Studies (ICLARS), a founding member of the African Consortium for Law and Religion Studies (ACLARS), and a former President of the European Consortium for Church and State Research.

Marianna Napolitano (Università degli Studi di Modena e Reggio Emilia, Italy) is Junior Assistant Professor (Rtd-A) at the University of Modena and Reggio Emilia working within the ITSERR project, and affiliated researcher at the Fondazione per le Scienze Religiose (Italy). Her dissertation, to be published with Brill, focuses on the history and policy of the Department for External Church Relations of the Moscow Patriarchate in post-soviet Russia. She has been a visiting fellow at the Russian State University for the Humanities. She is the academic assistant of the Italian UNESCO Chair on Religious Pluralism and Peace. Her research interests are church-state relations in Russia, and Russian and Ukrainian history and religion.

András Sajó (Central European University, Austria) is University Professor at Central European University, Vienna, and a research associate of the CEU Democracy Institute, Budapest. He is a former vice-president and judge of the European Court of Human Rights. He has been extensively involved in legal drafting throughout East Central Europe and participated and/or advised in drafting the Ukrainian, Georgian and South African constitutions. His latest books include *Ruling by Cheating: Governance in Illiberal Democracy* (2021) and the *Routledge Handbook of Illiberalism* (co-edited with Renáta Uitz and Stephen Holmes, Routledge 2021).

Fernando Simón-Yarza (University of Navarra, Spain) is Professor of Constitutional Law at the University of Navarra. He has widely published and lectured on several issues in the fields of Constitutional Law and Legal Philosophy. His book *Medio ambiente y derechos fundamentales* (Madrid, 2012), was the recipient of the prestigious "Tomás y Valiente Prize 2011", given by the Center for Political and Constitutional Studies and the Constitutional Court of Spain to the best work on constitutional law. He has been a Visiting Fellow at the University of Münster, Boston, Princeton and Oxford. In the field of philosophy, he has translated into Spanish several works of the German philosopher Robert Spaemann. He is a member of the James Madison Society (Princeton University).

Renáta Uitz (University of London, United Kingdom) is a professor of law and government at Royal Holloway, University of London, and senior research fellow at the Central European University, Democracy Institute, Budapest. Her research interests include transition to and from democracy, and the impact of illiberalism on constitutions, government and liberty. Her latest book is the *Routledge Handbook of Illiberalism* (co-edited with András Sajó and Stephen Holmes, Routledge 2021).

Mirjam van Schaik (Open University, The Netherlands) is an assistant professor of constitutional law and legal theory. She has previously worked as a lecturer and researcher at Leiden University. She holds a Ph.D. (Leiden University), an LL.M. (cum laude, Vrije Universiteit Amsterdam) and an M.A. in Philosophy (Vrije Universiteit Amsterdam). Van Schaik has published in the fields of law and legal theory. Her research focuses on fundamental rights, particularly freedom of religion or belief, and democratic legitimacy. Van Schaik is co-editor of the book *Religious Ideas in Liberal Democratic States* (2021), and she co-authored the Dutch country report for the international project Lex-Atlas: Covid-19 (2022). She is a member of the Netherlands Network for Human Rights Research, an editor of Nederland Rechtsstaat and an editor of the *Journal for Religion, Law and Policy*.

1 Human dignity, religious pluralism and reasonable accommodation

An introductory overview

Mark Hill KC

Introduction

Without question, 'human dignity' and 'religious pluralism' are both slippery and elusive concepts. Anyone turning to this volume expecting clear definitions and bright line distinctions will be disappointed. But they have become increasingly significant elements in the study of law and religion, often hitched to the idea of reasonable accommodation and the carving out of exceptions to laws and practices which allow multiple belief systems to flourish. One of the guiding principles of the International Consortium of Law and Religion Studies (ICLARS) has been providing an opportunity for different viewpoints and conflicting opinions to be voiced respectfully in an academic environment. Nowhere has this been more evident than in its conference convened in Córdoba in September 2022. This volume is the first of two books which harvest the best of the papers delivered at the conference, some from well-established professors within the field of law and religion, others from early career academics and researchers who are mentored and supported within the ICLARS structure. Individually and collectively, they make a substantial contribution to our understandings of human dignity and pluralism within the framework of contemporary law and religion scholarship.

Human dignity

In December 2018, a group of experts met in Punta del Este, Uruguay, at the invitation of Senator Carmen Asiaín, to discuss the issue of human dignity in preparation for the 70th anniversary of the Universal Declaration of Human Rights (UDHR). There, they signed a declaration on human dignity, which became the *Punta del Este Declaration on Human Dignity for Everyone Everywhere*, calling for a stronger focus on human dignity as a force to revitalise efforts to ensure human rights for all. As a follow-up to the adoption of the declaration, recognising the need for greater international engagement on human dignity as a value to strengthen human rights protection and implementation globally and as the ultimate goal of the implementation of human rights, Brett Scharffs, Jan Figel', Mark Hill KC and Ewelina Ochab, all

DOI: 10.4324/9781003502845-1

members of the International Religious Freedom or Belief Alliance (IRFBA)[1] Council of Experts, started working on practical initiatives to help revive the international focus on human dignity.

Among these initiatives is the proposal to establish an annual United Nations Day promoting Human Dignity for Everyone Everywhere (also referred to as the UN Human Dignity Day).[2] Human dignity is the foundation as well as the taproot of human rights. Pausing to focus on human dignity will help create cultures of dignity and reinforce human rights. Human rights and human dignity are inextricably linked. They appear together in every important human rights instrument, including the preamble and Article 1 of the UDHR.

The UN Human Dignity Day will create an opportunity for the world to pause and focus on human dignity as a foundation of human rights, as the goal or objective of human rights and as a way of measuring progress on the realisation and implementation of human rights. The focus on human dignity is an important way to emphasise that the UDHR is based upon principles that are truly universal. As such, human dignity is a way of building bridges and starting conversations in places where human rights are controversial or have become politicised. Our equal dignity is a basis of equal citizenship within each country.

In a world with so many centrifugal forces pulling us apart, we need to concentrate on some genuinely shared values, such as human dignity, that can serve as a centripetal element in bringing us together. Establishing such a UN Day is not an end in itself, but a means to encourage reflections and dialogue on the topic of human dignity and joint action. Among the joint actions are initiatives to raise awareness in schools, the better to equip the next generation with patterns of respect and generosity.

The focus on human dignity could further help to strengthen the understanding of human rights and duties (obligations, responsibilities) stemming from dignity, and the deep and strong nexus between freedom of religion or belief and human dignity. The UN Day would be an opportunity for educational initiatives on human dignity as a means of affirming human rights and human dignity for everyone the world over.

The concept of human dignity is already embedded in the constitutional architecture of the European Union and many of its member countries. Article 1 of the EU Charter of Fundamental Rights is clear and unambiguous: "Human dignity is inviolable. It must be respected and protected."[3] The right to human dignity constitutes the real basis of fundamental rights, as expounded in the Universal Declaration of Human Rights of 1948. It exists independently of the Charter and is said to be a general principle of EU law predating the

1 Now renamed the Article 18 Alliance, referencing the provision in the Universal Declaration of Human Rights which sets out the right to freedom of thought, conscience and religion.

2 Many have rightly pointed out the irony of identifying a single day in the year to focus on human dignity when it should be a primary concern every day of every year. But an annual reminder of its huge significance can only be beneficial.

3 European Union Charter of Fundamental Rights, Article 1.

coming into force of the Charter.[4] Only a handful of EU Member States do not refer to dignity in their constitutional instruments. In Germany, Romania and Portugal, dignity is given a position of primacy as the first article of their constitutions. In Bulgaria and Spain, dignity appears in the preamble. The constitution of Belgium states that fundamental rights are guaranteed in order that everyone has the right to lead a life with human dignity. Similarly, Article 30 of the Polish constitution says that dignity constitutes the "source of freedoms and rights of persons and citizens".

Some national constitutions engage with the obligation to respect dignity with a greater degree of specificity, identifying particular contexts where the legal and political systems create risks to a person's dignity: detention (Austria and Slovenia), deportation (Finland), procreation (Portugal), freedom of expression (Romania), misuse of information and technology (Portugal) or even business and commerce, as is the case in Article 41 of the Italian constitution or Article 106 of the Greek constitution which states: "Private economic initiative shall not be permitted to develop at the expense of freedom and human dignity."

Several chapters in this volume expressly engage with the topic of human dignity. The duty of reasonable accommodation,[5] and conscientious objection more generally,[6] are both practical outworkings of ascribing dignity to the views of other people. Similarly, the reform of weddings law in England and Wales is rooted, in part at least, in respecting the dignity of couples irrespective of their religious or ethnic backgrounds or their sexual orientation.[7]

At the heart of human dignity lies respect for diversity and difference, and these social goods are promoted through the deployment of various exceptionist tools such as conscientious objection and reasonable accommodation. But is exceptionalism the best way of advancing human dignity?

Fernando Simón-Yarza identifies what he describes as a "conceptual trap" in his study of Conscientious Objection to Unconstitutional Duties.[8] A new Spanish law established a register for health professionals who object to performing abortions and required them to register their objection. In consequence they are exempted from doing so, in a similar manner to those who have a conscientious objection to compulsory military service. But what precisely is conscientious objection and how does it preserve and protect human dignity? Simón-Yarza suggests that it is articulated as the law providing an exception from the performance of a duty out of respect for "a belief that is not widely shared by society". This conceptualisation of it, Simón-Yarza argues, especially where conscientious objection rests on religious grounds, dilutes the nature of the objection. Conscientious objection is a part of the manifestations of one's religion, which is part and parcel of freedom of conscience. Treating the belief as an exemption

4 See by way of example, *Netherlands v Parliament and Council* (Case C-377/98).
5 Chapter 3.
6 Chapter 4.
7 Chapter 5.
8 Chapter 3.

from a constitutional duty presupposes the legitimacy of the duty: that of doctors to carry out medical procedures. This conceptualisation, says Simón-Yarza, trivialises conduct which is dictated by conscience by normalising the posture of the state in condoning abortion (terminating the life of the unborn child).

He argues that the approach of the Spanish law has the effect of distorting freedom of conscience as a fundamental right; in other words, it ceases to be a constitutional limit to which the legislator's mandates must be submitted in order to qualify as legal duties. Rather than a refuge for objectors, freedom of conscience as recognised by Article 16.1 of the Spanish Constitution should be a limit on the legislator. This shift in the perception and realisation of conscientious objection, he argues, would facilitate a genuinely liberal society, in the most classical sense, showing a sensitivity to the consciences of minorities, weighing the relative importance of religious sensitivities against uniform compliance with a given set of rules. Whilst a utopian ideal should not lightly be set aside, a law of general application which did not permit of exceptions on the grounds of conscience would be an affront to human dignity and redolent of an authoritarian regime which gave scant regard to the concept of pluralism.

Similar considerations arise in Stefano Testa Bappenheim's study of State Law or Religious Precepts: The Right to Asylum.[9] Bappenheim categorises conscientious objection as a means of limiting state action by making us aware of the permanent tension and intimate connection between law and morals and acts as a bastion against a totalitarian state. The German government had initially opposed recognising conscientious objection to laws regulating the deportation of illegal immigrants. However, as the number of Catholic and Protestant priests and religious personnel who refused to comply with deportation orders of illegal immigrants in their pastoral care increased, so did tensions within civil society. Thus, the Federal Ministry of the Interior, to avoid further escalations, decided to recognise a *de facto* legitimacy to conscientious objection to the deportation of illegal immigrants, thereby affirming the human dignity of those otherwise being compelled to act against their conscience, and also, but to a lesser degree, that of the immigrants.

Recognising a legitimate objection of conscience allows people of faith to signal to society their values and significance, rather than having them obliterated in favour of a perceived greater good as expressed in a universal law of general application. This recognition, he argues, can lead to greater political and social cohesion, essential ingredients of functional religious pluralism. The use of conscientious objection as a "tactical tool" to express with non-violent methods the voice of one's conscience against the dictates of state law constitutes a moment of confrontation and growth. In this way a liberal, pluralist state accommodates the dignity of the person who can exercise fully the right conscientiously to dissent. Whereas Simón-Yarza considers that a conscience clause diminishes the individual, who is merely tolerated (in the negative sense of

9 Chapter 8.

that term) as a second-class citizen, Bappenheim detects the value of such provision in giving state legitimacy to minority opinions which are afforded recognition and protection as a bulwark against rampant majoritarianism.

Something of a *via media* emerges from the joint contribution of András Sajó and Renáta Uitz in A Secular Liberal Defence of Freedom of Religion: The Case for a Duty of Reasonable Accommodation.[10] They argue that individuals ought to be given exemptions, or accommodations, against generally applicable laws to allow for the free manifestation of religion, conscience and belief. They direct attention to the loss of respect for religion and resulting indifference to religious freedom which is increasingly evident in secularised democracies. This loss of respect for religion is exemplified in cases such as those in the European Court of Justice concerning ritual slaughter cases. For example, in the Flemish case, the Court held that slaughter without lethal stunning (in the interests of the animal's welfare) was not permitted because the corresponding limitation on Jewish and Muslims dietary practices (i.e., halal and kosher meat) was categorised as minimal. Sajo and Uitz argue that there is a trend in European courts of confusing the standard of strict proportionality with a balancing exercise of majoritarian civil practice with regard to butchery against the fundamental right to freedom of religion, as if these were rights (or interests) of equal value.[11] The balancing of rights has morphed into weighing rights against interests including those of individuals, commercial operators and the community. This was not previously a part of the jurisprudence of the pan-European Courts in Strasbourg and, latterly, Luxembourg.[12] The impact on freedom of religion is considerable. Self-styled secular states, in attempting to be neutral towards all religions, can end up imposing a burden such as when a generally applicable rule unduly favours a traditional or majority religion and is insensitive to the needs of other faith groups. In the West, Sunday has become a traditional secular rest day, notwithstanding that many other religions have a different holy day. Exceptions or accommodations should not be seen as diminishing those who claim the advantage of them, but as a living-out in the real world of both religious pluralism and human dignity. The accommodation or exception is an essential part of the right itself defining its ambit and reach, as opposed to a departure from the right.

Sajo and Uitz postulate their own version of a balancing test for determining when a religious exemption or accommodation to a generally applicable rule should apply. The first stage is to assess whether the general rule limiting freedom of religion is a necessary and proportionate restriction or serves a

10 Chapter 2.

11 For a general discussion of the 'weighted neutrality' increasingly applied in cases of religious freedom, see M. Hill, 'A Dance of the Veils: The Approach of the Luxembourg and Strasbourg Courts to Religious Dress', in C. Barnard, A. Lazowski and D. Sarmiento (eds.), *Pursuit of Legal Harmony in a Challenging World: Essays in Honour of Eleanor Sharpston* (Oxford: Hart Publishing, 2024).

12 Hill (n 11).

compelling (or at least important) state or public interests. If the limitation is justifiable, the second stage is assessing whether an exemption from a generally applicable rule is appropriate, to ensure that the burden on conscience is not excessive.

The deployment of this balance is an element of Fabio Balsamo's technical analysis in Leaving or Changing Religion in European Union Law: The impact of Data Protection Regulation.[13] He specifically explores a person's right to convert or to leave a religion against the right to privacy together with the right of religious institutions to proselytise as an expression of their religious freedom. These all come into conflict under Article 9(2) of the European Data Protection Regulations (GDPR). Balsamo notes that freedom of religion in EU law also includes the freedom of religious propaganda, namely the right to evangelise and share a message, which allows for and facilitates conversion from one faith to another. Today, proselytising often requires using personal data to better target one's activities. The GDPR allows religious entities to use former members' personal data for the performance of their own institutional activities, even without their consent. This means that religious institutions can use the personal data of former members and of those who have expressed a desire to leave, to target religious messages at them, impeding the right freely to leave one's religious group, through psychological and emotional pressures. Balsamo argues that in balancing these contrasting rights, the GDPR has wrongly prioritised the institutional right to manifest one's religion through proselytism over the fundamental right to change one's religion and freely leave a particular religious group.

Religious pluralism

The jurisprudence of the European Court of Human Rights repeatedly reminds us of the challenges engendered by religious pluralism.[14] In a much-criticised speech, British Home Secretary Suella Braverman stated that multiculturalism makes no demands of the incomer to integrate. She continued:

> It has failed because it allowed people to come to our society and live parallel lives in it . . . And, in extreme cases, they could pursue lives aimed at undermining the stability and threatening the security of society . . . We are living with the consequence of that failure today. You can see it play out in the streets all over Europe, from Malmö to Paris, Brussels to Leicester.[15]

13 Chapter 7.

14 For a recent study see M. Hill and L. Papadopoulou (eds.), *Islam, Religious Liberty and Constitutionalism in Europe* (Oxford: Hart Publishing, 2024).

15 Rt Hon Suella Braverman, UK Secretary of State for the Home Department, speech to the American Enterprise Institute, 26 September 2023.

British Prime Minister Rishi Sunak, himself a second-generation immigrant from India, swiftly dissociated himself from those remarks.[16] Self-evidently, multiculturalism and religious pluralism pose challenges for civil society, but the Strasbourg court is robust in its plea for the challenges to be overcome and for states to recognise the societal benefits which can accrue from a variegated pattern of religiosity.

> Respect for religious diversity undoubtedly represents one of the most important challenges to be faced today; for that reason, the authorities must perceive religious diversity not as a threat but as a source of enrichment.[17]

These remarks are reflected, for the United Kingdom at least, in some recent remarks of King Charles III, in some of the earliest pronouncements of his reign. Somewhat counterintuitively, despite having an established church, England's proud – albeit recent – tradition of religious pluralism is rightly celebrated. In remarks to faith leaders on 16 September 2023, King Charles observed:

> [T]he Sovereign has an additional duty – less formally recognized but to be no less diligently discharged. It is the duty to protect the diversity of our country, including by protecting the space for Faith itself and its practise through the religions, cultures, traditions and beliefs to which our hearts and minds direct us as individuals. This diversity is not just enshrined in the laws of our country, it is enjoined by my own faith. As a member of the Church of England, my Christian beliefs have love at their very heart. By my most profound convictions, therefore – as well as by my position as Sovereign – I hold myself bound to respect those who follow other spiritual paths, as well as those who seek to live their lives in accordance with secular ideals.[18]

He returned to this theme in a speech at Mansion House, London, on 18 October 2023:

> I have often described the United Kingdom as a "community of communities"; an island nation in which our shared values are the force which

16 'Rishi Sunak Rejects Braverman Claim Multiculturalism Has Failed', *The Guardian*, 28 September2023.www.theguardian.com/politics/2023/sep/28/rishi-sunak-rejects-braverman-claim-multiculturalism-has-failed.

17 *Handyside v United Kingdom*, (1979–80) 1 EHRR 737 at para 37. See also M. Hill, 'Locating Freedom of Religion within the Qualified Rights of the European Convention on Human Rights and in the Jurisprudence of Strasbourg', in P. Babie, N. Rochow and B. Scharffs (eds.), *Freedom of Religion of Belief: Creating the Constitutional Space for Fundamental Freedoms* (Cheltenham: Edward Elgar, 2020), pp. 283–297.

18 King Charles III, 'Remarks to Faith Leaders', 16 September 2023. www.royal.uk/kings-remarks-faith-leaders accessed 21 October 2023.

> holds us together, reminding us that there is far, far more that unites us than divides us. . . . There is the breathing space we afford one another, leaving us able to think and speak freely. This well carries the politeness and respect we owe to one another; our willingness to put others first and treat them as we would wish them to treat us. To listen to their views and, if we do not agree, to remind ourselves to engage in a way which is passionate, but not pugnacious. This includes the practice of our religious faiths, in freedom and mutual understanding.[19]

The concept of a nation being a community of communities finds expression in many of the contributions to this volume. But religious pluralism is not the only aspect of constructive diversity worthy of academic discussion. Burkhard J. Berkmann introduces us to Legal Pluralism in German Scholarship[20] and addresses its application for religious freedom. The concept concerns two or more legal systems which operate simultaneously.[21] The multiplicity of laws can encompass the laws of the state on one hand, but also the laws of religious bodies, indigenous law and other sub-legal systems that regulate different aspects of human life. How can the state deal with this legal pluralism, specifically the "small" pluralism, as Berkmann calls it, that results when religious law and state law are acting on citizens simultaneously, in ways that might be contradictory?

Berkmann analyses the discussion of this question by a number of contemporary German commentators. He notes that some authors like Schuppert analyse the relationship between the state and religion in terms of a "negotiated order of coexistence," driven by mutual recognition. For the state, this means recognising the centrality of religion via state-church legal treaties (a common instrument in German law) and for the church (or other religious communities) recognising the importance of other religions, the Constitution and the state. Other authors, like Shachar, propose a "joint governance" model, where no single entity has exclusive jurisdiction, but where both the religious order and the state share in governance of citizens. For other authors like Seinecke, legal pluralism is a deep-seated feature of society. It "not only grants a space for autonomous rule-making to religious, indigenous, or social communities within the modern nation-state, but also protects the inner connection between law and social identity". Reflecting the language of enrichment deployed by the European Court of Human Rights, Seinecke reveals how it enables social tolerance and ensures peace between religious communities.

19 King Charles III, 'Speech at Mansion House', 18 October 2023. www.royal.uk/mansion-house accessed 21 October 2023.

20 Chapter 4.

21 Lord Williams of Oystermouth, when he was Archbishop of Canterbury, received unjustified criticism when he made some anodyne remarks in a public lecture in 2008: 'Civil and Religious Law in England' subsequently published in R. Griffith-Jones (ed.), *Islam and English Law: Rights, Responsibilities and the Place of Shari'a* (Cambridge: Cambridge University Press, 2013), pp. 20–33.

This interaction between religious law and state law emerges in the context of marriage, which can be both contractual and sacramental. Frank Cranmer writes about a current proposal under consideration by the UK Parliament with regard to Reforming Weddings Law in England and Wales.[22] The Marriage Act of 1949 is the primary statute governing the solemnisation of marriage in England and Wales and prescribes two separate mechanisms for confecting a marriage: civil and religious. Religious ceremonies are then divided up into four types: weddings solemnised in the Church of England and the Church in Wales; Jewish weddings; Quaker weddings; and "everyone else" weddings (which Cranmer notes includes everyone from Ahmadi Muslims to Zoroastrians). Cranmer draws out the complex religious and historical roots of this categorisation: the Marriage Act 1949 replaced the Marriage Act 1836 and includes elements of Lord Hardwicke's Act of 1753, which in turn borrowed elements from the Church at the time, such as the publication in parish churches of banns of marriage inviting objection to a proposed union.

However, as a progeny of these older laws, the current Marriage Act makes demands that have become untenable in today's pluralistic society. The main issue Cranmer identifies is that, with the exception of Quaker and Jewish weddings, the Act requires that a religious wedding be conducted in an authorised building. And while many long-established and largely Christian faith groups tend to have churches or other designated places of worship, minority faith and new religious movements, such as Pagans and Parsees, may not. Other jurisdictions achieve a more fluid and practical pluralism by registering individual officiants who can conduct and register marriages, as opposed to the physical building within which the ceremony is permitted to take place.

But what do we mean when we speak of religious pluralism? In her discussion of Refugee Law, Atheism and Religious Persecution,[23] Silvia Baldasarre emphasises that the idea also includes the protection of theistic, non-theistic and atheistic conceptions. Although no comprehensive definition of religion is possible, over the years, the concept has been expanded to include the binominal of theism/atheism. For example, the Concluding Document of the Vienna Meeting (1989) affirms that states need to ensure "effective equality between believers and non-believers". Similarly, in *Kokkinakis v Greece* (1993), the European Court of Human Rights observed that the freedom of thought, conscience and religion guaranteed by Article 9 of the Convention is a precious asset not only for believers, but also for "atheists, agnostics, sceptics and the unconcerned", something which the Court has reiterated several times since.

That the religious topography of our increasingly global and interconnected world is changing is undeniable. For Baldassarre, this means that states need to develop adequate legal instruments to protect not only freedom of religion, conscience and belief in its historic and traditional sense, but also non-belief

22 Chapter 5.
23 Chapter 9.

and scepticism. This becomes particularly relevant in the context of asylum seeking by non-religious people, with a fear of persecution in consequence of their secular or humanist world view. Baldassarre argues that, although "international normative and jurisprudential developments have progressively included nontheistic and atheistic conceptions in the concept of 'religion,' there is some resistance to considering nontheism as an integral part of the religious phenomenon". For example, a Sudanese woman's asylum application in the UK was rejected because the authorities considered that there was "insufficient evidence" of her atheism, without considering that in Sudan and other countries, the free expression of atheism is punishable by death or other harsh penalties. Similarly, Joseph Moradi's asylum application in Norway was rejected on the basis that Afghanistan only punishes a manifestation of atheism and not atheism itself. Moradi's case had to go through several layers of review before the Norwegian courts recognised that not being able to express or manifest one's atheism is part and parcel of the protections of freedom of religion or belief. With non-religious, secular and humanist organisations facing growing persecution, the lack of harmonisation of national laws and policies threatens the equal treatment of religious and non-religious asylum claimants. This chapter sits at the intersection of religious pluralism and human dignity.

Religious pluralism occasionally extends to the accommodation of difference within the same tradition, as Marianna Napolitano points out in The Greek Catholic Church in Ukraine, the Russian Orthodox Church (ROC) and Catholic Proselytism.[24] The multifaceted nature of religious pluralism can include deep differences and conflict within one religion. Napolitano recounts the difficulties and strained relationships between the Russian Orthodox and non-Orthodox churches after the fall of the Soviet Union. The Russian Orthodox Church, worried about losing its position of primacy as the church with the largest number of believers in the Universal Orthodox Church, was particularly worried about the impact of aggressive proselytism from other churches and the possibility of sects and schisms emerging within its canonical territory. Napolitano details the strained relations between the ROC and the Vatican especially with respect to proselytism, commenting that although in an official document published in 1992 the Vatican asserted that it did not intend to conduct missionary activity and much less proselytise in the area of the former Soviet Union, the Russian Orthodox Church formed the view that the Catholic Church's acquisitive posture posed something of a threat to Orthodoxy in Russia and other former Eastern bloc countries.

Finally, Mirjam van Schaik and Jasper Doomen in their piece on Challenging the Right to Change Religion or Belief make detailed reference to the interpretation of Article 18 of the International Covenant on Civil and Political Rights (ICCPR).[25] Their chapter invites consideration of the expansiveness

24 Chapter 10.
25 Chapter 6.

of the right to freedom of religion, conscience and belief within the context of the ICCPR. Whereas the aspirational Universal Declaration of Human Rights includes the clear and direct language that freedom of religion "includes the right to change his religion or belief", as respect for human dignity demands, the ICCPR adopts a different formulation, stating that it includes "the freedom to have or to adopt a religion or belief of his choice". Van Schaik and Doomen track the legislative history of the ICCPR's language, noting the contentious debates over apostasy and the different iterations through which the language evolved. They argue that the language ultimately adopted in the final text leaves Article 18 conceptually ambiguous and lacking legal certainty. This in turn reduces the significance of apostasy's fight for religious freedom.

Conclusion

This collection is an embodiment of the breadth and variety of meanings that can be attached variously to the expressions 'human dignity' and 'religious pluralism' and the range of concepts with which they are freighted, especially reasonable accommodation. One chapter extends into legal pluralism, examining multiple overlapping systems to which individuals are called simultaneously to give their allegiance. Whilst for many religious pluralism remains aspirational, the conflicts and contradictions which remain the world over are tending towards a rejection of the sentiment of the Strasbourg Court and others that multiculturalism is a source of enrichment. Whilst that may be our direction of travel, the destination remains a long way off. Religious pluralism does not carry with it the goal of equality. Majority and minority religions will continue to coexist but for reasons of history, tradition and culture one will dominate and the others will be tolerated: a community of unequal communities, to take a more pessimistic reading of the words of King Charles. One thing that emerges from the exciting new scholarship in this volume is the welcome idea that many of the negative implications of toleration are beginning to be lost. For the most part, accommodations and exemptions from general laws are given readily and willingly as a positive means of promoting the dignity of all persons. Simón-Yarza is something of an outlier in arguing that the classification of accommodation diminishes the humanity of the intended beneficiary.

What this volume does demonstrate, in keeping with the ethos of ICLARS, is the liveliness of the field of study of law and religion as a distinct discipline set apart from constitutional law and the sociology of religion. Each chapter contains a closely argued analysis of a single thread in a large tapestry, without which the whole is incomprehensible. Individually and collectively, they mark the enrichment of the comparative study of law and religion for this and future generations.

2 A secular liberal defence of freedom of religion

The case for a duty of reasonable accommodation

András Sajó and Renáta Uitz

Introduction

In 2020, the Court of Justice of the European Union (CJEU) endorsed a Flemish decree that provides that slaughter without lethal stunning, including ritual slaughter, could be prohibited.[1] According to the CJEU, the least onerous means of protecting animal welfare is stunning, as it is "the optimal means of reducing the animal's suffering at the time of killing,"[2] and the resulting inconvenience to the manifestation of the religion is scientifically proven to be minimal.[3] Muslim and Jewish believers are able to obtain kosher or halal meat from abroad. Consequently, freedom of religion and animal welfare were properly ('fairly') *balanced* in national law.[4]

The minimization of the burden on religious freedom is related to the structure of fundamental rights protection in the EU. The prohibition of ritual slaughter originates in a generally applicable neutral law. The EU Charter of Fundamental Rights permits all proportionate restrictions which serve "objectives of general interest recognised by the Union or the need to protect the rights and freedoms of others" (Art 52(1)).[5]

The CJEU is aware that this prohibition can specifically burden a religious practice, but a religious dietary command has little weight in the balancing inquiry. In its 2018 on ritual slaughter, the CJEU took into account a 2000 judgment of the European Court of Human Rights (ECtHR) in *Cha'are Shalom*.[6] There, the ECtHR found that a restriction on ritual slaughter imposes such a minimal burden on believers that it does not interfere with religious freedom, considering that believers are able to easily import Glatt Kosher meat

1 Case C-336/19, *Centraal Israëlitisch Consistorie van België and Others v Vlaamse Regering*, ECLI:EU:C:2020:1031 (17 December 2020).
2 Case C-336/19 (n 1), para 72.
3 *Ibid.*, para 76.
4 *Ibid.*, paras 65 (generally), pp. 71, 80.
5 *Charter of Fundamental Rights of the European Union*, [2016] OJ C 202/389.
6 C-426/16, *Liga van Moskeeën en Islamitische Organisaties Provincie Antwerpen VZW and Others*, ECLI:EU:C:2018:335 (29 May 2018), para 45, referring to *Cha'are Shalom Ve Tsedek v France*, Application no. 27417/95, Judgment of 27 June 2000.

DOI: 10.4324/9781003502845-2

from abroad.[7] The ECtHR reached this conclusion while acknowledging that "to provide Jews with meat from animals slaughtered in accordance with religious prescriptions, . . . is an ***essential aspect*** of practice of the Jewish religion" (emphasis added).[8] Yet, the CJEU left the latter consideration out of the equation when it "took into account" Article 9 of the European Convention on Human Rights.[9] And while the CJEU noted the increasing societal awareness of animal welfare,[10] it was silent about the fact that – in an effort to minimize animal suffering – more and more countries prohibit the export of meat that meets ritual slaughter requirements.[11] In practice it is relatively easy for *any* interest (such as animal welfare) to be recognized as general interest to the detriment of fundamental rights (such as religious freedom). The proliferation of rights and the culture wars further exacerbate this phenomenon.

Although in principle liberal secularism stands for tolerance and respect of free *personal* choice (individual autonomy),[12] in many liberal democracies freedom of religion, especially as an *individual* right, does not always receive sufficient protection (respect),[13] even if religious organizations are overprotected.[14] The ritual slaughter cases of the European apex courts indicate that

---

On the case law of the ECtHR more generally see András Sajó and Renáta Uitz, 'Individual Religious Freedom under the European Convention of Human Rights', in Susanna Mancini (ed.), *Constitutions and Religion* (Cheltenham, UK: Edward Elgar, 2020), p. 286.

7 *Cha'are* (n 6), para 81 (importation).

8 *Ibid.*, para 73.

9 Case C-336/19 (n 1), para 56 ('Since it is apparent from the explanations relating to Article 10 of the Charter that the freedom guaranteed in paragraph 1 thereof corresponds to the freedom guaranteed in Article 9 of the ECHR, that freedom must be taken into account for the purpose of interpreting Article 10(1) of the Charter.')

10 Case C-336/19 (n 1), para 79, also C-426/16 (n 6), para 64. Change, however, is not a value *per se.* Germany changed its legal system into a racist one, and the ban on ritual slaughter was the first Nazi law, reflecting 'change' originating in the people. And change it was!

11 Shortly after this chapter was presented at the ICLARS conference in Cordoba in 2022, a Hungarian parliamentary party, *Mi Hazánk* (most often described as extreme right wing and antisemitic) declared its intention to ban ritual slaughter with reference to the CJEU judgment. A 'neutral' law adopted following this initiative would be most likely unconstitutional for racially discriminatory intent.

12 Liberal is used here in the European sense of the term (classical liberalism).

13 There are well-known reasons given in the literature justifying why freedom of religion deserves strong and even special protection. Benjamin Constant considers religions valuable as long as the moral dimension (the other-directed enthusiasm) prevails. Tzvetan Todorov, *Benjamin Constant: La passion démocratique* (New York: Hachette, 1997), p. 142. See in this sense also Douglas Laycock, 'Religious Liberty as Liberty', *The Journal of Contemporary Legal Issues* 7 (1996), 313, 326.

14 At the same time in the same countries religious groups receive generous overprotection, as a matter of positive state obligation to promote a liberty (see e. g. financial support and endorsement of certain religious ethical and cultural practices in public life). Religious majority practices are turned into general norms in the name of national or communal tradition. Here neutrality becomes a fig leaf.

at least in some contexts religious freedom is given limited weight,[15] so generally applicable laws do not have to bother with it. This invariably results in treating religious believers who seek to follow the imperative commands of their conscience as second-class citizens. This outcome may easily be avoided by exempting adversely affected believers from the general legal measure (*accommodation*).[16] Accommodation refers here to exemptions granted from generally applicable laws to essential *individual* religious manifestations (even though these are often inseparable of collective exercise of religion.).[17] The duty of reasonable accommodation is a key expression of the prohibition of coercion in matters of conscience; compliance with this positive obligation is made all the more pressing by the propensity of the regulatory state to cover every aspect of public and private life.

Simple as this sounds, the accommodation of religious freedom claims remains controversial.[18] Constitutions tend to be silent on reasonable accommodation; consequently, courts often derive this obligation from a web of general provisions and underlying principles, including equality/non-discrimination, human dignity, private life, personal autonomy and premises associated with living in a diverse society. For the ECtHR the "highly valued"[19] freedom of reli-

15 Cases C-157/15, *Achbita, Centrum voor Gelijkheid van kansen en voor racismebestrijding v G4S Secure Solutions*, ECLI:EU:C:2017:203 (14 March 2017) and C-188/15, *Bougnaoui and Association de défense des droits de l'homme (ADDH) v Micropole Univers*, ECLI:EU:C:2017:204 (14 March 2017).

The US Supreme Court is of the opposite view on statutory grounds. See *Equal Employment Opportunity Commission v Abercrombie and Fitch Stores, Inc.*, 575 US 664 (2015).

Even the Supreme Court of Canada, famous for its protection of pluralism, has disregarded the existence of the interference in religious exercise in the case of a non-Western religion: *Ktunaxa Nation v British Columbia (Forests, Lands and Natural Resource Operations)*, [2017] 2 SCR 386.

Denying the existence of interference under the pretext that a specific opportunity to practice does not preclude practice in general was also the preferred approach of the ECtHR for decades. *X v United Kingdom, Commission*, Application no. 8160/78, Decision of 12 March 1981, DR 22, 27 (a teacher's claim for 45 minutes off at the beginning of the afternoon on Fridays to pray at the Mosque rejected, as he accepted restriction of his own free will (para 9).

16 András Sajó and Renáta Uitz, 'Freedom of Religion', in Michel Rosenfeld and András Sajó (eds.), *The Oxford Handbook of Comparative Constitutional Law* (Oxford, UK: OUP, 2012), pp. 909, 919–922.

17 The accommodation of religious organizations (allowing them to run what they believe are their internal affairs) is a different matter, though church autonomy is indispensable to individual freedom of religion and is protected by the collective aspect of freedom of religion (worship and manifestation in community with others). In matters of church autonomy, however, the prohibition of entanglement remains an additional limit in a secular liberal state. Most of the practical accommodation occurs in the form of exemptions from general laws.

18 In this text, accommodation and reasonable accommodation are used interchangeably and in a broader sense than in employment law.

19 *Eweida and Others v United Kingdom*, Application nos. 48420/10, 59842/10, 51671/10 and 36516/10, 27/05/2013, Judgment of 15 January 2013, para 80. Freedom of religion is 'one of the most vital elements that go to make up the identity of believers and their

gion does *not necessitate* accommodation. Although at one point the ECtHR recognized that "failing to introduce appropriate exceptions" is contrary to the Convention (as a matter of discrimination),[20] exceptions to general rules are granted only exceptionally where the government is compelling someone to choose between conscience and a secular imperative. The ECtHR recognized a *de facto* duty of legislative accommodation only in respect of very serious conscience-based conduct (conscientious objection to military service) where the restriction originated in a general legal duty contrary to a familiar religious tenet and the person demonstrated that he is ready to make serious sacrifice. Additional considerations limited the scope of accommodation: the exemption from armed military service was granted because it concerned a minority religion and was understood to serve social pluralism.[21]

Outside such exceptional instances, the ECtHR assesses the extent to which the interference with religious freedom was balanced on the national level and concludes that "too much" (or too little) weight had been attributed to it, without explanation for this judicial assessment.[22] The ECtHR – without accepting a general duty of accommodation at the workplace – held in *Eweida*[23] that there is a certain positive obligation of the state to enable freedom of religion even where the interference is not directly attributable to the State, making a kind of accommodation a matter of occasional balancing.[24] The ECtHR said expressly that special religion protective legislation is not required for the protection of religious freedom, and the Convention obligation is satisfied if the religious concern is seriously considered.[25]

conception of life' and one of the foundations of a 'democratic society,' and pluralism depends on it. *Bayatyan v Armenia*, Application no. 23459/03, Judgment of 7 July 2011 (Grand Chamber), para 118. Respect of conscience plays a central role here.

20 *Thlimmenos v Greece*, Application no. 34369/97, Judgment of 6 April 2000, para 48. (This formula was not used in later cases.) Exceptionally the Commission too recognized the duty to accommodate in respect to a court hearing: *SH and HV v Austria*, Application no. 18960/91, Commission, Decision of 13 December 1993 (inadmissible).

21 *Bayatyan* (n 19), para 126.

22 *Eweida* (n 19), para 94.

23 The Court could have used its earlier caselaw which was less permissive: 'Article 9 does not, however, protect every act motivated or inspired by a religion or belief and does not always guarantee the right to behave in the public sphere in a manner which is dictated by one's religion or beliefs' (see, for example, *Arrowsmith v the United Kingdom*, Application no. 7050/75, Commission, Decision of 12 October 1978, DR 19, 5; *Kalaç v Turkey*, Application no. 20704/92, Judgement of 1 July 1997, para 27 and *Leyla Şahin v Turkey*, Application no. 44774/98, Judgment of 10 November 2005 (Grand Chamber), paras 105 and 121.

24 The *Eweida* court (n 19) while reiterating these common sense requirements, suddenly and without justification provided and applied a standard contrary to earlier Grand Chamber precedent under the guise of burden of proof. See para 82 '. . . there is no requirement on the applicant to establish that he or she acted in fulfilment of a duty mandated by the religion in question', with references to *Cha'are* (n 6), *Leyla Sahin* (n 23) and *Bayatyan* (n 19), among others. The authorities cited do not contain the quoted sentence and indicate the opposite.

25 *Eweida* (n 19), paras 91–92.

Although in many cases accommodation is sought by members of minority groups, it is unfortunate to justify accommodation as a question of minority protection.[26] What is protected is conscience, irrespective of a person's belonging to a religious minority or majority. Neutral laws of general applicability by their very generality disadvantage (at least some) religions and people who would like to follow the imperative command of their conscience.

This chapter argues from a liberal secularist perspective that freedom of religion deserves more respect, including a kind of positive obligation (duty) of the state to provide reasonable accommodation to religious exercise both at the level of general legislation and in specific individual situations. The chapter applies a theory of liberal secularist constitutionalism to problems emerging in European freedom of religion, as exemplified in the case law of European apex courts. In order to indicate larger trends it looks also at some model solutions developed outside Europe.[27] It does not provide a systematic comparative analysis of the law and therefore it uses terms like freedom of religion and free exercise, as well as reasonable accommodation, accommodation and undue burden interchangeably, except when it comes to the discussion of specific cases.

The duty of reasonable accommodation of essential manifestations of religious belief (hereinafter: essential religious manifestation) is compatible with the premises of a liberal secular order. Secular here means a legal order where the state remains neutral in matters of religion, where the source of law is 'the people' and no supreme alternative legal sources are accepted.[28] Secularism as a precondition of the constitutional order does not have a position on the role of religious freedom: it can be for or against religious manifestations or recognize these freedoms only in certain, primarily private spheres. "What secularism does rule out, however, is any attempt to use the religious views of one part of the community to exclude from consideration the values of other members of the community."[29] *Liberal* secularism intends to maximize religious liberty within the arrangements of the secular state, while non-liberal versions of secularism can be insensitive to religious liberty.

Part II reviews the legal causes of the underestimation of individual religious rights. Part III discusses the extra-legal causes of the disadvantage, focusing on the myopia of the secular state that is concerned with the appearance of neutrality and adulates generally applicable laws. Part IV argues for countering

26 For a typical treatment of accommodation as minority protection see Martha Nussbaum, *Liberty of Conscience* (New York: Basic Books, 2008), p. 117. This minority concern is part of the contemporary trend that replaces human rights protection with minority protection.

27 The manuscript was closed before the US Supreme Court's unanimous judgments in *Goff v DeJoy*, 600 US 447 (2023).

28 András Sajó, 'Preliminaries to a Concept of Constitutional Secularism', *ICON* 6 (2008), 605. The focus on religious belief is not intended to imply that secular beliefs central to a comprehensive world view are not to be protected at the same level.

29 *Chamberlain v Surrey School District no. 36*, [2002] 4 SCR 710, para 19.

the resulting structural disadvantage by overprotection, in the form of a duty of reasonable accommodation (understood in a non-technical, broad sense). This requires religious persons and communities to act in the spirit of mutual accommodation (incorporating to a reasonable extent the constitutional val ues of the liberal secular order, relying on their overlapping values). Part V reviews the terms of and limits to accommodation, to ensure that proper (non-trivializing) weight is attributed to essential religious manifestations in adjudication and social interactions.

The legal causes of diminishing respect for religious freedom

The trend exemplified in the European ritual slaughter cases is sometimes related in the literature to the arguable loss of respect for religion and resulting indifference to religious freedom in secularized democracies. The diminishing respect for religious freedom is surprising. After all, the scope of legally protected religious manifestation rights was extended in the last decades in democracies, as it has become accepted that following religious commands was a matter of personal belief (see II.1 on the 'subjective approach').[30] The US Religious Land Use and Institutionalized Persons Act (2000) redefined the exercise of religion to include "any exercise of religion whether or not compelled by, or central to, a system of religious belief."[31]

The diminishing respect for freedom of religion is partly due to a general attack on classic political and civil rights, as one-sided, bourgeois, oppressive, or – even worse – "neoliberal" constructs. The increasingly popular Western cult of identity is also diminishing the weight of religious liberty claims. This is paradoxical, because the protection of religious self-expression was key to extending the liberal, subjective understanding of what counts as "religious" in the first place.

The prevailing judicial methodology in matters of fundamental rights also contributes to the diminished protection of classic fundamental rights. In principle, interference in the exercise of a fundamental rights is the exception (to be narrowly interpreted), and it must be shown convincingly that the limitation is necessary and proportionate (or least restrictive), or – in the US approach – that there is a compelling reason for the restriction. These approaches used to contribute to the superior position of classic, enumerated fundamental (human) rights. Today in Europe, balancing and proportionality are used as if they were interchangeable, and classic human rights are routinely balanced against the rights of others (and other legitimate aims resulting in limitations) as if these were rights of equal value.

30 BVerfGE 108, 282 (297) (*Kopftuch*). International courts were slower in this respect. Ute Sacksofsky, *Religiöse Freiheit als Gefahr? Vereinigung der Deutschen Staatsrechtslehrer* (Berlin: De Gruyter, 2008), p. 20, fn 69.

31 42 US Code § 2000cc-5(7).

The subjective understanding of religious manifestation

Thomas Aquinas was concerned about enabling the work of "erring conscience" (which he attributed to non-Christians only). In diverse contemporary societies, public authorities are increasingly wary (for good reasons) of determining what constitutes religion and religious command, because this would run the risk of state-imposed religious views, a matter of partiality and state imposition with all its historically proven oppressive consequences. For the same reason, judges refrain from considering the centrality of particular beliefs or practices to a faith.[32] Many courts accept a sincere personal (subjective) religious belief and manifestation claim at face value, irrespective of whether it is required by an established religious belief system, accepted by some religious authority or amounts to standard (even minority) community practice.[33] This is the polar opposite of the 'essential religious practices' doctrine that has been followed by the Indian Supreme Court since 1954[34] with considerable difficulty and disagreement on the bench,[35] subjecting the Court to intensifying criticism for becoming an arbiter in questions of religion under the guise of settling constitutional issues.[36]

The subjective understanding of religious belief and conduct is not just a matter of legitimate judicial deference related to state neutrality and an endorsement of identity claims. It can also be defended on the basis of liberal individualism that intends to maximize respect for individual choice. "With the *Charter*, it has become the right of every Canadian to work out for himself or herself what his or her religious obligations, if any, should be."[37] Admittedly, the subjective standard gives too much credit to such (allegedly) irresistible conscience claims which appear trivial, idiosyncratic or delusional for a reasonable external observer. Even Pastafarianism received some judicial endorsement.

Perhaps being concerned about trivialization or unreasonable positive discrimination, some courts (including those which accept that sincerity, consistency, seriousness etc. of belief are sufficient and stand for a subjective understanding of religious claims) try to limit the sphere of protected manifestations by restricting the subjective or deferential understanding of belief, especially if it is not central to identity in an objective sense. It was in this sense

32 See e.g. *Hernandez v Commissioner*, 490 US 680, 699 (1989). See, however, the essential content doctrine following this.

33 E.g. *Syndicat Northcrest v Amselem*, [2004] 2 SCR 551, paras 42, 47 (See further, *Eweida* (n 19)).

34 *Commissioner, Hindu Religious Endowments, Madras v Shri Lakshmindar Tirtha Swamiyar of Shri Shirur Mutt*, (1954) SCR 1005.

35 *Law Society of British Columbia Appellant v Trinity Western University*, (2018) 2 SCC 32.

36 For an overview: Dushyant Kishan Kaul, 'The "Essential Practices" Doctrine, Examining the Constitutional Impact of Inordinate Judicial Intervention on Religious Freedoms', *International Journal on Minority and Group Rights* 29 (2022), 350.

37 *R v Big M Drug Mart*, [1985] 1 SCR 295, 351 (Dickson CJ).

that the UK Supreme Court rejected the claim that supervisory tasks in abortion clinics (that did not entail participation in the medical procedure itself) are part of a conscience claim, stating (that as a matter of statutory interpretation) this is not "facilitation" (of sin) and therefore it does not fall under the statutory exemption granted in the parliamentary conscience clause.[38] The US Supreme Court was of the opposite view in *Hobby Lobby*.[39]

The proliferation and inflation of rights

Like other classic fundamental rights mentioned in the 1789 French Declaration of Rights of Man and Citizen and in the US Bill of Rights, freedom of religion suffers from the prevailing proliferation of rights (*rights inflation*). All the rights voted into the Hall of Fame of human rights are understood to be of equal abstract weight following an interpretation based on the Vienna Declaration and Programme of Action of 1993: "All human rights are universal, indivisible and interdependent and interrelated."[40] Indivisibility and the interdependence are understood to mean that all human rights are equal, and their priority can be determined only situationally.[41]

The number of fundamental human rights and constitutional rights is constantly growing. Collective interests and communitarian expectations are transformed into the right of others, and the direct negative effect on an identifiable individual right is replaced with the *potential* effect of, and expressive harm to, non-specific rights of non-specific groups. The argument is that "once it is recognized that acts of discrimination undermine the dignity of individuals even when they do not result in deprivation of a service, it must be legitimate for states to seek to prevent such attacks from occurring."[42]

The more rights of equivalent importance exist, the higher the likelihood of conflict to the detriment of religious rights. As rights are not absolute (except some prohibitions like torture) fundamental human rights can be and often must be restricted for the sake of protecting ever-increasing 'rights of others.' Once on equal footing, these non-universal rights can be used in a balancing exercise to the detriment of freedom of religion. In this atmosphere

> [t]here is good reason to worry that the prodigious expansion of human rights has weakened rather than strengthened the claims of human rights and left the most disadvantaged more vulnerable. More rights do not

38 *Greater Glasgow Health Board v Doogan & Anan*, [2014] UKSC 68, para 38.

39 *Burwell v Hobby Lobby Stores, Inc.*, (2014) 573 US 682.

40 Endorsed by UN General Assembly Resolution 48/121, 20 December 1993.

41 This equivalence is not fully supported in international human rights law. Freedom of religion is the only 'active' non-derogable right: International Covenant on Civil and Political Rights, (adopted 16 December 1966, entered into force 23 March 1976) 999 UNTS 171), Art 4 (others concern state violence: torture, the principle of *nullum crimen* etc.).

42 Ronan McCrea, 'Religion in the Workplace: *Eweida and Other v United Kingdom*', *Modern Law Review* 4 (2013), 277.

> always yield more justice. Transforming every worthy political preference into a claim of human rights inevitably dilutes the authority of human rights.[43]

In this new (quasi-socialist) gospel classical rights lose their lexical priority.[44]

In the immediate context of religious freedom, the proliferation of rights appears as the expansion of the scope of conscience claims and the expansion of notion of coercion that warrant exemption from generally applicable laws. Conscience claims are increasingly stretched to cover complicity in the (allegedly) sinful actions of others[45] (such as a hospital clerk refusing to fill out paperwork for a woman seeking a legally available abortion). As such, complicity-based conscience claims interfere with the fundamental human rights of others. Even if the emotional commitment and conviction of a baker or a hairstylist is as firm as that of the *refusnik* who faces imprisonment for rejecting compulsory military service, in the worst-case scenario (in order to avoid confrontation) the *refusnik* baker can always limit the bakery's services to baking bread, paying a fine or moving to another profession. The risk of inflation of conscientious objection claims calls for a nuanced approach to accommodation, and not for abandoning accommodation in the name of neutrality or judicial deference.

Freedom of religion as an identity claim

Religious rights claims are more and more frequently presented (and very often felt) by rights holders as an expression of "adherence to a faith."[46] Such personal identity claims of belonging exceed the traditional understandings of religious manifestation, as used in the text of international human rights instruments and many constitutions. As the US Supreme Court noted, the fundamental rights found in the Fourteenth Amendment's Due Process Clause "extend to certain personal choices central to individual dignity and autonomy, including intimate choices that define personal identity and beliefs."[47] The protection of 'religious identity as belonging' became a tool for bypassing the judicial doctrine which held that "[f]reedom to manifest one's religion' does not mean

43 'Report of the US Commission of Unalieanable Rights', 26 August 2020, 39. https://2017-2021.state.gov/wp-content/uploads/2020/07/Draft-Report-of-the-Commission-on-Unalienable-Rights.pdf accessed 10 September 2023.

44 For a critical discussion of these developments see András Sajó, 'The Fate of Human Rights in Indifferent Societies – (i.e. in More and More Constitutional Democracies)', in András Sajó and Renáta Uitz (eds.), *Critical Essays on Human Rights Criticism* (The Hague: Eleven Publishing, 2020), p. 15.

45 Douglas NeJaime and Reva Siegel, 'Conscience Wars: Complicity-Based Conscience Claims in Religion and Politics', *The Yale Law Journal* 124 (2015), 2516.

46 *Ebrahimian v France*, Application no. 64846/11, Judgment of 26 November 2015, para 47.

47 *Obergefell v Hodges*, 576 US 644 (2015).

that one has the right to manifest one's religion at any place and in any manner that accords with one's beliefs."[48]

The new trend is exemplified in the French burqa case decided by the ECtHR.[49] The applicant spoke about her desire to wear a burqa depending on her mood, pointing to a matter of personal construction and not a matter of imperative commands of conscience. As the ECtHR put it: "the wearing of the full-face veil in public places . . . is the expression of a *cultural identity* which contributes to the pluralism that is inherent in democracy."[50] This "freedom is, in its religious dimension, one of the most vital elements that go to *make up the identity of believers*" and is valuable for its contribution to pluralism[51] (emphasis added). As the ECtHR stated: "the women concerned, [because of the ban] are thus obliged to give up completely an element of their identity *that they consider important*, together with their *chosen* manner of manifesting their religion or beliefs."[52]

In part, the acceptance of the subjective understanding of religious manifestation is related to an attitude of liberal secularism. Yet when an identity claim (the right to belonging) is used as a proxy for religious freedom, the spiritual dimension of religious belief is turned into a matter of personally curated kinship. This is the predicament of religion in a post-modern society. "[I]f religion is to be meaningful in postmodernity, each person must arrive at a personal and highly subjective understanding of it. People can no longer be expected simply to accept purportedly objective religious 'truths' that are handed down by their traditions."[53]

The prevailing legal methodology undermining freedom of religion

As more and more rights are being elevated to fundamental rights, balancing among equal rights and even interests have become the preferred methodology in the name of equality of rights.[54] As the example of the ECtHR indicates, this (rather *ad hoc*) balancing[55] was quickly extended to situations where technically strict proportionality should have applied (see the terminology

48 *R (SB) v Governors of Denbigh High School*, [2007] 1 AC 100, para 86 (Lord Scott of Foscote).
49 *SAS v France*, Application no. 43835/11, Judgment of 1 July 2014 (Grand Chamber).
50 *SAS* (n 49), para 120.
51 *Ibid.*, para 124.
52 *Ibid.*, para 139, emphasis added.
53 Victoria S. Harrison, 'Postmodern Thought and Religion: Open Traditionalism and Radical Orthodoxy on Religious Belief and Experience', *The Heythrop Journal* 51, (2010), 962, 967 with reference to the classical formulation of Don Cupitt, *The Sea of Faith: Christianity in Change* (London: BBC, 1984), p. 19. See also Marcel Gauchet, *Un monde désenchanté?* (Ivry-sur-Seine: Éditions de l'Atelier, 2004), p. 169.
54 This is less of a problem in the US where the list of constitutional rights is relatively short. However, because generally applicable laws can disregard religious considerations without strict or even intermediate scrutiny, the effect is somewhat similar.
55 Karl-Heinz Ladeur, 'The Myth of the Neutral State and the Individualization of Religion: The Relationship Between State and Religion in the Face of Fundamentalism', in Susanna

used in the aforementioned slaughter cases). Balancing is the source of uncertainty – and uncertainty is visible also within the inconsistencies, fragmentation, sudden changes in freedom of religion law. Balancing makes deference to the choices of the legislature and public administration easy, as long as that choice is not manifestly arbitrary. This is what happened in the ritual slaughter cases: the law allowed putting animal welfare interests not only on par with but above freedom of religion.

New considerations, absent in the text of the ECHR emerge in balancing: "regard must be had in particular to the fair balance that has to be struck between the competing interests of the individual and of the community as a whole."[56] Community interests refer to the interests of the many against the 'selfishness of the individual.' This shifts the balance automatically in favour of the interests of the many (even where the prevailing ideology does not state expressly the supremacy of the collective). This a favour rendered to truth in numbers, contrary to the idea of human rights. As a result, the internationally acknowledged list of fundamental rights that became the common heritage and foundation of liberal democracies is relativized, without taking into consideration that these rights proved to be quintessential for liberal democracy and for defending individual freedom (i.e., foundational values that are left, so far, not much contested).

Religious and non-religious conscience-based action deserves special protection because it responds to "transcendent moral obligations – . . . obligations that transcend [the nontheist's] self-interest and his personal preferences and which he experiences as so strong that he has no choice but to comply – is analogous to the transcendent moral obligations that are part of the cluster of theistic beliefs that we recognize as religious."[57] From the perspective of the secular (liberal constitutional) justification it is not the transcendental *origin* of the moral obligation that matters, but the intensity of genuine moral obligations related to a comprehensive life plan ("no choice"). Interestingly, with the subjective turn in the legal understanding of religious manifestations, the transcendental element seems to have lost its importance.

Neutral laws and secular myopia

Troubled by the priests' usurpation of power, Spinoza admitted that "the external Form of Public Religious Worship, ought to be accommodated to the Peace of the Commonwealth,"[58] and obedience to laws is quintessential to any order. General laws in contemporary societies are acts of the sovereign. Today

Mancini and Michel Rosenfeld (eds.), *Constitutional Secularism in an Age of Religious Revival* (Oxford: OUP, 2014), p. 47.

56 *Eweida* (n 19), para 84.

57 Laycock (n 13).

58 Title of Chapter XIX in Spinoza, *A Treatise Partly Theological, and Partly Political* (London: n.p., 1689), p. 412. The same chapter title is translated as 'the external cult of religion must be

the liberal belief is that the sovereign's power is not absolute: it has to respect, to a degree, fundamental rights and the rule of law. Regrettably, the secular effort to prevent religious strife, together with the aspiration to recognize the equal dignity of all human beings, inevitably make the liberal constitutional order short-sighted.

In principle, the laws of a neutral secular state have to keep equal distance from religions. As such, general laws in a neutral state are meant to be indifferent to specific considerations of one or another religion. In several modern democracies the public domain is institutionally structured along non-religious values. In some respect this secularization reduces burdens on religious conscience: oath-taking is less common, military conscription is abolished, etc. At the same time, secularist indifference introduces a systemic flaw into the legal order: for the secular decision-maker the religious motivation informing a behaviour is invisible, and therefore irrelevant. The indifference of the neutral state puts religious conscience in an "asymmetrical" position.[59] This secularist flaw is in the fabric of the liberal constitutional order.

Religion-based conflicts are to be avoided, and this experience is often reflected in constitutions. In a society of equals, generally applicable laws are also needed to counter harm to others, for social coexistence and for coordination. The prohibition of harming others burdens those religions whose doctrines require (or justify) harmful conduct. There is nothing wrong with general laws of this kind. In fact, beyond safeguarding equality, one of the main justifications of having generally applicable laws is that religions as factions, following a non-secular, partial vision of the community, tend to destroy the public order with excessive passion. Equal respect for all and tolerance that is indispensable for living together may disadvantage religions. At least in some instances, the real or alleged needs to maintain "religious harmony"[60] or living together result in a kind of "repressive tolerance" to the detriment of individual free exercise. In such socio-cultural environment freedom of religion may become structurally disadvantaged, and this is reflected in law.[61]

The adverse effect of secular myopia on religion, and on minority religions in particular, is a fact of life in constitutional democracies even in the best of times. Not all general laws serve the community, the interests and values of all, and as such, general laws can be the tool of persecution, disregarding in their generality different believers. Legislation often simply presents longstanding

---

consistent with the stability of the state' in Spinoza, *Theological-Political Treatise*, ed. Jonathan Israel (Cambridge: CUP, 2007), p. 238.

59 Kathleen M. Sullivan, 'Religion and Liberal Democracy', *University of Chicago Law Review* 59 (1992), 195, 211.

60 *Leyla Sahin* (n 23), paras 104–111.

61 Sometimes religions disadvantage themselves by being harmfully intolerant towards others (sometimes even to co-religionists) or being otherwise incompatible with public order. In such instances the tolerant state rightfully disadvantages such religious activities. See Thomas M. Scanlon, *The Difficulty of Tolerance* (Cambridge: CUP, 2003), p. 197.

('historic') majority traditions presenting them as neutral common practice – to the detriment of minorities, be they religious or not. In a secular democracy, claims that religious arguments are 'special' because they originate in some supreme, transcendental truth – while certainly permitted and politically relevant – are considered intellectually dubious and legally irrelevant. At the same time, religious behaviour that used to be politically or culturally irrelevant may receive new meaning and become politically suspect from the perspective of the secular public order (especially with growing pluralism and religious fundamentalism).

The anti-religious insensitivity of general rules which favour uniform solutions requires corrections. Such corrections are not only needed because generally applicable rules as determined by the majority tend to be biased in favour of a traditional or majority religion or are insensitive to religious needs of all religions. Having in mind an abstract citizen of the secular political community, general rules answer specific problems without considering the possibility that when applied in practice the general legal solution may have disparate impact on the religious conduct of a particular individual.

If Sunday is the day of rest, those who observe the Sabbath on another day of the week are disadvantaged by the disparate negative effect of the general rule. This harm is not fixed by offering a truly neutral, secular reason ("Sunday is simply the traditional common day of rest"). Sometimes the neutral law poorly hides prejudicial intent, and courts are ready to review and reject legislation with anti-religious animus.[62] Disguised intent fundamentally differs from the structural bias of secular myopia. While prohibitions of Kosher slaughter were historically related to antisemitic public sentiment and some religious practice restrictions in Europe reflect anti-Muslim bias,[63] it is obvious that this was not the case with the CJEU's endorsement of the Flemish decree in 2020 (given that the "political work" is done by national legislation).

Be that as it may, it remains the case that at times even the mere burden on religion (interference) is denied.[64] Like in a leading case in the UK, where the believer "voluntarily accepted an employment or role which does not accommodate that practice or observance and there are other means open to the person to practise or observe his or her religion without undue hardship or inconvenience."[65] In such an environment the fundamental right of religious

62 *Church of the Lukumi Babalu Aye, Inc. v Hialeah*, 508 US 520 (1993).

63 All religious movements with a visibly unusual form of life (and not only Muslims) are at a disadvantage, simply because the general rules reflect a normalization of historical, traditional life forms. As long as the Universal Declaration's world view prevails, those who for whatever reason do not adopt to it will be at a disadvantage.

64 *R (Begum) v Governors of Denbigh High School*, [2006] UKHL 15. The school dress code (that has already accommodated mainstream Muslim sensitivities) is not contrary to freedom of religion, given the availability of a school where the wearing of the jilbab is permitted. (The same logic is applied in employment relations, endorsed by the ECtHR).

65 See e. g., *Denbigh High* (n 64), para 23 (per Lord Bingham). The powers of the employer are even more respected in government service: *Goldman v Weinberger*, 475 US 503 (1986).

freedom is not protected, *unless* it receives special legal support. The insensitivity of neutral generally applicable laws can be and shall be countered by exceptions. Such an exception may be granted by courts in individual cases. Ideally, general laws themselves should leave an opportunity for seeking a religious exemption. The Flemish decree upheld by the CJEU in 2020 (and later by the Belgian Constitutional Court[66]) removed such an exemption from the Belgian national law.

Lawyers and society at large must accept the world consensus of international human rights law as a normative social fact. Freedom of religion is an undeniable black-letter fundamental right. The secular state must guarantee that the dignity of others is not factually denied, especially by state action. The classic negative approach to rights protection (non-interference of the state) became insufficient in a densely regulated world. Had the slaughterhouse not been subject to regulation ritual, slaughter would have been left alone as a negative freedom. Once the modern regulatory state creates a situation where pre-regulation liberty is of little practical relevance and the structural flaws of the liberal constitutional order are perpetuated by secular myopia, *reasonable accommodation is a state duty.*

Countering secular myopia: the duty of reasonable accommodation

Manifestations of religion dictated by a believer's conscience (personal beliefs) are at disadvantage in secular European legal orders. Recognizing the proper weight of religious rights vis-à-vis other rights, interests and values is the first avenue leading to the genuine protection of religious freedom as an individual right. Such proper recognition is not a plea for special treatment. It means that religious rights are given what is due to a fundamental human right (constitutional right) without the trivialization that was noticeable in the European ritual slaughter cases. In the words of Justice O'Connor of the US Supreme Court: "Religious needs can be accommodated through laws that are neutral with regard to religion."[67] Accommodation is not just compatible with secularism: it is dictated by the robust interest in liberty that fills the shell of secularism.

To overcome the structural flaws – the myopia – of the secular legal order, religious freedom is due *enhanced protection* in the form of a duty of reasonable accommodation. To overcome the structural myopia of the secular legal order, religious freedom is due *enhanced protection* in the form of a duty of reasonable accommodation afforded to the essential religious manifestations.

66 Judgement no. 117/2021 (30 September 2021).
67 *Board of Education of Kiryas Joel Village School District v Grumet*, 512 US 687, 714 (1994).

Proper recognition for religious freedom: enhanced protection through the duty of reasonable accommodation

The secular plea for taking religious freedom seriously is not to be mistaken for the kind of "religious exceptionalism" that is increasingly recognized in the United States.[68] Fundamental rights are treated with utmost care because they concern extremely valuable but vulnerable values. A liberal society respects central personal choices stemming from a comprehensive life plan. Without such overprotection, religious rights would be systematically disadvantaged.

Consider freedom of expression. Exceptions to generally applicable rules are granted in favour of particularly valuable classes (categories) of speech. When it comes to political speech, speech about public figures or on matters of public interest, liberal courts find that exceptions to general rules are to be granted because these categories of speech are of particular importance for democracy. Religious freedom serves similar, particularly important public interests and values (e. g. autonomy and self-determination, pluralism, antidiscrimination, social peace) and deserves similarly strong protection.

Richard Posner has demonstrated that (one of) the reasons for such overprotection of freedom of expression is that there is little return on the production of ideas and people are not willing to stand up to protect speech, while governments have an interest in curtailing it, especially in the context of political speech that criticizes the government. Overprotection is intended to rectify this imbalance.[69] A similar reasoning applies to freedom of religion where the individual believer may not have sufficient motivation to stand up for religious rights in public (especially where the secular constitutional order enables worship at the private level) and where secular considerations and the desire of uniformity do not favour the generation of religious goods. Pietism is the normal answer in a modestly unfriendly world, not individual action or litigation.

From the perspective of a fundamental right to freedom (as of religion) what has to be justified is the restriction (even by generally applicable laws) and not the need for an exemption from restrictive rules (accommodation). In principle, once a believer has established that a right (conduct) that is genuinely related to an important requirement of a religion is substantially burdened by a generally applicable law or (to a lesser extent) a private power, the

68 This is exemplified in *Hosanna-Tabor*, where the pastoral exception was extended to a degree that would deny disability benefits and anti-discrimination – a matter of discrimination in Europe. *Hosanna-Tabor Evangelical Lutheran Church and School v Equal Employment Opportunity Commission*, 565 US 171 (2012).

For a strong version of accommodation see Michael W. McConnell, 'Accommodation of Religion: An Update and a Response to the Critics', *G Wash Law Review* 60 (1991), 685 (individual or group decides which practice is engaged, government facilitates it). The US counterargument is that accommodation endorses religion and thus violates the Establishment Clause of the First Amendment.

69 Richard Posner, *Economic Analysis of Law*, 5th ed. (Boston, MA: Aspen, 1998), p. 730.

burden is on the restricting party to show that the measure was necessary and justify the interference with reference to an important right or constitutional value. The state should prove the necessity of prohibiting ritual slaughter.[70] This logic is reversed in the world of equal rules to all, where equality dictates generally applicable laws and where the honesty and reasonableness of legislation is presumed. This is to be rectified by a state duty for granting an exemption not only via judicial protection, but also in generally applicable laws.

As it was made clear early on by the US Supreme Court, accommodation is not a license to seek the governmental endorsement of particular religious values or commands:

> The Free Exercise Clause simply cannot be understood to require the Government to conduct its own internal affairs in ways that comport with the religious beliefs of particular citizens. Just as the Government may not insist that appellees engage in any set form of religious observance, so appellees may not demand that the Government join in their chosen religious practices by refraining from using a number to identify their daughter.[71]

Secularist myopia and the duty of reasonable accommodation revisited

This chapter follows the idea expressed by Justice Albie Sachs that "the State should, wherever reasonably possible, seek to avoid putting believers to *extremely painful and intensely burdensome choices* of either being true to their faith or else respectful of the law" (emphasis added).[72] The neglect of religious freedoms (together with some other foundational rights for modern, enlightened democratic society) can be countered only if taken seriously, ensuring the robust protection of essential religious manifestations. This requires legislative exceptions, not just considerations at the level of expensive, ex post judicial balancing in individual cases, and it is a matter of degree.[73] The need for accommodation depends both on the nature of the religious conduct and the governmental prescription. Our understanding of reasonable accommodation goes beyond Sachs' formula, as it extends the positive obligation (duty) of the state to all regulated area, where a private party exercises power created or endorsed by government (as an employer, school administrator, etc.)[74]

70 The level of necessity remains another contested matter.

71 *Bowen v Roy*, 476 US 693 at 699 (1986). See further in this sense Michael McConnell, 'Religious Freedom at a Crossroads', *University of Chicago Law Review* 59 (1992), 115, 127.

72 *Christian Education South Africa v Minister of Education*, [2000] 9 BHRC 53, para 35.

73 Gérard Bouchard and Charles Taylor, *Building the Future: A Time for Reconciliation, Consultation Commission on Accommodation Practices Related to Cultural Differences* (Quebec: Government of Quebec, 2008).

74 Strictly private entities (such as a private association or family) are subject to anti-discrimination law only to the extent this subject is afforded consideration in a legal system.

Historically, accommodation was considered in situations where a person was forced by her conscience to choose between secular norms and religious commands, resulting in an impasse. Arguably, at the time of the making of the US Constitution broadly understood accommodation was the accepted practice and principle in America.[75] This position resulted from a proto-liberal and very religious understanding of the demands of conscience. At the same time the regulatory power of the secular state was very limited. The classical liberal position (at least under Protestant influence), as in the case of arch-liberal Benjamin Constant, considered freedom of religion to exist in the impenetrable private sphere, off-limits to state interference. Over time the strict division between public and private became unsustainable and the boundaries got blurred. The state increasingly entered into the private sphere (i.e. family, workplace and private social services) and it colonized spheres of liberty which were previously left more or less to private determination.

At the same time, historically the dominant (established or majority) religion was very much present in the public (and even in the political) sphere and therefore the conduct required by religion was seen as "normal." For its part, the secular state continuously tried to squeeze religious organizations out from the public sphere. In consequence, public conduct that used to be taken for granted under the umbrella of the dominant religion gradually found itself unprotected and defenceless in the face of ever-expanding governmental regulation and secular private ordering. Gradually, religious believers and their organized forces felt forced to leave their religious beliefs at home. Many of them also felt like second-class citizens in the public square. Whatever the reality of this sentiment, such a situation is certainly problematic for the liberal ideal of inclusive, respectful society. Ignoring religious needs in public life would contribute to state omnipotence,[76] hence the need for a more robust protection of freedom of religion, including reasonable accommodation.

Save for instances of anti-religious animus, in most democracies generally applicable laws do not generate special duties to protect religious conduct and do not call for exemptions.

In the US, religious accommodation has routinely been associated with the Free Exercises Clause of the First Amendment.[77] In 1990, the US Supreme Court concluded that generally applicable laws "incidentally" restricting freedom of religion did not deserve the highest level of scrutiny that affords accommodation to religious freedom, claiming that such a system "would be

75 Michael McConnell, 'The Origins and Historical Understanding of Free Exercise of Religion', *Harvard Law Review* 103 (1990), 1409.

76 Peter Badura, 'Staatskirchenrechtals Gegenstand des Verfassungsrechts', in Joseph Listl and Dietrich Pirson (eds.), *Handbuch des Staatskirchenrechts I*, 2nd edn (Berlin: Duncker & Humblot, 1994), p. 222.

77 Michael McConnell, 'Accommodation of Religion', *Supreme Court Review* 1985 (1985), 1 and Kent Greenawalt, *Religion and the Constitution, Volume I: Free Exercise and Fairness* (Princeton, NJ: Princeton University Press, 2006).

courting anarchy" in a religiously diverse society.[78] The Supreme Court of Canada is known for its rather generous reasonable accommodation doctrine,[79] although more recently the Court has become divided on the issue of religious accommodation in individual cases.[80] Also, the Canadian Supreme Court does not require legislative accommodation when it comes to generally applicable laws restricting religiously mandated conduct;[81] indirect religious discrimination has to be remedied unless the remedy imposes an undue burden.[82] The Constitutional Court of deeply religious South Africa makes the reasonable accommodation of difference "a question of principle central to the whole constitutional enterprise,"[83] yet it does not require accommodation for religious freedom at the level of generally applicable laws. In litigation about the local application of the general law, a "least burdensome on religious rights" approach applies in South Africa.[84]

For reasons mentioned here, generally, applicable laws were mostly immune to religious exceptionalism, but anti-discrimination laws require minimal accommodation where this does not impose *undue burden* on other parties. The term "reasonable accommodation" originates in US anti-discrimination law and in disability law. In the US, the undue burden test that is applicable in (non-public) employment law under Title VII today means "more than a *de minimis* cost,"[85] although courts differ as to what constitutes disproportionate burden. In Canada, "[e]mployers . . . must demonstrate that it would have been impossible to modify or eliminate a particular requirement without incurring undue hardship."[86]

In this chapter, accommodation is not used in the narrow sense that applies in employment/anti-discrimination law; rather, it refers to all generally

78 *Employment Division, Department of Human Resources of Oregon v Smith*, 494 US 872, 888 (1990).

79 *R v Edwards Books and Art Ltd* [1986] 2 SCR 713.

80 *Syndicat Northcrest* (n 33) (5:4); *Alberta v Hutterian Brethren of Wilson Colony*, 2009 SCC 37 (4:3); *R v NS*, 2012 SCC 72 (3-way split). Generally: Rosalie Jukier and José Woehrling, 'Religion and the Secular State in Canada', in Javier Martinez Torrón and W. Cole Durham, Jr. (eds.), *Religion and the Secular State. National Reports* (Madrid: International Center for Law and Religion Studies, 2010), pp. 155, 167–169.

81 See Ch J. MacLachlin in *Alberta v Hutterian Brethren* (n 80), para 36 (fear for the universality of general laws).

82 See, however, *Central Okanagan School District no. 23 v Renaud*, [1992] 2 SCR 970 (under a provincial human rights code).

83 *Prince v President of the Law Society of the Cape of Good Hope (CCT36/00)*, [2002] ZACC 1 (25 January 2002). J Sachs, concurring, para 171, also para 172: 'The test of tolerance as envisaged by the Bill of Rights comes not in accepting what is familiar and easily accommodated, but in giving reasonable space to what is "unusual, bizarre or even threatening"'.

84 *Christian Education South Africa v Minister of Education*, [2000] 9 BHRC 53, para 31.

85 A contrario, in the absence of clear statutory language, *Trans World Airlines v Hardison*, 432 US 63 (1977). The Americans with Disabilities Act defines undue hardship as an 'action requiring significant difficulty or expense'. 42 USC 12111 (10).

86 *British Columbia (Public Service Employee Relations Comm) v BCGEU*, [1999] 3 SCR 3, para 54.

applicable laws.[87] Reasonable accommodation in employment law promotes full participation of all in social life.[88] Unrelated to the merits and achievements of the anti-discrimination approach,[89] we argue for a liberal approach intended to maximize individual liberty, including religious liberty, and not social inclusion.[90] The perspective on accommodation familiar from anti-discrimination law is problematic for the equal religious freedom of all. Affording accommodation only to members of vulnerable religious groups would be unfair towards other beliefs and believers. For liberalism, the issue is not the disadvantage suffered by a (minority) religious person, but the right of all to follow deeply held convictions and imperative commands of conscience in conduct at all places where this is reasonably possible. Conscience is not a matter of belonging to (or identifying with) a group.

The need for accommodation is particularly pressing in cases of governmental coercion, where the generally applicable law requires conduct that is manifestly contrary to an essential dictate of (religious) conscience. Conscience is sometimes understood as an inner imperative command, while other religious commands may be imperative but external and therefore remain a matter of choice for the believer. (Do I pray today? If I miss it, there are ways to remedy it and I can remain a faithful believer.)

Sometimes the accommodation measure is hardly visible because it reflects a certain liberal understanding of secularism without reference to specific religious commands. For example, where a policy intends to erase the use of alcohol or drugs, the legislator – knowing that such intoxicating substances are required in a minimal amount for sacramental purposes – will prohibit personal consumption only above a certain limit. As a general rule the minimum amount of intoxicating substance will be accessible to all. While this may not be a very practical solution, it has the advantage of avoiding the accusation of privileging certain religious conducts in a secular world.

Legislative accommodation is even more important in the age of the procedural turn in judicial review: courts try to avoid taking substantive positions

87 A different dimension of accommodation refers to collective accommodation claims. Here, special collective legal regimes are requested in the name of pluralism, as in the case of religious personal law applied by religious courts. States tend to resist such legal pluralism, at least to the extent it would be contrary to constitutional values.

88 See e.g. Pierre Bosset and Marie-Claire Foblets, 'Accommodating Diversity in Québec and Europe: Different Legal Concepts, Similar Results?', in Council of Europe (ed.), *Institutional Accommodation and the Citizen: Legal and Political Interaction in a Pluralist Society* (Strasbourg: Council of Europe, 2010), p. 37. Equality means substantive equality. See e.g. Kristin Henrard, 'Duties of Reasonable Accommodation in Relation to Religion and the European Court of Human Rights: A Closer Look at the Prohibition of Discrimination, the Freedom of Religion and Related Duties of State Neutrality', *Erasmus Law Review* 5 (2013), 59.

89 Not all equality theories embrace reasonable accommodation: see Lori Beaman, *Deep Equality in the Age of Religious Diversity* (Oxford: OUP, 2017), p. 131.

90 On this see Emanuelle Bribosia, Julie Ringelheim and Isabelle Rorive, 'Reasonable Accommodation for Religious Minorities: A Promising Concept for European Antidiscrimination Law?', *Maastricht Journal of European and Comparative Law Review* 7 (2010), 137, 147–148.

in constitutional value conflicts and are also concerned about the economic possibilities. This means that instead of proposing specific solutions, courts increasingly find comfort in the proper formal conduct of the legislative process and require a dialogic approach for implementing remedies, namely that all the concerned parties be duly involved in the spirit of genuine respect.[91]

The duty of mutual accommodation

The inbuilt anti-religion bias of the secular state triggers the duty of the state to engage in accommodation in matters of government-imposed obligations, in government-regulated areas of public life and even in private relations (to the extent this subject merits constitutional consideration). The duty of accommodation is not unilateral, it is not limited to the legislator or the person in the position of authority[92] and it is not only an obligation falling on the liberal secular state. As a citizen of a plural society where mutual respect applies, the religious rights holder also has certain responsibilities (though she is not obliged to respect the state, only to obey it within limits). In a plural society, religious believers are expected to make an effort to enable equality and the effective realization of legitimate, democratic state goals and policies reflected in legislation. They should also accept solutions that seek to protect their *direct* religious rights.[93]

Living together in a plural, tolerant constitutional order is premised on mutual respect.[94] Thus, while living together is not listed among the formal reasons that justify the limitation of freedom of religion, it is the premise of the daily functioning of a diverse society as a constitutional democracy. This requires that efforts of *accommodation be mutual and reciprocal* (in relations among fundamental rights holders).[95] Living together presupposes not only that the state and the majority be respectful (or at least tolerant), but also that all affected parties make efforts to uphold the fundamental constitutional

91 Note, however, the disadvantage of the believer at a workplace where a trade union negotiates on the believer's behalf.

92 See *Ontario (Human Rights Commission) v Simpsons-Sears Ltd*, [1985] 2 SCR 536 (obligation to take reasonable measure to reach agreement in the anti-discrimination context).

93 In *Dewey v Reynolds Metals Company*, 429 F2d 324 (6th Cir. 1970) (upheld by an equally divided Supreme Court) the believer stubbornly refused to accept voluntary replacement 'grounded in his belief that working on Sunday is inherently wrong and that it would be a sin for him to induce another to work in his place'.

94 'Pluralism and democracy must also be based on dialogue and a spirit of compromise necessarily entailing various concessions on the part of individuals or groups of individuals which are justified in order to maintain and promote the ideals and values of a democratic society'. *Leyla Sahin* (n 23), para 108.

95 See in a similar vein the importance of religious harmony and tolerance between opposing or competing groups and of the value of pluralism and broadmindedness as grounds for the restriction of freedom of religion, *Leyla Sahin* (n 23), paras 104–111.

tenets of the liberal secular order.[96] The intransigency of all participants makes coexistence and accommodation difficult (if not impossible) and results in self-exclusion from reasonable accommodation.

The state may be duty-bound to provide accommodation, but in many situations reasonable accommodation could be reached through dialogue and compromise among the concerned parties[97] without state intervention. The legally mandated solution or judicial intervention is needed only because of the inability (or lack of willingness) of the parties to agree. This problem of accommodation has become politically ultra-sensitive in some democracies. Unfortunately, in a world where the "narcissism of small differences" prevails. the search for compromise is perceived as the betrayal of identity, a moral shortcoming. All this goes against the ideal of a tolerant society where reasonable people apply gestures of tolerance and recognition. In the culture wars minor issues become symbolic crusades, and law and courts are routinely instrumentalized. Compromise becomes difficult when what used to be a fuzzier matter of habit is turned into sharp questions of rights and law.[98]

Historically, religions tend to move towards an overlapping consensus envisioned as a minimalist constitutional program. Of course, it would be contrary to state neutrality to allow legislation or courts to impose or express a preference for an interpretation of religious precepts that conforms to the secular order and the rights of others. At the same time, all parties shall seek secularly acceptable positions in religious conduct and – as far as the believer is concerned – make amends where this is *religiously reasonable* (according to the terms and conventions of a given religion).[99] While conscientious objection to military service deserves exceptional treatment, it requires the state as well as the believer to actively seek compromise. For example, the state shall provide an opportunity for non-armed alternative service, while the objector is expected to comply with the requirements of that non-armed service.[100] Even in matters of dictates of conscience the believer is expected to sincerely revisit her conscience claims, given the human propensity of error.

96 The flipside of accommodation in public and regulated private relations is the immunity of the internal organization of religious organizations. The scope of religious autonomy remains contested.

97 Accepting that a communal religious tent is as good as an individual one (as many other believers did) or enduring for nine days the sight of tents on balconies built in violation of building bylaws is not a big deal, unless the issue is perceived as quintessential for religious freedom (see *Syndicat Northcrest* (n 33). J Binnie dissented, claiming that Amselem failed his constitutional duty to respect other owners' rights, having determined himself what his religious duty entails.

98 Raymond Plant, 'Religion, Identity and Freedom of Expression', *Res Publica* 17 (2011), 7, 9.

99 Nussbaum provides an early example of voluntary concession: in 1793 a Jew was subpoenaed for refusing to testify on a Saturday, and the other party waived the benefit of the testimony during the appeal process. Nussbaum (n 26), p. 126.

100 *Bayatyan* (n 19), para 124. American Seventh Day Adventists provided 'equivalent service' in World War II.

The limits of reasonable accommodation claims

In the eyes of many people minorities are continually getting "exemptions or other 'extras', . . . [and this] may in the long run undermine the appreciation of diversity in a society."[101] A person with sincere religious beliefs and resulting religious obligations differs from a person without such beliefs, and this difference can be relevant in certain life situations, allowing or necessitating different treatment. Nonetheless, accommodation runs the risk of abuse, suspicions of favouritism and discrimination, and it may endanger public order and cooperation where personal belief becomes personal law. Consider Kant's warning: "Enthusiastic religious delusion is . . . the moral death of the reason without which there can be no religion, because, like all morality in general, religion must be founded on principles."[102]

Although *forum internum* is unconditionally protected, not all subjective religious claims deserve the same equally high respect and protection in a liberal secular order – and this does not deny respect of the believer *qua* believer. In a secular liberal state, the manifestations of *sincere* comprehensive beliefs must be accepted, even without the backing of communally established religious positions or practices. Yet sincerity alone cannot determine the level of legal protection, especially when it comes to exemptions from general laws. Whether based on constitutional or human rights norms or statutory exemption, the duty of accommodation has to be translated to the specific conditions of individual claimants. In such cases, the threshold issue is whether a particular conscience claim merits protection based on a set of subjective and objective assessment criteria.

Respect for sincerely held beliefs should not encourage *delusional* conduct.[103] The duty of accommodation cannot become an opportunity to endorse trivial or whimsical dictates of putative religious beliefs, idiosyncrasies or identitarian claims (even when presented as or believed to be dictates of conscience), especially when such a recognition would aggravate the culture wars or foment anti-democratic sentiments.[104] Individuals presenting idiosyncrasies as compelling dictates of conscience cannot expect the state to serve their caprice via actively granting them an exemption from general laws, although their sincerely held consistent belief will most likely be still protected as an instance of negative liberty (as protection from state interference).

101 Heiner Bielefeldt and Michael Wiener, *Religious Freedom Under Scrutiny* (Philadelphia, PA: Pennsylvania University Press, 2019), p. 76.

102 Immanuel Kant, 'Religion within the Boundaries of Mere Reason', in Allen Wood and George di Giovanni (trans and eds.), *Religion within the Boundaries of Mere Reason, and Other Writings* (Cambridge: CUP, (1793) 1998), pp. 37 194.

103 Mari Stenlund and Pamela Slotte, '*Forum Internum* Revisited: Considering the Absolute Core of Freedom of Belief and Opinion in Terms of Negative Liberty, Authenticity, and Capability', *Human Rights Review* 19 (2018), 425.

104 *Kalaç* (n 23).

To counter the systemic disadvantage woven into the fabric of the secular legal order proper respect for the essential manifestations of sincerely held religious beliefs calls for a *two-stage inquiry*. The first stage assesses whether the general rule limiting freedom of religion is a necessary and proportional restriction and whether it serves compelling or at least important state (public) interests (depending on the legal tradition of the different jurisdictions). Exceptionally, relying on a substantive review of legislation the ECtHR found that restricting freedom of religion by generally applicable (criminal) law without reasonable and objective justification is unacceptable.[105] The ECtHR also considers the necessity of the general law that restricts freedom of religion. This does not necessarily mean a compelling state reason in the US sense but at least requires a serious interest that cannot be achieved with lesser restriction.

If the limitation is justifiable, the second stage is devoted to assessing whether an exemption from generally applicable rules is appropriate, to ensure that the burden on conscience is not "particularly painful" (Justice Sachs) or "substantial" (RFRA). The second stage of the accommodation inquiry is not about assessing religious compliance or doctrinal knowledge, as that would violate the secular non-involvement (neutrality) requirement. Ultimately, judicial approaches investigating the sincerity of essential manifestations tend to focus on assessing the objective importance of a religious belief for the applicant. The disregard of trivial beliefs cannot cause extreme pain by objective standards. Here the emphasis is often on preventing abuse and mockery by the claimant under the guise of a conscience claim. Special treatment in the form of reasonable accommodation is appropriate in the sense of requiring the applicant to show that a religious manifestation is rationally connected to the protected belief.[106]

This can be determined, for instance, by taking the consistency requirement seriously and requiring the applicant to show that the manifestation is indeed required by the teachings or tenets of her religion or is a standard practice in her faith community. The religious reasonableness (justification) of the personal view becomes dubious when a religious conscience claim is not supported by hard evidence of community standards or authoritative text/interpretation (authoritative by the community's own standards) and where the connection between the alleged command of conscience and the religious position is convoluted. A judicial consideration of the existence of a rational connection between the existence of moral principles and the desired rule-breaking exception is not a matter of religious doctrinal knowledge. The ECtHR looks for a "sufficiently close and direct nexus" between the precept of faith and the applicant's conduct (act or omission).[107] A "remote connection" is not sufficient.

105 *Thlimmenos* (n 20), para 44.
106 *Eweida* (n 19), para 82.
107 *Eweida* (n 19), para 82, with references to earlier case law: 'the existence of a sufficiently close and direct nexus between the act and the underlying belief must be determined on the

While the assessment of these criteria draws most attention (and disagreement), there are several important considerations at this state that mitigate the risk of an absolutist accommodation.

Firstly, the nature of the generally applicable law (e. g. the attached sanction, the intensity of the governmental coercion, the choice left) and the resulting burden on the believer matter for avoiding excessive accommodation. Paradigmatic conscience cases like refusal of armed military service are about very heavy government-imposed coercive burdens. Being ready to face imprisonment gives a strong impression of the sincerity and determination of the applicant. Social acceptance has normative effects in law. Conscience claims that "merit" accommodations are made socially credible by the weight of personal sacrifice (as with Jehovah's Witnesses going to jail and concentration camps). Finally, the gravity of the sanction is one of two elements of the nexus requirement.

A second line of limiting considerations comes from the specific context (employment, supply of goods and services, health, education, etc.) in which the believer seeks accommodation. The legal characterization (nature) of the environment matters, too (i.e. whether a public or a private authority commands the situation). Public interests (diffuse interests of a community, of users, etc.) do generate different common needs and expectations and determine whose rights, values and interests are to be taken into consideration when a religious right is limited. Although the horizontal effect of the constitution remains contested, liberalism (or at least liberal constitutionalism) had to accept that interference in the private sphere is legitimate for the public interest to maintain public order and even for sustaining constitutional values.

The standard logic of human rights protection is reversed every time a believer has to assert a claim for religious accommodation. Normally, the restriction of a fundamental right is an exception that has to be justified by the party that imposes a limitation. In the case of reasonable accommodation, the believer carries the burden of justifying a request for an exemption. The private (voluntary or contractual) nature of employment relations is used to justify the reversal of the burden of justification. Yet employment relations are rarely ever freely undertaken contractual relations: there is a power imbalance and – given hard economic constraints – a job is not necessarily taken as a matter of free choice of vocation. Given the governmental regulation of employment – and in many jurisdictions, the horizontal applicability of the constitution in private relations – this reversal of burdens is not convincing.

It follows that while the principle of accommodation is still valid, as private relations cannot force individuals to forego their religion, the level of such protection depends on the impact of the religious conduct on other rights

facts of each case . . . . [A]cts or omissions which do not directly express the belief concerned or which are only remotely connected to a precept of faith fall outside the protection of Article 9 § 1'.

at stake in concrete (special) situations. Religious freedom is a fundamental right exactly because of its negative spill-over effect: it inevitably burdens others. (Offensive speech is protected; demonstrations and strikes are lawful nuisances.) Requiring an employer to prove that individual accommodation would impose a more-than-minimal burden on the business does not afford sufficient weight to religious freedom. More importantly, once the state enters into regulating these private and semi-private relations, it has a duty to ensure accommodation at the level of generally applicable rules *wherever possible.* At a minimum, the state must specifically signpost religious considerations applicable to the situation it regulates, not leaving the matter up to individual conflicts and litigation that will inevitably burden the believer.

Finally, there are instances where the duty of accommodation simply does not apply. Accommodation is appropriate only where religious manifestation respects the public order (i.e. it can be assumed that the followers of a religious command will not engage in large-scale civil disobedience, just like free speech will not result in sedition and mutiny). A related precondition of accommodation is that the religious commands should not go against the fundamentals of liberal order (no human sacrifice is allowed).

1. Under no circumstances should accommodation become the source of public power contrary to the separation of church and state or state neutrality.[108]

As the *Refah Partisi* case (the ban on an Islamic Party in Turkey) indicates, there is no place for accommodation for political conduct where religion motivates political action or creates a parallel legal system incompatible with the democratic order. In *Leyla Sahin*,[109] where an exception was claimed for a politically innocent matter (wearing a headscarf at a university exam), accommodation would not be an issue. In *Refah Partisi*, the crux of the problem was that the religiously motivated conduct was clearly related to a politicized religion and promoted, often violently, a religious political movement. The activity of the applicant political party was found incompatible with the democratic constitutional order. While this is not present in the judgment, the same Islamist interpretation of the alleged religious command regarding female modesty and the political movement that insisted on this interpretation forced women to wear the headscarf in Eastern Turkey in schools, and teachers were regularly attacked on the street for not wearing the headscarf. A religion and the beliefs inspired by religion must not be contrary to what is minimally necessary for coexistence in a democratic society.

2. Further, enhanced protection should not entail discriminatory advantage to religious persons.

108 In this spirit under the Establishment Clause see *Kiryas Joel* (n 67) (religious community was granted municipal powers enabling exclusively religious education. The Constitution allows the State to accommodate religious needs by alleviating special burdens, but the scheme crosses the line from permissible accommodation to impermissible establishment).

109 *Leyla Şahin* (n 23).

For example, there is no right for more protection against expressions of disapproval or displays of dislike than against non-religious dislike. If people motivated by religious convictions can protest in front of an abortion clinic, they cannot claim that people who consider religion harmful or irrational cannot express such views in front of a temple or church.

3. In the liberal tradition, harm to others resulting from religious command is ultimately unacceptable, even if it follows religious precepts. Only conduct that is not actually (demonstrably) harmful to others (or violates their rights)[110] shall be accommodated. A neutral state cannot refuse to recognize the Church of Flat Earth. Yet, a parent who sincerely believes in Flat Earth cannot deny her child's attendance of science classes that explain that the Earth is round and revolves around the Sun.

Beyond harm, other third-party effects are also to be considered, particularly direct and actual restrictions of the rights of others, especially fundamental rights. When granting a religious exception, the effect on third parties is to be taken in consideration.[111] "Granting an exemption from social security taxes to an employer operates to impose the employer's religious faith on the employees," and more importantly it deprives them of a statutory benefit.[112]

The effect on third parties is an important consideration, although fundamental rights imply the acceptance of a certain level of burdening third parties: a demonstration is a traffic inconvenience, offensive speech is endured, etc. General laws on road traffic cannot disregard freedom of assembly, and traffic and commuters must accept the disadvantage they suffer due to this right. A general law on monument protection cannot be used to ban demonstrations in the historic city centre simply because each building is protected there. Reasonable *legislative* accommodation means that the monument protection act should specify that peaceful assembly is one of the activities permitted in historic heritage sites where traffic restrictions are otherwise necessary.[113]

110 This is what makes *Hobby Lobby* (n 39) highly problematic: the conscience-based claim, based on a weak indirect effect on the taxpayers' religious conviction, restricted (indirectly) the reproductive rights of others at a time when these others had a constitutionally recognized privacy (reproductive) right.

111 See in this sense John Locke, *A Letter Concerning Toleration and Other Writings*, ed. Mark Goldie (Carmel, IN: Liberty Fund, 2010), p. 43. Locke refers to 'being of other church' but this can be replaced with other fundamental identity markers (e.g. gender).

112 *United States v Lee*, 455 US 252, 261 (1982). *Hobby Lobby* (n 39) goes beyond what is reasonable in its accommodation: the conscience-based claim, based on a weak indirect effect on the taxpayers' religious conviction, restricted (indirectly) the reproductive rights of others. (At the time the case was decided these 'others' had a constitutionally recognized privacy (reproductive) right.)

113 On the enormous potential of general laws to discriminate and being abused in the context of 'anti-extremist' legislation see *Taganrog LRO and Others v Russia*, Application nos. 32401/10 and 19 others, Judgment of 7 June 2022. Criminal laws on racism often have exceptions favouring special forms of expression (like art) and similar treatment is due to religious manifestation.

In most cases, granting a religious exception is not discriminatory against the non-believer *as such*, as there is no significant burden: allowing the sacramental consumption of peyote does not impose any *additional* burden on drug users who are subject to criminal sanctions (they are not worse off). Accommodation satisfies Pareto optimality, even if other drug users feel that they are less respected than religious drug users. A reorganization of working days in favour of Sabbath observers that imposes extra burden of Sabbath work on others within the limits of labour law can be justified, as the underlying contractual employment relation grants the employer the power to set working conditions in line with the general needs of the workplace. This is Pareto suboptimal, but a matter of lawful and justified discretion.

4. Accommodation does not apply where the religious claim would prescribe the behaviour of others (especially non-believers and those who are not part of the religious community). "Accommodation of religion upholds the religious freedom of the person accommodated but may simultaneously undermine the freedom of religion and belief of another."[114]

5. Accommodation is impermissible where the general law enforces a constitutional imperative. This was, at least arguably, the case with the prohibition of polygamy,[115] but not in the case of unemployment benefit[116] (*Sherbert*).

With all these caveats, reasonable accommodation remains the proper standard regarding genuine religious belief claims, rooted in conscience for liberal secularism.

Conclusion

Legislation and judicial decisions in many liberal democracies give limited weight to freedom of religion when it comes to balancing it against other social concerns. Moreover, accommodations are gradually denied to religious believers in certain areas where they used to be traditionally granted. Animal welfare protection to the detriment of ritual slaughter is the current paradigmatic example in Europe. This trivialization and reluctant protection of individual religious freedom result from the structure of the secular legal order which relies on and trusts neutral laws of general applicability. Quite often, when a general law is enacted its impacts on religious freedom are not considered, or the burden on religious freedom is treated as incidental by the "neutral" legislator. Restrictions of individual freedom of religion are handled as collateral damage at best if they are registered at all.

Non-liberal secularism normalizes the disregard of religious concerns in generally applicable laws, holding that neutrality requires a religion-blind

114 Lucy Vickers, *Religious Freedom, Religious Discrimination and the Workplace*, 2nd edn (London: Bloomsbury, 2016), p. 225.

115 *Reynolds v US*, 98 US 145 (1879).

116 *Sherbert v Verner*, 374 US 398 (1963).

approach within government[117] and wherever the state is engaged in enforcing its policies (unless it concerns a majority religious organization). Some form of balancing takes place only where the general law singles out a religion (having a disparate effect).

Such disregard often stems partly from non-religious (secular) social mentalities, although the structure of the law and adjudication are not negligible, either. Moreover, the liberal order does not live up to its promises:[118] it favours collective religious rights, mostly within churches, thereby tolerating illiberal enclaves (values) and at the same time disregarding individual rights. Liberal myopia has well-known negative practical consequences for minority and non-traditional religions. Given the structural disadvantages inherent in a modern secular legal order, the secular liberal legal order is obliged (and capable) to afford proper recognition to religious freedom and provide enhanced protection to individual freedom of religion (including exceptionalism in the form of reasonable accommodation).

Deference towards generally applicable laws and locally imposed solutions reverses the standard methodology of fundamental rights protection: where the law or other local acts (e.g. workplace rules and decisions) interfere with a fundamental right, the burden is on the state to prove the necessity of the interference. Free exercise rights should not be squeezed into discrimination law, and reasonable accommodation shall apply both at the legislative and local level, as the possibility of local accommodation does not eliminate the burden of rights enforcement that disadvantages the believer. The current standards of accommodation centring on undue burden do not grant proper weight to individual religious freedom.

Undeniably, there can be no rule of law and equality without laws being generally applicable. But fundamental rights and human rights are recognized as being above the power of the state and the general laws and the structure of law must respect them. To avoid a situation where accommodation

117 See e.g, Quebec Religious Accommodation Law (Bill 62, 2017), Explanatory Note: 'The purpose of this Act is to establish measures to foster adherence to State religious neutrality. For that purpose, . . . personnel members of public bodies must demonstrate religious neutrality in the exercise of their functions'. The law singles out face coverings and applies to those who seek government services (students, patients, etc.) Religion-based exceptions can be negotiated at the service level upon request.

118 At the same time practical illiberal historical concessions favouring traditionally powerful religious organizations provide (collective) accommodation and counter the disadvantages of secularism. The autonomy of churches provides space for religiously inspired conduct. Collective accommodation is the name of the game, raising genuine concerns of discrimination. If believers wish to educate their children in the faith, the state will guarantee denominational schools. If the religion dictates that people help co-religionists, they can do it within their community; if they wish to provide health services for the poor they can work in denominational hospitals, etc.

would permit every citizen "to become a law unto himself," the state's duty to provide accommodation for religious freedom shall apply only where

- the choice between the two commands is intensely burdensome (substantial burden) to raise an assumption that this is a matter of conscience;
- the dictate of conscience is not trivial (or "delusional") and is demonstrably related to a religion (or other comprehensive life plan);
- a direct nexus exists between the religious command and the individual conduct;
- the conduct does not impose a disproportionate burden on the fundamental and statutory rights of others and is not destructive to constitutional order.

3 Conscientious objection to unconstitutional duties

A conceptual trap

Fernando Simón-Yarza

Introduction

In recent years, there has been a proliferation in Spanish legislation of conflicts of conscience in the face of legislation that raises serious bioethical concerns. Thus, for example, Article 16 of Organic Law 3/2021, regulating euthanasia, provides for the creation of a register of physicians that places severe restrictions on freedom of conscience. Along the same lines, Article 19, paragraph 1, of the Organic Law 2/2010 of 3 March on sexual and reproductive health and voluntary termination of pregnancy (introduced by Organic Law 1/2023 of 28 February), has also provided for the creation of a register of objectors in the following terms:

> For organisational purposes and for the proper management of the service, a register shall be created in each autonomous community and in the National Institute for Health Management (INGESA) of health professionals who decide to object for reasons of conscience with respect to direct intervention in the practice of voluntary termination of pregnancy.

The establishment of a register of health professionals objecting to abortion has given rise to an important political and legal debate in the past, and such a register was endorsed by the Spanish Constitutional Court Judgment (CCJ) 151/2014 of 2 September,[1] and more recently, by CCJ 44/2023 of

1 Article 19.2 of *Organic Law 2/2010 of 3 March, on sexual and reproductive health and voluntary termination of pregnancy* originally regulated conscientious objection to abortion as follows: 'health professionals directly involved in the voluntary termination of pregnancy will have the right to exercise conscientious objection without access to and quality of care being impaired by the exercise of conscientious objection. The refusal to perform the termination of pregnancy for reasons of conscience is always an individual decision of the health personnel directly involved in the performance of the voluntary termination of pregnancy, which must be expressed in advance and in writing'. In development of this regulation, the Parliament of Navarra approved the *Foral Law 16/2010, of November 8, creating the register of professionals objecting to abortion*. This statute was challenged before the Constitutional Court by 50 deputies of the Popular Group in Congress. Over three years later, the Constitutional Court issued a

DOI: 10.4324/9781003502845-3

9 May.[2] Nevertheless, the debate should not be considered closed because of these decisions. On the contrary, the content of the rulings presents an opportunity to reflect on the very meaning of conscientious objection. As is well known, it is an institution originally linked to military conscription, in which it was originally conceived as an exemption from the constitutional civic duty to defend one's country. According to this understanding, conscientious objection is explicitly protected in the Spanish Constitution.[3] This is also how it has been understood in comparative law.[4]

Inevitably, considering the circumvention of a mandate for reasons of conscience in this way – as a circumvention of a juridical duty – is very problematic when the conduct imposed is not a *constitutional* duty – that is, a duty expressly recognised by the Constituent and, therefore, legally unquestionable – but a *legal* mandate, subordinate to the Constitution. In this case, the very idea of considering resistance to the law as exceptional conduct *per definitionem* runs the risk of subordinating freedom of conscience to the imperative of the legislator, regardless of its content. Conscience must then pass the test of reasonableness in order to be exempted from legal mandates, while the legislator is excused from passing any test of respect for freedom of conscience when defining the duties of citizens. The definition of the objection as an "exemption from a legal duty" implies what we could call a "conceptual presumption" of the legitimacy of the objected mandate. Insofar as the existence of the "legal duty" is assumed as a precondition of the objection, the objector can only aspire to request the exemption from it, but cannot go so far as to question, as an objector, the legitimacy of the said "duty".

In the case of a legal mandate, in order to speak of an objection, the constitutional legitimacy of the duty itself must first be examined – even when the duty is purportedly imposed to civil servants who are subordinated to the

ruling on September 25, 2014, which *dismissed almost all the claims of the appellants*. However, a dissenting opinion by Judge Ollero Tassara asserted that the Register of objectors violates freedom of conscience. For a more detailed commentary on CCJ 151/2014, see my own essay: '¿Exención de un *deber* de abortar? Sobre el registro navarro de objetores y el concepto de objeción de conciencia', *Revista Jurídica de Navarra* 58 (2014), 159–180.

2 CCJ 44/2023, Gr. n. 9.

3 Art 30 CE: '1. Spaniards have the right and duty to defend Spain. The law shall establish the military obligations of Spaniards and shall regulate, with due guarantees, conscientious objection, as well as other causes for exemption from compulsory military service, being able to impose, where appropriate, a substitute social service'.

4 *Vid.* e.g. K. Greenwalt, *Religion and the Constitution* (Princeton: Princeton University Press, 2009), pp. 49–67; *see* also P. Bock, 'Conscientious Objection', in N. J. Young (ed.), *The Oxford International Encyclopedia of Peace* (Oxford and New York: Oxford University Press, 2010), online version at: www.oxfordreference.com; Ö. Heval Çinar, *Conscientious Objection to Military Service in International Human Rights Law* (New York: Palgrave MacMillan, 2013), pp. 21ff; and K. Brownlee, 'Conscientious Objection, Civil Disobedience', in A. Marmor (ed.), *The Routledge Companion to Philosophy of Law* (New York and London: Routledge, 2011), pp. 531–532. The use of the term began to spread in the late nineteenth century, and especially during World War I, to describe peaceful resistance to military conscription.

Administration by a specific principle of hierarchy (art. 103.1 Spanish Constitution). In order to admit an objection to a legal duty, we must first verify the constitutionality of the said duty. Thus, treating as an objection any kind of opposition to the law for reasons of conscience is plainly unacceptable. If we admit this, freedom of conscience is distorted as a fundamental right, or, in other words, it ceases to be a constitutional limit to which the legislator's mandates must be submitted in order to be qualified as legal duties. Rather than a refuge for objectors, freedom of conscience as recognised by Article 16.1 of the Spanish Constitution is a limit to the legislator.

This is, in my opinion, the main shortcoming of several analyses of the so-called "conscientious objection to abortion", including that of the Constitutional Court Judgments 151/2014 and 44/2023. Starting from an inadequate analogy with the exemption from a constitutional duty such as that of defending one's own nation, resistance to abortion is treated as if it were an exemption from a constitutional duty, that is, presupposing the legitimacy of such a duty.[5] But as I have said, according to the very meaning of fundamental freedoms,[6] it is not the conscience of the individual, but the state power, which must first justify itself. Furthermore, in a pluralist society, when the public authorities establish obligations whose content is morally repugnant to a broad sector of the population, the reasons of conscience of those who refuse to observe such conduct cannot be given an underprivileged *status*, even when those who refuse to observe it are civil servants subject to a special subordination to the State.[7] We cannot concede – as the Spanish Constitutional Court Judgments 151/2014 and 44/2023 did – a legal duty to perform abortions, since such a duty collides with what, for countless physicians, constitutes a multi-secular obligation of conscience that it would be gravely unjust to

5 Understandably, some authors are reluctant to speak of conscientious objection in cases such as abortion (*see,* in this regard, the opinions expressed in M. Cebriá García, 'Objeción de conciencia del personal sanitario y reformas legislativas en España', *Revista General de Derecho Canónico y Derecho Eclesiástico del Estado* 27 (2011), 11 ff.). Other authors criticise the conception of objection as an exceptional event (in this sense, *e.g.,* R. Navarro-Valls and J. Martínez-Torrón, *Conflictos entre conciencia y ley* (Madrid: Iustel, 2011), pp. 34 ff.). Underlying both reactions, we can perceive a rejection of the idea that any legal duty can be imposed and, therefore, that resistance to the law must necessarily be presented as an exception to a duty.

6 On the asymmetry between 'juridically constituted' freedoms and 'juridically attributed' public powers, *see* E. Schmidt-Aßmann, *Das allgemeine Verwaltungsrecht als Ordnungsidee*, 2nd edn (Heidelberg: Springer, 2004), pp. 13–15.

7 The expansion of conscientious objections – some authors have spoken of a *'big-bang'* – cannot be attributed simply to the fraud of those who seek to circumvent legislation, but is mainly due to other factors relevant to making a value judgment regarding rights: the growth of the legislator's intervention in social life, cultural and religious pluralism, the *de facto* adoption of many political decisions at the supranational level, etc. In this regard, *see* R. Navarro-Valls and J. Martínez-Torrón, *Conflictos entre conciencia y ley* (Madrid: Iustel, 2011).

transgress.[8] In the words of one of the founders of modern liberal political thought, "if society issues wrong mandates instead of right, or any mandates at all in things with which it ought not to meddle, it practices a social tyranny more formidable than many kinds of political oppression . . . penetrating much more deeply into the details of life, and enslaving the soul itself".[9]

Conscientious objection and political judgment on subjective beliefs

As Joseph Raz has stated, the defence of the right to conscientious objection is linked to a reflection on the nature of liberalism, since a liberal State necessarily takes into account the ethical convictions of its citizens and considers it a moral good not to require them to adopt attitudes that would betray their own principles, as long as such principles are deemed worthy of some consideration and respect. Notwithstanding the necessary nuances, Raz has pointedly said that, at least *a priori*, it seems that "a state is liberal only if it includes laws to the effect that no man shall be liable for breach of duty if his breach is committed because he thinks that it is morally wrong for him to obey the law on the ground that it is morally bad or wrong totally or in part".[10] Though related to the natural law tradition, the right to conscientious objection does not entail an immediate appeal to natural law, as is sometimes assumed. When conscientious objection is defended, it is not a supra-positive right that is invoked, but a safeguard that, enshrined as a fundamental right in the positive-legal order, exempts the objector from fulfilling another normative mandate which would otherwise be imposed. It is, therefore, a genuinely liberal institution, whereby positive law – based on moral reasons – declares the inviolability of certain dictates of individual conscience, even over and above other norms of the legal system.

Conscientious objection as a general (not absolute) right

Obviously, making the objection absolute would on the one hand allow its abusive use in order to avoid any duty that may be deemed as onerous, and on the other hand, it would bestow on subjective sensitivity an inadmissible weight, even when society has a legitimate interest in demanding uniform

8 Such obligation was solemnly fixed by Hippocrates in the 5th century BC. Since then, countless physicians honor it as a most serious obligation *of conscience:* 'I swear by Apollo, physician, by Asclepius, and by Hygieia and Panacea, and by all the gods and goddesses of Olympus, taking them as witnesses, to keep this oath according to my ability and my conscience: . . . I will never provide any woman with an abortifacient pessary, even if she asks me for it'.

9 J. Stuart Mill, *On Liberty* (Boston: James R. Osgood & Co., (1859) 1871), pp. 13–14.

10 J. Raz, 'A Right to Dissent? Conscientious Objection', in *The Authority of Law*, 2nd edn (Oxford: Oxford University Press, 2009), p. 276.

compliance with the law.[11] Nevertheless, the right to conscientious objection constitutes a guarantee included in article 16.1 of the Spanish Constitution. As the Constitutional Court has stated in its Judgment 53/1985, "it is part of the content of the fundamental right to religious freedom recognised in art. 16.1 of the Constitution" and is therefore "directly applicable".[12] The fact that it is not an absolute right does not make it more problematic than any other fundamental right. Its application must be preceded, of course, by a weighing that considers both the social importance of the legal mandate and the authenticity and seriousness of the convictions of those who oppose its observance. But this weighing and these value judgments are not entirely exclusive to conscientious objection: the recognition of a constitutionally protected freedom of expression, for example, also requires a value judgment on the content of what is expressed and on the social costs of admitting certain types of expression. Just as the fact that not all expression is constitutionally protected does not require us to make freedom of expression *a priori* problematic, neither can conscientious objection be questioned on the grounds that it may be exercised abusively. *Abusus non tollit usum.*

Some authors have pointed toward a dangerous – and in my view wrongly construed – *reductio ad absurdum*: we should not admit a general right to conscientious objection, for it would lead to the dissolution of the whole legal system. This *reductio ad absurdum* was suggested in the eighties by the Spanish Constitutional Court itself: "conscientious objection in general, that is, a right to be exempted from the fulfilment of constitutional or legal duties for being that fulfilment contrary to one's convictions, is neither recognised nor imaginable to be recognised in our legal system nor in any legal system, since that would mean the denial of the very idea of state. What could happen is that it may be exceptionally admitted, with respect to one particular duty."[13]

In my opinion, the Constitutional Court mistakes here an "absolute" right with a "general" right; that is, with a right *simpliciter*, without any further specification in its abstract *prima facie* formulation. All legal mandates are subordinated to multiple constitutional "general" rights which, absolutely affirmed, would lead to "the denial of the very idea of state". If, by declaring that a *general* right to conscientious objection does not exist, the Court wants to express the view that an *absolute* right to conscientious objection does not exist, we could simply reply that this must be applied to any abstract constitutional right. An absolute right to conscientious objection – the same as an absolute right to freedom of speech, or to privacy, or to freedom and

11 In the same sense, e.g., Raz himself, op. cit., pp. 282 et seq.; and J. Rawls, *A Theory of Justice* (Cambridge: The Belknap Press of Harvard University Press, 1971), p. 370.

12 CCJ 53/1985, Gr. n. 14. On the jurisprudential evolution in relation to the so-called objection to abortion, *see* M. Domingo Gutiérrez, 'La objeción de conciencia al aborto. Evolución jurisprudencial', *Revista General de Derecho Canónico y Derecho Eclesiástico del Estado* 23 (2010).

13 Constitutional Court Judgment 161/1987, Ground 3.

security, or to equality, etc. – "is neither recognised nor imaginable to be recognised". By contrast, a general right to conscientious objection is perfectly imaginable, and does not necessarily lead to the disappearance of the idea of state. Between the postulate of an "absolute" right to conscientious objection and the postulate of a "general" right (or a right "*simpliciter*") there is a great difference that the Constitutional Court seems to overlook. All legal mandates are subordinated to multiple fundamental rights "of a general nature" which, if affirmed as absolute rights, would lead to "the very denial of the idea of the State". Thus, if by arguing that there is no general right to object, the Court intends to establish the non-existence of an *absolute* right to object, we must reply that this is true of almost all fundamental rights. An absolute right to object – just like an absolute right to freedom of expression, or to privacy, or to liberty and security, etc. – "is neither recognised nor can it be imagined to be so", but a general right to object is perfectly imaginable and need not lead to the disappearance of the idea of the State.

In fact, the general right to "conscientious objection" is becoming increasingly important in our pluralist societies, given the serious division among questions of conscience. Western societies are going through a profound crisis of values that leads many to seek refuge in religion in the face of the pressure of the dominant relativistic ideology. To this we must add that a genuinely liberal society, in the most classical sense, must be sensitive to the conscience of its minorities, weighing the relative weight of this sensitivity against the importance of uniform compliance with a given set of rules. In recent years, the U.S. Supreme Court has become increasingly respectful towards freedom of conscience. By way of example, in the important case *Burwell v Hobby Lobby*, it has prevented the federal government from forcing employers to fund abortifacient drugs for their employees. This decision has had a major impact in other countries, although it has not failed to find critics who – I think wrongly – consider more important the "right" to the abortion pill – lacking any constitutional coverage – than the guarantee of indemnity of one's own conscience.[14] Another interesting issue, decided not long ago, was the U.S. Supreme Court decision to protect the right to religious liberty of a Denver cake baker who refused to perform a personalised cake service – a custom artistic cake – for a same-sex wedding.[15]

A general right to conscientious objection is not only practicable, but increasingly necessary in our pluralist societies. The just measure of such a

14 *Burwell v Hobby Lobby Stores Inc.*, of 30 June 2014 (573 US 682). In Spain, the Constitutional Court has declared unconstitutional a €3300 fine imposed to a pharmacist by the Government of Andalucía for refusing to deliver emergency contraceptives (CCJ 145/2015, of June 25). The same freedom has been recognised in other countries of the Council of Europe, although its relevance for the Convention has been denied, strikingly, by the European Court of Human Rights *(Decision Pichon and Sajous v France*, of 2 October 2001).

15 *Masterpiece Cakeshop, Ltd., et al., Petitioners v Colorado Civil Rights Commission, et al.*, of 4 June 2018.

right depends ultimately on the structure and content of the reasoning that leads from the *prima facie* positions – the abstractly formulated right – to the definitive positions – the concretely recognised fundamental-legal power. It is the task of legal theory to channel, through conceptual forms, the structure of reasoning that advances from *prima facie* rights to definitive legal positions, without it being possible, obviously, to completely eliminate the value judgment.[16] If we accepted the thesis denying the existence of an abstract or general right to conscientious objection, the collision between subjective conviction and legal mandate would inexorably be solved in favour of the legislator, regardless of the seriousness of the objection and the social importance of a uniform compliance with the legal obligation.

It is appropriate to recall Hegel's comment on the value of the "tribunal of conscience" *(Tribunal des Gewissens)*, commenting on the trial of Socrates. The great philosopher of German idealism maintained that "no people" can recognise such a tribunal above the State: "If you are conscious of having fulfilled your duty, we [the people] too must be conscious of having fulfilled it."[17] Strictly speaking, this statement by Hegel in no way contradicts the existence of a right to conscientious objection as a liberal institution, since such a right consists precisely in the fact that the state recognises, due to the seriousness of someone's convictions, that he has not failed in his duty by exempting himself from a legal duty. In this sense, "conscientious objection" is essentially different from "civil disobedience", which is characterised precisely by the fact that it is not recognised by the legal system. Civil disobedience is based on the appeal to natural law *above and against* positive law. In compliance with natural law, the citizen who invokes "civil disobedience" refuses to observe positive law. The citizen who disobeys chooses not to betray his or her own conscience.[18]

16 See in this vein R. Alexy, *Theorie der Grundrechte* (Frankfurt am Main: Suhrkamp, 1986), pp. 90–92.

17 Hegel, *Vorlesungen über die Geschichte der Philosophie*, in Hegel's Werke, Vol. XIV (Berlin: Dunker & Humblot, 1833), p. 114: 'Aber kein Volk, am wenigsten ein freies Volk (und von dieser Freiheit wie das athenisches Volk) hat ein Tribunal des Gewissens anzuerkennen; dies kennt kein Bewußtsein, seine Pflicht erfüllt zu haben, als das Bewußtsein, das *es* hat. "Wenn du das Bewußtsein hast, deine Pflicht erfüllt zu haben, so müssen auch wir dies Bewußtsein haben, daß du sie erfüllt hast"'.

18 There are famous historical and literary examples of this type of resistance, from Sophocles' Antigone to the story of Chapter VII of the Second Book of the Maccabees, the episodes of resistance to the Nazi regime, the peaceful resistance of Gandhi and Luther King, or the clandestine activities of the persecuted Catholic Church in China. Against the opinion of those who say that in a democracy there is no room for examples of disobedience such as those described, it is worth recalling a beautiful passage from the famous philosopher of democracy Alexis de Tocqueville: 'A nation is like a jury charged with representing universal society and applying justice, which is its law. Should the jury, which represents society, have more power than the very society whose laws it applies? Thus, when I refuse to obey an unjust law, I do not deny to the majority the right to command; I do nothing but appeal against the sovereignty of the people before the sovereignty of the human race'. *(Democracy in America* I, Part II, Ch. 7)

This is not the case with conscientious objection, which is a general (not absolute) right, duly recognised by the legal order.

The specific complexity of conscientious objection

The peculiarity of conscientious objection lies, as Rawls has pointed out and Raz has clearly indicated, in the fact that the law exempts a person from fulfilling a *duty* out of respect for a belief that is *not widely shared by society*. By doing this, the State takes seriously the private beliefs of an individual who is morally compelled not to fulfil an otherwise valid legal obligation.[19] What distinguishes conscientious objection compared to other constitutional rights is that *the value judgment it entails is particularly complex*. On the one hand, it must be admitted that the legal duty to which the objection is invoked is legitimate, i.e., that it constitutes an imposition that, as such, does not infringe on any right of citizens – in particular *freedom of conscience*. On the other hand, however, it must be recognised that, despite not being socially shared, the moral scruples of those who object have such *subjective* strength and seriousness that the legal mandate must give way in their case. The objection is recognised *despite* the objective implausibility – from the perspective of society – of the moral reservations invoked. That is precisely the reason why it constitutes a genuinely liberal institution. Thus, the logic of the objection can be analytically examined as follows:

a) *If the moral reservation of the objector were socially considered to be true*, it would not be possible to speak of conscientious objection, because the obligation would be plainly considered unjust by the whole of society. Therefore, such an obligation would directly violate the right to moral integrity of the citizens.

b) *If the moral reservation of the objector were socially considered objectively plausible (although not necessarily true)*, it would not be possible to speak of conscientious objection either, because it would not be possible to impose a legal duty on a matter about whose morality serious objections can be raised, with well-founded reasons. In a liberal society, such a "legal duty" would violate *freedom of conscience* and would be unconstitutional. As I will argue, this is the framework in which – at the very least – the refusal to perform an abortion should be analysed, and that is why we should not speak of "conscientious objection".

c) The discourse of "conscientious objection" always implies the possibility of imposing such a legal duty. Thus, it entails a positive social judgment regarding the morality of the conduct required by this duty and, consequently, an openly sceptical social judgment regarding the objector's

19 J. Raz, op. cit. In a similar sense, Rawls says that 'conscientious refusal' is distinguished by the fact that the objector does not appeal to the convictions of the majority (*A Theory of Justice*, op. cit., p. 369).

reservations. If, notwithstanding this, the fundamental right to object is recognised, this is because in a liberal, pluralist state, respect for subjective sensitivity is sometimes more pressing than the uniform fulfilment of the legal duties objected to. The weighing that precedes the concrete recognition of a right to object consists precisely in discerning whether the scruples of the objectors are worthier of protection than the mandate of a uniform rule for everybody. Needless to say, the paradigmatic example is the objection to military service, although there are many other analogous cases. Thus, for example, the famous American *salute flag cases*, in which the Supreme Court of the United States upheld the claim of Jehovah's Witness students who refused to say the "pledge of allegiance" for religious reasons.[20] What makes it possible to consider this type of case as a "conscientious objection" is the fact that the pledge of allegiance may legitimately be imposed as a civic duty. Another similar case is found in *Wooley v Maynard*,[21] in which the Supreme Court protected the right of Jehovah's Witnesses not to include their state motto – in this case that of New Hampshire: "*live free or die*" – on their car license plates because it clashes with their religious convictions. Here again, Jehovah's Witnesses appeal to reasons not shared by the general public, but the *subjective seriousness* of their belief contrasts with the *objective insignificance* of the consequences of non-compliance, and therein lies the justification for the objection. Of particular difficulty are those cases in which both serious *subjective* moral reasons and serious *objective* social reasons compete. Thus, for example, in the controversial decision *Employment Division v Smith*, the U.S. Supreme Court held that it was lawful to deny unemployment benefits to a person dismissed from his employer for using *peyote*, a drug that certain native tribes use as part of a religious ritual. The Supreme Court held that the State was *entitled*, but not *required*, to accommodate the *subjective* reasons of native Americans who use peyote as part of their rituals.[22]

20 *West Virginia State Board of Education v Barnette*, of 14 June 1943 (319 US 624). This Judgment overruled a previous decision in the case *Minersville School District v Gobitis*, of 3 June 1940 (310 US 586). *West Virginia* contrasts with the Judgment issued by the European Court of Human Rights in the case *Valsamis and Efstratiou v Greece*, of 18 December 1996. Here, the Strasbourg Court held that the refusal of two Jehovah's Witness girls to participate in the national parade – which led to their expulsion from the school for one and two days respectively – was not covered by their right to religious freedom.

21 *Wooley v Maynard*, of 20 April 1977 (430 US 705).

22 *Employment Division Department of Human Resources of Oregon v Smith*, of 17 April 1990 (494 US 872). On this decision and its consequences, see S. Girgis, R. Anderson and J. Corvino, *Debating Religious Liberty and Discrimination* (New York: Oxford University Press, 2017), pp. 14 ff.

The refusal to perform abortions: an exemption from a legal duty?

The reflections developed in the previous section allow us to question the entire approach of CCJs 151/2014 and 44/2023 to the problem of the conscientious objection to abortion. The very qualification of resistance to abortion as an "exemption from a legal duty"[23] obscures the reality of the situation, ignoring the broad sector of the population that considers abortion to be morally inadmissible, as well as the reasons why doctors have been refusing to perform abortions. Such considerations are essential to formulate the value judgment that inevitably precedes any recognition of a "definitive position" of a fundamental right. By avoiding them, the case can only be falsely closed.

It should be added that the very idea of "conscientious objection" disguises the problem, since it sounds like an individual guarantee even when it involves a trap for the right-holder. An analytical effort is needed to detect linguistic deviations and erroneous use of the categories. In fact, the Constitutional Court Judgments 151/2014 and 44/2023 never speak openly of a "legal duty to perform an abortion", nor does it even say, in a single sentence, that "refusing to perform an abortion is an exemption from fulfilling a duty". All this is implicitly maintained by the decision, which, starting from the fact that the objection *is* an exemption from a legal duty, it reproduces the language used by the legislator – thus avoiding the horrible expression "duty to perform abortions".[24] However, the fact is that (1) performing the abortion is assumed to be the legal duty of the physician; (2) objecting to the performance of the abortion is assumed to be an exemption from an obligation; and (3) the right not to collaborate in performing abortions is therefore excluded from the principle *favor libertatis* and subjected to burdens like the duty of registration.

The right not to perform abortions against unnecessary and disproportionate burdens

Considering such an inalienable right as the right not to perform abortions – which, according to the *lex artis* of Hippocrates, is also a moral duty, as countless physicians still consider it to be – to be an exemption from a legal duty, violates the "essential content" of freedom of conscience (*see* art. 53.1 Spanish Constitution). However, even supposing that articles 19bis and 19ter LO 2/2010 did not reach its "essential content", both these precepts and the laws creating registers of objectors would, at the very least, constitute an interference with the *prima facie* content of the right. They would have to overcome,

23 STC 151/2014, Gr. n. 5.

24 The greatest clarity of exposition – not free of circumlocution – is found in Grounding 5: 'The exercise of the right [to conscientious objection] implies an exemption from a legal duty linked to the provision of health care for the voluntary interruption of pregnancy in the cases provided for by law'.

therefore, the "principle of proportionality" *(Übermaßverbot)*,[25] which obliges restrictions on rights, as is well known, to be subject to a triple *test* of "suitability" *(Geeignetheit)*, "necessity" *(Erforderlichkeit)*, and "proportionality" in the strict sense *(Verhältnismäßigkeit)*:

a) The *suitability* of the measure to ensure its purpose – the effectiveness and quality of abortion – is beyond dispute. Of course, considering the refusal to have an abortion as an exemption from a legal duty and registering objectors contributes, overall, to ensuring the effectiveness of abortion. The question is, therefore, the *necessity* of the measure and its *proportionality in the strict sense.*

b) The principle of *necessity* requires that the measures restricting fundamental rights be minimally harmful to them; that is, that there are no less burdensome measures that might achieve the end pursued by the restriction. The register of objectors would never have passed the necessity test if it had been applied by the Constitutional Court, since it is not necessary to exercise the objection "in advance and in writing" – as required by the Spanish abortion law.[26] Neither is the declaration "in advance and in writing" – which also interferes with the right to freedom of conscience, since it prevents the so-called "supervening objection"[27] – necessary to ensure its own purpose, namely the effectiveness of the abortion. An alternative to previous declaration and registration of objectors would be, for example, the creation of a register of doctors willing to perform abortions. In the face of this alternative, it cannot be argued that, in that case, few physicians would take the step. The fact that there are no doctors willing to take the step *motu proprio* only confirms the seriousness and objective social truth of the moral reasons of those who refuse to perform an abortion and, therefore, reaffirms the fundamental thesis of this chapter, namely, that the duty to perform an abortion violates the "essential content" of freedom of conscience – which calls into question the constitutionality of both the previous declaration and the register of objectors. If the legislator really believes that abortion is harmless and that the reasons for not performing abortions are objectively implausible, creating a register of doctors willing to abort cannot pose any problem.

25 The character of the *Übermaßverbot* as a constitutional parameter was postulated by Peter Lerche in an important work of the early sixties *(Übermass und Verfassungsrecht*, Heymanns, Cologne – Berlin – Munich – Bonn, 1961) and was expressly assumed, a few years later, by the German Federal Constitutional Court. Today, it is a principle in common use, both in doctrine and in constitutional jurisprudence.

26 I agree with the *opinion of the Council of Navarra* 54/2010, of October 18: 'It is obvious that the lack of a public register does not prevent the exercise of the right, which is why the anticipated formulation of conscientious objection does not necessarily have to be made through the formula of the register'.

27 *See* Cebriá García, op. cit., pp. 23–24, and the bibliography cited therein.

c) Having explained the unnecessary nature of the register, as well as the violation of the "essential content" of freedom of conscience by the norms that subordinate this right to the effectiveness of abortion, it does not seem necessary to analyse the *proportionality in the strict sense of the* challenged norms.

Conclusion: taking rights seriously, but some rights more seriously than others

Throughout these pages, I have tried to illustrate the meaning of conscientious objection through the register of objectors to abortion. Yet, the conceptual problem posed by the objection to legal duties whose constitutionality has not been analysed is not limited to this issue and is very topical. In the field of bioethics, for example, the so-called objection to euthanasia raises exactly the same problems. The refusal to cooperate with euthanasic practices has been subjected to similar burdens, including the duty of registration (see art. 16 of the Organic Law 3/2021).

This kind of register raises additional problems, i.e., the right not to manifest one's convictions. It is worth remembering, in this regard, that the "register of non-Catholics" was removed as unacceptable from the 1967 Religious Freedom Bill, passed during the Francoist regime. Despite being an authoritarian political regime, several ministerial reports regarding that Bill stressed that the register of non-Catholics was contrary to human dignity and freedom.[28] In my opinion, the register of objectors to abortion or euthanasia is much more repugnant in legal terms, given its potential to persecute nothing less than the defence of human life and respect for the Hippocratic oath. The President of the College of Physicians of Madrid, Manuel Martínez-Sellés, recently said that "the new law on euthanasia" treats doctors as having an "obligation" to "kill patients";[29] and, with regard to the new register of objectors to abortion, he said that physicians are "obviously very concerned, because this could be used in the future to decide on hirings, promotions, etc.".[30]

In addition to the violation of freedom of conscience, there is also an obvious discrimination based on religious convictions and conscience, which is a direct violation of the principle of equality before the law (art. 14 Spanish Constitution). It is clear that the rules subjecting to burdens the refusal to perform abortions have a "disparate impact"[31] on persons who hold religious

28 *Vid.* M. Blanco, «La primera ley de libertad religiosa. Génesis de la ley de 1967», *Anuario de Derecho Eclesiástico del Estado*, 14, 1998, pp. 119–186.

29 *Vid.* www.elmundo.es/papel/2021/01/11/5ff48e95fdddff75748b458a.html (interview of 11 January 2021; last accessed 29 November 2021).

30 *Vid.* www.hispanidad.com/sociedad/martinez-selles-sobre-registro-medicos-objetores-aborto-puede-utilizarse-dia-manana-decidir-contrataciones-ascensos-etc_12036595_102.html (interview of 5 September 2022; last accessed 29 November 2022).

31 See T. Khaitan, *A Theory of Discrimination Law* (Oxford: Oxford University Press, 2015), pp. 73 ff.

convictions associated with the sanctity of life. Such rules, therefore, are untenable from the point of view of discrimination law, and their constitutionality is subject to a strict scrutiny test.

I would like to conclude by referring to one of the leading contemporary theorists associated with the conception of rights that underlies the idea of a right to abortion: Ronald Dworkin. According to Dworkin, rights prevent society from interfering with the freedom of individuals on the basis of what he describes – in a remarkably ambiguous and obscure way – as "moral preferences".[32] From this optic, moral reasons that oppose conducts such

32 *Vid. e.g.*, the language used by Dworkin in the following fragments: 'If someone is denied liberty of sexual practice in virtue of a utilitarian justification that depends critically on other peoples' moralistic *preferences*, then he suffers disadvantage in virtue of the fact that his concept of a proper life is already despised by others'. (R. Dworkin, 'Is there a Right to Pornography?', *Oxford Journal of Legal Studies* 1, no. 2 (1981), 207, emphasis mine; note that the moral reasons reduced to desires and preferences are placed by Dworkin in the sphere of utilitarian calculation). *Vid.* also, in the same article, and also in defense of a purported 'right to pornography:' 'Suppose we assume that the decision to prohibit pornography altogether does, in fact, meet that test, because the *desires* and *preferences* of publishers and consumers are outweighed by the *desires* and *preferences* of the majority, including their *preferences* about how others should lead their lives' (p. 201, emphasis mine; *vid.* also, by the same author, the section 'The Right to Liberties', in *Taking Rights Seriously* (Cambridge: Harvard University Press, 1978), pp. 272 and following). From this conception of morality, Dworkin concludes that treating the moral *preferences* of individuals differently is a form of *discrimination of persons*, a thesis whose weakness is highlighted, among others, by R. P. George, 'The Concept of Public Morality', *American Journal of Jurisprudence* 45 (2000), pp. 27 ff. It should be added that such a use of language contradicts the ordinary experience of *moral* discourse, which appeals to non-instrumental reasons not reducible to subjective *preferences* lacking general validity. Few people criticise pornography only because they 'do not like it'; they do so because it is 'unworthy', because it 'debases' the person and society, because it is 'destructive' of the moral ecology. On the abandonment of the classical political discourse of natural *ends* and the political consequences of such abandonment, *vid.* R. Spaemann, 'Zur Ontologie der Begriffe "Rechts" und "Links"', in *Grenzen. Zur ethischen Dimension des Handeln* (Stuttgart: Klett-Cotta, 2001), pp. 260 ff; *see* also, by the same author, *Rousseau: ciudadano sin patria*, Centro de Estudios Políticos y Constitucionales, Madrid, 2013, especially pp. 7 ff; as well as the lucid critique of A. MacIntyre, *After Virtue* (Indiana: University of Notre Dame Press, 1981), chaps. 2 and 3. Dworkin faces the discussion on abortion with the same relativistic background. For him, 'the crucial question' – that is, the first thing to be *asked* – is whether a state can impose a canonical interpretation on the intrinsic value of (human) life (see i. a. R. Dworkin, 'What the Constitution Says', in *Freedom's Law* (Cambridge: Harvard University Press, 1996), p. 104). The negative answer cannot rest on ethical *disagreement*, as Dworkin suggests (*see e.g.* '*Roe* in Danger', in op. cit., p. 45; and 'What the Constitution Says', op. cit., p. 93), since, disagreement not being a sufficient basis for denying the existence of a correct answer in relation to a discussion, basing the right to abortion on disagreement about the intrinsic value of human life means *privileging one of the positions in dispute* and removing it from the political debate. In another passage, however, Dworkin seems to approach the positions that deny the moral status of 'person' to the *unborn* and even to the newborn because they lack *subjective self-consciousness* (*see 'Roe* in Danger', in *Freedom's Law*, op. cit., 1996, p. 50; and *Life's Dominion. An Argument About Abortion, Euthanasia, and Individual Freedom* (New York: Random House, 1993). See a penetrating critique of this thesis – which identifies personhood and dignity with a quality, with something that 'one has' at a given moment,

as abortion or euthanasia are not treated as authentic "reasons" that *bind* one's conscience, but as purely individual interests with no other basis than any other desire or impulse. This has serious consequences, as illustrated by the non-application of the "*favor libertatis*" principle to the regulation of the refusal of abortion. When all rights and freedoms are treated as preferences and mere desires or preferences are taken too seriously, freedom of conscience – that is, not the freedom to do what one *wants* to do, but the freedom to do what one *ought* to do – loses its pedigree. Thus, there is no guarantee that the rights of conscience – the most important rights according to classical liberal thought – take precedence over other preferences, desires, or whims.

and not with the *being* who possesses these qualities – in R. Spaemann, 'Are All Human Beings Persons?', in *Persons. The Difference Between 'Someone' and 'Something'* (Oxford: Oxford University Press, 2006 (repr. 2012)), pp. 236 ff.

4 Legal pluralism in German scholarship

Its application for religious freedom

Burkhard J. Berkmann

Introduction

Outline of topic and method

Religions have several dimensions: for example, doctrines of faith, worship, ethics, and often legal norms. Just think of Jewish and Islamic law, Hindu law, or the church laws of various Christian denominations. Until now, the legal dimension has received little attention when it comes to pluralism. Yet it would be of particular interest. While faith refers to an inner conviction, legal norms aim at an outer behaviour. If the norms of various religions demand different, even opposing actions, conflicts that affect living together in society could easily arise. What dietary rules should be observed in hospitals and schools? What visual and acoustic signals are permitted in public? While religious studies are devoted to religious pluralism, legal studies are increasingly concerned with legal pluralism. At the intersection of the two disciplines lies the pluralism of religious laws. The study of this phenomenon, therefore, suggests an interdisciplinary approach.

Lampe defined legal pluralism as follows: "Legal pluralism is the heterogeneous multiplicity of laws in the same social field" (Lampe 1995, p. 8). Today, there is a growing awareness that, there are other legal orders in addition to state law which communities and organizations, independent of state borders, give themselves: the law of transnational commercial enterprises, Internet law, sports law, the law of indigenous peoples, and certainly the law of religious communities.

The aim of this article is to analyse theoretical conceptions of legal pluralism that have been developed recently by researchers in Germany. This regional scope is interesting for several reasons. So far, Germany has not been known for legal or religious pluralism, nor for theories reflecting it. This situation is changing, however, in light of the contemporary transformation of society. According to the Pew Research Center, religious diversity in Germany is high. It has a diversity index of 5.3 (Report 2014, p. 15). Nevertheless, pluralism is perhaps more deeply rooted in Germany than it seems. After all, Protestants and Catholics have lived together here for centuries. The two churches have

DOI: 10.4324/9781003502845-4

their own legal orders. The state has had to learn to deal with this small pluralism. In contrast, the population in other European states was, for a long time, religiously more homogeneous. Today, the question in Germany is whether the structures that have proven successful for the coexistence of Catholics and Protestants can be extended to other religions. Therefore, legal scholars are increasingly concerned with religious pluralism in Germany. This development deserves academic analysis. This chapter presents the pluralistic conceptions of seven scholars affiliated with German academic institutions. The central research question is whether and in what way their approaches take religious law into account. Further questions are: Do they describe pluralism only as an existing fact or do they welcome it in normative terms? Which opportunities and which dangers do they see in pluralism? What kind and degree of pluralism do they advocate?

As for the method, the following steps are taken. First, the initial situation must be presented. This includes the state of research to date, the legal situation and the theoretical background. Subsequently, the seven approaches are presented in the main part. Thereafter, the results are systematically evaluated by highlighting the opportunities and risks of pluralism. Finally, in the discussion of the results, attention will be drawn to a paradox that exists between the view of pluralistic theories and the view of individual religions. It will become apparent that religious law is considered to varying degrees and that its specific nature is not always recognized.

Preliminary remarks on legal pluralism and its impact on state law, religious groups, and individual religious freedom

It seems useful to make some preliminary remarks, starting with the question of what legal pluralism means. There are different notions of legal pluralism. Legal pluralism is the existence of two or more legal systems within the same population or geographical area. Legal pluralism in the strict sense would mean the recognition not only of internal rules of religious communities, but of sub-legal systems that regulate a considerable part of human life together. Legal pluralism means that several legal systems apply simultaneously within the territory of a state, which may include the internal law of religions. Ferrari distinguishes states with "weak legal pluralism" from such a system: "They try to accommodate some specific religious rules within the State legal system but are far from recognizing an autonomous or semi-autonomous religious legal order" (Ferrari 2016, p. 14).

An important question is how legal pluralism affects state law. For a long time, state law in Germany was based on the cooperation of the state with the two "major churches". As far as the continuation of this model is concerned, various positions are held in view of the increasing religious plurality. According to one view, the cooperation should be extended to other religions, precisely in order to promote the integration of their members (Cf. Hecker 2019, p. 122). This position can be based on the right to self-determination of religious societies. In contrast, others warn against a pluralistic overload of state-church-law, because the new religious communities are not comparable with the traditional churches (Cf. Jestaedt 2012, p. 151f.).

On the other hand, there is the question of how legal pluralism affects religious groups. In a pluralistic system it is easier to justify the legal traditions of such groups. With all its specific theological features, it easily finds a place in the diversity of contemporary legal phenomena. Its peculiarity is no longer disruptive, but welcome. However, it must be noted that religious law does not always receive equal attention in legal pluralist models.

Finally, the implications for individual religious freedom must be considered. The European Court of Human Rights does not cease to emphasize that religious freedom promotes pluralism. Freedom of religion is anchored in Art. 9 of the European Convention on Human Rights. Observance of religious law is not explicitly mentioned there; however, according to established case law, being able "to manifest his religion or belief, in worship, teaching, practice and observance" is considered a part of religious freedom. Therefore, freedom of religion forms a gateway by which religious law can penetrate the sphere of secular law (Wittreck 2016, p. 94), leading to some kind of legal pluralism.

The starting situation

The state of previous research

The newly developed approaches need not start from scratch; rather, they can draw on antecedents in history. As early as the 20th century, there were German researchers who broadened the view towards legal pluralist phenomena.

Based on his studies in Indonesia, the ethnologist Franz von Benda-Beckmann (1941–2013) discovered a legal-pluralistic triangular constellation of Adat, Islam, and state (Cf. Benda-Beckmann 2009, p. 170). Rüdiger Schott (1927–2012), another ethnologist, studied segmentary cultures in Africa, where he found a strong intertwining of law and religion (Cf. Schott 1995, p. 41). Sanskritologist Werner Menski, born in Germany in 1949, is an expert on Hindu law and the law of other religions in Southeast Asia. Wolfgang Fikentscher (1928–2015) presented a history-of-religions approach in the 1970s, following the then-widespread idea of the Axial Age. Among the bodies of "early and religious law" he includes both the law of religions in the "true sense", which links people with numinous conceptions, and what in his view are a-religious, early totemistic moral orders (Fikentscher 1975, p. 149).

It is noticeable that they primarily conducted research of foreign peoples and cultures. They were more active in the field of ethnology than in the field of jurisprudence and researched legal pluralism mainly in distant countries, not in Germany. The more recent research, on the other hand, which will be presented in this chapter, has a predominantly legal background and relates to the situation in Germany.

State law

Furthermore, the "starting situation" includes the current state law. For centuries, Germany has been characterized by the coexistence of two large churches, the Catholic and the Protestant, both of which also have their own church law. The state has long had to learn to deal with this small form of legal pluralism. Three particularities of German state law favour the accommodation of different religious laws.

The first particular feature is the right to self-determination of religious societies. This right is quite extensive compared to other European countries[1] and covers the freedom to regulate and administer their own affairs independently (Art. 140 GG in conjunction with Art. 137 para. 3 WRV),[2] which includes making, interpreting, and applying one's own law (Robbers 2019, p. 115). This is the constitutional basis for the recognition of religious law by state law.

The second particular feature is treaties with religious communities. They are of particular interest for religious law because they usually refer to it, which implies a recognition by the state (Berkmann 2020a, p. 148). The treaty instrument is used in Germany primarily in relation to the Catholic Church (treaties under international law, "concordats") and to the Protestant regional churches (treaties under public law). Some German federal states have also concluded treaties with other Christian communities and with Jewish communities (cf. Lutz-Bachmann 2015, p. 439). A recent development is treaties with Islamic communities (cf. Rohe 2014, p. 384; Scheffler 2012, p. 10f.; Müller 2021, p. 19f.) and the Alevi Community.[3] However, the treaty system is not as extensive as in Italy.

The third particular feature in German law is a certain form of private international law. If rules on conflict-of-laws adduce the law of a foreign state and the latter refers to partial religious legal systems, then the religious law is to be applied by German courts as well (Berkmann 2020a, p. 140). However, foreign law is only applied to the extent that it does not contradict public order, i.e. the fundamental principles of the domestic legal system. In Germany, violations of public order are not examined in the abstract ("abstrakte Prüfung"), but with regard to the particular case in question ("konkrete Prüfung"). In other words, it is not a question of whether the foreign legal rule as such, but whether the result that occurs in the specific case complies with the standard

1 However, the guidelines issued in the area of the OSCE are also quite extensive: European Commission for Democracy through Law/OSCE Office for Democratic Institutions and Human Rights (ODIHR). 2014. Guidelines on the Legal Personality of Religious or Belief Communities.

2 'GG' (Grundgesetz) refers to the 'Basic Law for the Federal Republic of Germany' of 23 May 1949; 'WRV' (Weimarer Reichsverfassung) refers to the 'German Constitution of 11 August 1919' ('Weimar Constitution').

3 Freie Hansestadt Bremen, Treaty dated 14 October 2014; Bundesland Rheinland-Pfalz, Treaty dated 9 April 2019; Bundesland Schleswig-Holstein, Treaty dated 24 November 2021.

of the domestic fundamental values (Helms 2019, p. 310). This means that religious law is applied more frequently than if the examination were in the abstract.

Luhmann's systems theory

Finally, the starting situation also includes the tradition of thought of the country in question. In Germany, Luhmann's systems theory plays a major role. It is therefore not surprising that some researchers try to build on it, although at first glance, this theory does not seem to be favourable for religious law. For society as a whole can be understood as a system according to this theory and the social sub-areas of law, economy, politics, religion, etc. as social subsystems (see Braun 2001, p. 342). Each subsystem demarcates itself from its environment by means of a binary code and in this way maintains the process of *autopoiesis* (self-reproduction). In terms of religion, the binary code is transcendence/immanence; in terms of law, lawful/unlawful. In this view, the subsystems appear almost entirely isolated, so that the possibility of interaction between law and religion would be severely limited. In order for this theory to be fruitful for religious law, it must first succeed in establishing a connection between the subsystems of law and religion. This is precisely what Teubner, Günther, and Augsberg attempt in different ways.

Analysis of theoretical approaches

Having illuminated the starting situation, we now turn to the more recent theoretical approaches, of which I will briefly introduce seven. The order is based on two principles: from the older to the more recent, and from the more general to those that focus specifically on religious law.

Teubner

Gunther Teubner, born in 1944, was Professor of Private Law and Sociology of Law at the Goethe University in Frankfurt am Main. He concedes that only nation-states can develop constitutions that claim to cover all spheres of life, but he points out that this constitutional totality breaks down anyway because social subsystems establish themselves worldwide in discrepancy to the politics left behind on the intergovernmental level (Teubner 2012, p. 85). In this regard, Teubner observes the emerging phenomenon of self-constitutionalization of global orders without a state. He demonstrates this with case studies that, according to him, represent types of legal pluralism (Ibidem, p. 88). One of them concerns indigenous law.

In this context, religion also plays a role for Teubner, because there is a danger to knowledge about religion, culture, and lifeworld, which is essential for the survival of indigenous peoples (Cf. Teubner 2012, p. 246). According to him, indigenous legal norms are genetically and structurally inseparable from religious, political, economic, and traditional knowledge-based systems of interaction (Cf. Teubner and Korth 2009, p. 167). For him, the appropriate solution does not consist in "species protection" aimed at preserving the cultural stock, but in the creation of a basic legal framework to enable an independent development of indigenous cultures in confrontation with modernity (Ibidem, p. 162). His re-entry approach pursues the goal of reconstructing the foreign in the own. In reality, there is no "indigenous law" as formal law in the modern sense, but it is reconstructed by modern law as customary law in order to be protectable in the first place (Ibidem, p. 159).

Teubner does not examine the law of religious communities as supra-territorial, non-state law. Rather, he considers fundamental rights – which include religious freedom – as a model for conflict norms that set limits to the hyper structures of world society in their expansion into regional-cultural realms (Ibidem, p. 156). In this respect, he draws on Luhmann's theory of fundamental rights.

Günther

Klaus Günther, born in 1957, is Professor of Legal Theory, Criminal Law, and Criminal Procedure Law at the Goethe University in Frankfurt am Main. For him, legal pluralism is a factually existing, describable phenomenon (descriptive legal pluralism), but he furthermore questions whether it would be a preferable alternative also in normative terms (normative legal pluralism) (Cf. Günther 2016, p. 49). He sees both merits and dangers. Ultimately, according to him, what matters is how legal pluralism is managed. By this he means the coordinating impulses and mechanisms that are both strong enough to prevent re-feudalization and weak enough not to promote or justify hegemonic efforts to establish a homogeneous global law with a world state (Ibidem).

Günther demonstrates the phenomenon of legal pluralism above all in the growth of international organizations such as the World Trade Organization or the EU, as well as non-governmental organizations such as Amnesty International, Greenpeace, etc. (Günther 2001, p. 539). But he also reflects on autonomous norm-setting processes in the realms of the Internet, sports, and science (Günther 2016, p. 44). He mentions religious regulatory systems of social behaviour only briefly, to point out their complex and conflicting relationship with pluralized national and international legal systems (Günther 2001, p. 554).

Günther does not seem to include religious norms among legal norms but points out that there are dynamic processes of exchange and interaction between the two fields (Cf. Günther 2001, p. 553). On the other hand, he is aware that there are many non-state communities, be they religious, ethnic, or cultural, which, with the articulated conviction of autonomy in some matters central to their respective identities, give themselves their own rules (Cf. Günther 2016, p. 44). While distinguishing between legal and other normative orders that are moral, ethical, religious, or social in nature, he notes that the actors involved often seek to have their norms recognized as law because they associate at least a symbolic surplus value with it (Günther 2016, p. 45).

Schuppert

Gunnar Folke Schuppert, born in 1943, held the Chair of Political and Administrative Studies, in particular Constitutional and Administrative Law, at the Humboldt University in Berlin and was Professor of New Forms of Governance at the Social Science Research Centre Berlin. He uses governance research as his starting point. Governance collectives are collectives such as groups, associations, states, ethnic minorities, and territories that give themselves rules to order their group-specific problems and to stabilize themselves as collectives (Cf. Schuppert 2017, p. 169). According to Schuppert, "everything speaks in favour of subsuming religious communities under the term governance collective: Religion is not an individual private matter, but a collective phenomenon, which leads to the formation of religious communities that – this is at least true for Christianity, Islam, and Judaism – see themselves as legal communities, which also tend towards institutional consolidation – from the institutional church to transnational networks, and which are also characterized by a distinct collective religious identity" (Cf. Schuppert 2017, p. 171). Finally, Schuppert examines the relationship between state and religion, which he understands primarily as a "negotiated order of coexistence" (Cf. Schuppert 2017, p. 231). In this order, two legal instruments play a special role: treaties under state-church law (Cf. Schuppert 2012, p. 56) and the fundamental right to religious freedom (Cf. Schuppert 2017, p. 239).

According to Schuppert, the state has no regulatory power over religions because the secular, ideologically neutral state is constitutionally prevented from any direct access to the religiously based creation of meaning (Sinnstiftung), as this falls within the competence of the religious communities (Cf. Schuppert 2012, p. 47). The order of coexistence can only be effective in the long term if it is understood and practiced as an order of mutual recognition (Cf. Schuppert 2017, p. 245). However, this implies that the religious communities, for their part, must do their share of recognizing others. More specifically, they must recognize the constitution, the right of other religious communities to exist, and the primacy of conflict resolution by the state (Cf. Schuppert 2017, p. 256). The latter means that non-state enforcement regimes must be addressed with caution, lest they erode the state monopoly of law enforcement too much, that is, with unforeseeable consequences (Cf. Schuppert 2017, p. 257).

Shachar

Ayelet Shachar, born in 1966, is the Director of the Max Planck Institute for the Study of Religious and Ethnic Diversity in Göttingen. She qualifies religious law as "law" straightaway: Religious law, Canon law, Jewish law, Sharia law, Hindu law (Cf. Shachar and Hirschl 2018, p. 432). She also notes that they predate state law and the constitutional domain and continue to impact a wide range of legal areas, from commerce law to family law (Cf. Shachar and Hirschl 2018, p. 432). However, she is very critical when she speaks of a "clash of orders", because she believes that the traditional Catholic Church, conservative Evangelical movements, Wahhabis Islam, or ultraorthodox Judaism are diametrically opposed to the liberal constitutional view (Cf. Shachar and Hirschl 2018, p. 427). The main problem for her is that religious groups curtail the rights of their members – especially women. Therefore, she is looking for a new way to respect both cultural diversity and individual rights (Cf. Shachar 2001, p. XI).

Following Robert Cover, she refers to a "nomos" as a normative universe in which law and cultural narrative are inseparably related (Cf. Shachar 2001, p. 2). Nomoi groups are consequently bearers of such a nomos. Yet Shachar observes that there are persons whose legal status derives from more than one source of legal authority because they belong to several communities insofar as they are, for example, citizens of a state and members of a nomoi group (Cf. Shachar 2001, p. 88f.). To deal with this situation, she proposes the approach of "joint governance". This means that no single entity has exclusive jurisdiction, but that powers are re-allocated in many possible ways between the state and the group (Cf. Shachar 2001, p. 90). Joint governance is associated with a repertoire of techniques designed to accommodate the various nomoi within the state (Cf. Shachar 2001, p. 89). Subsequently, she presents four possible solutions that are already practiced in some cases, and then adds a fifth model, newly developed by her, which she prefers.

She calls this model "transformative accommodation". While the other models assume a static view of the group nomos, it is now considered that it can and, if necessary, should alter. Group traditions are given public recognition, but at the same time, their leaders are spurred to amend them in ways that are loyal to the nomos but are also more compatible with the democratic standards (Cf. Shachar 2001, p. 117f.). The impetus of internal transformation is competition for the loyalties of those citizens who overlap both jurisdictions (Cf. Shachar 2001, p. 113). Shachar expects this to improve the situation of traditionally vulnerable group members without removing them from their nomoi groups (Cf. Shachar 2001, p. 118).

Augsberg

Ino Augsberg, born in 1976, holds the Chair of Philosophy of Law and Public Law and is Co-Director of the Hermann Kantorowicz Institute for Basic Legal Research at the Christian Albrechts University in Kiel. He explicitly touches on religious law or religious legal systems (Cf. Augsberg 2015, p. 126) and deals with Jewish law in more detail (Cf. Augsberg and Ladeur 2009, p. 434). He advocates a reflexive legal pluralism. With this term, he points to the need "for legal orders to adjust to each other and to competing interests" (Augsberg

2015, p. 126). He exposes a crucial problem associated with legally pluralistic constellations: actually, the individual citizen or believer, who is subject to both orders, can thereby be subject to opposing rules (Cf. Augsberg 2012, p. 299, 2015, p. 124). Consequently, he understands religious law primarily in the context of a conflict of laws scenario (Cf. Augsberg 2012, p. 296). Interpreting the central elements of constitutional law on religions in this sense (Cf. Augsberg 2015, p. 124), religious freedom functions as a legal technique that allows the application of religious rules within the state legal order (Cf. Augsberg 2012, p. 299) and the right of self-determination becomes an explicit rule of collision (Cf. Augsberg 2015, p. 124).

Augsberg presents tolerance as a mechanism of reflexion between law and religion. Tolerance does not level differences but affirms the other's otherness by upholding one's own position (Cf. Augsberg 2014, p. 91). This mechanism works both ways between the religious and the legal spheres. On the one hand, the legal system has to accept the self-conception of groups of people claiming to be religious communities, and on the other hand, the religions must not try to take over other social functions (Cf. Augsberg 2014, p. 92). Luhmann attributes to fundamental rights the function of preventing social subsystems from encroaching on one another and thus guaranteeing the functional differentiation of society (Cf. Luhmann 1965, p. 197f.). Accordingly, Augsberg regards religious freedom as a protective mechanism which, on the one hand, prevents law from interfering with the autonomy of religion and, on the other hand, prevents religion from undermining the process of differentiation through its own attempts at totalization (Cf. Augsberg 2009, p. 249). The neutrality of the state does not preclude differentiation between various religions based on quantitative or qualitative criteria, such as cultural achievements (Cf. Augsberg and Ladeur 2007, p. 17). Finally, the differentiation of subsystems also means that the neutral state may not seek to harmonize state and religious law (Cf. Augsberg 2015, p. 126). In this respect, there is a difference from Shachar's "transformative accommodation".

Viellechner

Lars Viellechner, born in 1976, is Professor of Public Law, in particular Constitutional Law, Constitutional Theory, Philosophy of Law, and Transnational Law at the University of Bremen.

In the eyes of Viellechner, it is clear that today, in view of the emerging world society, it is no longer possible to limit oneself to the constitution of the state. The two extreme alternatives would be a radical legal pluralism or a universal legal order. However, both seem likewise undesirable or impossible according to him (Cf. Viellechner 2012, p. 569). He sees the following problems with a radical legal pluralism: Lack of inclusion, loss of legal certainty and legal equality, democratic deficit, lack of protection of fundamental rights, and contradictory norms (Ibidem, p. 561). He sees the solution in a "responsive legal pluralism", i.e. through a horizontal coordination of the various legal orders, by taking each other into account on an internal basis (Cf. Viellechner 2013, p. 267). The principles of complementarity and subsidiarity help to achieve this (Cf. Viellechner 2013, p. 269). However, Viellechner does not address religious law in detail.

The establishment of responsivity in law requires a new type of "conflict of laws" modelled on private international law (Cf. Viellechner 2013, p. 270f.). This has the advantage that there is no need to agree on substantive standards, but only on single coordination rules (Cf. Viellechner 2013, p. 272). Another advantage is that it is not necessary to mediate between different social systems, but only between different legal systems (Cf. Viellechner 2013, p. 273). After all, social systems do not have a common language, while the coordination of different legal systems can be achieved without translation problems through a universal code of legality (Cf. Viellechner 2013, p. 274). It should be emphasized that Viellechner does not content himself with the separation of the different social systems but seeks a connection between them and finds it in law. Thus, law does not appear as one of various sub-systems between which there is no closer link. Rather, communication is possible insofar as they are legal systems which share the same legal language.

Seinecke

A recent monograph comes from Ralf Seinecke, born in 1981 and Academic Counsel at the Goethe University Frankfurt. He starts from the observation that legal pluralism was part of the order of society in the Middle Ages and in the early modern period, and that even the law of the 20th century would never have been merely positivist, monist, or even apolitical (Seinecke 2015, p. 1). Today, however, in his view the state-oriented theories of law would finally lose their plausibility, because the nation-states would have to share their power with various globally organized actors of the economy, politics, or religions (*Ibid.*, p. 20). Law is set and recognized by social communities, economic associations, religious communities, or other societies as genuine law apart from the law of the state. Seinecke readily recognizes social, religious, or economic norms as law, but is aware that this presupposes certain normative assumptions (Ibidem, p. 26).

Seinecke does not content himself with presenting various legal pluralist approaches, but also asks about possible justifications of legal pluralism. Among them are again ways of justification that take the religious aspect into account. One justification consists of reflexivity: legal pluralist reflections broaden the horizon of jurisprudence by forcing the recognition of alternative laws and discovering that state law is only one type of law among many social, economic, indigenous, religious, or ideological laws (Cf. Seinecke 2015, p. 316).

The cultural-ideological type of legal pluralism underlines the religious, philosophical, or ordinary meaning of law and removes the seemingly sharp division between law and religion or between law and culture (Cf. Seinecke 2015, p. 34). Seinecke finds a version of this type in Robert Cover, who starts from Jewish legal thought, according to which the legal text remains one and the same, while the many interpretations create new law, so that an infinite multiplicity of legal worlds and a radical legal pluralism emerge (Cf. Seinecke 2015, p. 36).

Another justification is socio-political. Legal pluralism not only grants a space for autonomous rulemaking to religious, indigenous, or social communities within the modern nation-state, but also protects the inner connection between law and social identity (Cf. Seinecke 2015, p. 320). "Pluralism of religions enables social tolerance and ensures peace between religious communities" (Seinecke 2015, p. 320). "The pluralistic contexts of law, i.e., the cultural, religious, social, or economic legal orders, increase the discursive possibilities and alternatives of decision-making" (Seinecke 2015, p. 322).

Systematic evaluation

In the next step, the seven approaches will be systematically evaluated according to various aspects.

Legal pluralism and validity of law

The first aspect is the question of validity. How can several partly contradictory legal systems apply simultaneously in the same territory? Although this question is an obvious one in legal pluralism, it is rarely treated in depth.

Günther and Kadelbach are among the few legal theorists in Germany to address this problem. However, they come to the sobering conclusion that from a legal theory perspective no solution is possible, whereas from a sociological perspective it is only possible by expanding or abandoning the concept of law in favour of a general concept of norms (Cf. Kadelbach and Günther 2011, p. 34).

As far as sociology is concerned, it is worth recalling Max Weber, who in his time put forward a concept of law that is open to legal pluralism (Cf. Seinecke 2015, p. 139). His gradual concept of validity enables him to assume the simultaneous validity of different, even contradictory orders, because they are valid to the extent that there is a chance that action will actually be guided by them (Cf. Weber 1980, p. 17). The validity can thus be stronger or weaker. According to him, canon law is law even where it comes into conflict with state law (Cf. Weber 1980, p. 184). He cites excommunication as an example of a sanction in religious law (Cf. Weber 1980, p. 693).

In contrast, the binary-coded legal concept of validity only admits the alternative that a legal norm either applies or does not apply (Cf. Seinecke 2015, p. 139). Günther and Kadelbach limit themselves to Kelsen's positivist concept of law, according to which a legal norm is valid if it can be derived from the basic norm (Cf. Kadelbach and Günther 2011, p. 34). However, since several basic norms cannot exist side by side, there cannot be parallel legal systems (Cf. Kadelbach and Günther 2011, p. 33f.). Furthermore, they are based on an understanding of law according to which legal norms are to be set autonomously for their legitimacy and are to be traced back to the will of the norm addressees (Cf. Kadelbach and Günther 2011, p. 36). The democratic legitimacy of state law serves as a model (Cf. Kadelbach and Günther 2011, p. 35 and 37). On the other hand, Günther and Kadelbach measure the coexistence of polycentric normative orders according to the standards of freedom, equality, and solidarity. Likewise, they want the principles of fairness, autonomy, equal treatment, and respect to be upheld (Cf. Kadelbach and Günther 2011, p. 40f.). Ultimately, they take a value-oriented view, from which they take a critical view of legal pluralism.

The concept of law in religions

The second aspect concerns the concept of law. By leaving this concept undefined, legal pluralist approaches may initially avoid the difficulty of having to examine the normative quality of what presents itself as law. However, problems arise elsewhere. Those who think they can do without a clarification of the concept of law are, in fact, operating with a non-reflected and inarticulate concept, which makes a factual and academic discussion of law more difficult (Cf. Valcke 2014, pp. 123–126). Donlan and Heckendorn-Urscheler, who are quite open-minded about legal pluralism, have recognized the problem and have outlined a concept of law that also does justice to legal diversity. They define law on the basis of two functions which it fulfills: "establishing a rational conceptual framework that allows solving all cases according to a consistent pattern" and "regulation of conduct and conflict resolution through institutionalized authority" (Donlan and Heckendorn Urscheler 2014, p. 9).

In religions, on the other hand, it is not a formal-functional concept of law that prevails, but a material one. For law to be spoken of, it must correspond to substantive standards. From the perspective of the religions, law must correspond to fundamental values, especially justice, or it is derived from nature, the cosmic order as well as revelation (Cf. Berkmann 2020a, pp. 85 and 129).

Not chaotic, but institutionalized legal pluralism

The third aspect of evaluation concerns the question of what kind and degree of legal pluralism is advocated. Seinecke distinguishes between chaotic and institutionalized legal pluralism. Chaotic legal pluralism is disorderly and hierarchy-free, has no standards for resolving legal conflicts and abandons general principles such as justice and the common good in favour of individual *ad hoc* preferences (Cf. Seinecke 2015, p. 37). In contrast, institutionalized legal pluralism translates the diversity of law into a legal order by using various instruments such as state recognition, a federalism, freedom of religion and association, private autonomy, or international law (Cf. Seinecke 2015, p. 40f.).

However different and innovative the approaches presented may be, it is clear that as soon as it comes to concrete legal implementation, they return to the familiar and classic legal instruments such as treaties, freedom of religion, or rules on conflict of laws and, at best, develop them moderately or bring them into a new systematic relationship with each other. Thus, the instruments already known in German law will not expand or alter. Personal statutes or subsystems of religious law, as they exist in other parts of the world, are not conceivable.

Significance of religious law

The fourth aspect concerns the question of the significance of religious law within these approaches. As it turned out, it does not always receive much attention. Some approaches focus on the law of indigenous peoples or transnational commercial enterprises, for example. Sometimes canon law appears only as a historical example of legal pluralism. The anthology by Kadelbach and Günther, for example, devotes an entire chapter to canon law, but its topic concerns the 16th century (Cf. Duve 2011, pp. 147–174). Other works are devoted to religious law, such as Jewish and Islamic law, but only touch on canon law in passing. Occasionally, individual provisions taken from religious laws, especially Islamic law, serve as examples of norms that cannot be accepted despite all esteem for legal pluralism. An example of this is the stoning of the adulteress (Cf. Kadelbach and Günther 2011, p. 37). Finally, however, there are authors like Schuppert, who devote broad space to the law of religious communities.

At first glance, legal pluralist approaches seem conducive to the justification of religious law. If, by contrast, one was to assume a monopoly on law-making by the state and regard only state law as true law, it would be difficult to justify the existence of religious law as an independent legal order. It would then either appear as an exotic exception, or it would somehow be derived from state law contrary to its self-understanding – even if only through the construction of some state recognition – or it would be relegated to the internal world of theology in order to prevent it from competing with state law. In contrast, legal pluralism has an almost liberating effect. The existence of non-state law now seems self-evident and even welcome. It is no longer seen as a relic of pre-modern societies, but as a post-modern legal phenomenon, so that religious law can join the good company of *lex mercatoria*, *lex digitalis*, and *lex sportiva*. Since the legal pluralist concept of law is defined very broadly, there is also no pressure to make religious law equal to state law. Rather, with all its theological specificity, it easily finds a place in the diversity of contemporary legal phenomena. Its peculiarity is no longer deemed disturbing but is appreciated (Cf. Berkmann 2020b, p. 85).

Finally, it should be noted that religious law itself is not a homogeneous bloc. The internal laws of the various religions also vary widely in terms of their origins, their juridical nature, and their scope of application (Cf. Berkmann 2018, p. 128).

Differentiation between the different legal orders

The fifth and final aspect concerns the distinction between the different types of non-state legal systems. There are considerable differences between them.

Just think of state law, internet law, transnational financial law, indigenous law, and religious law. These different manifestations of law require different approaches. Günther and Kadelbach concretize: "While for the various *leges oeconomicae* it will be important to know whether it is sufficient that the addressees recognize the norm and abide by it, for the law of ethnic minorities, indigenous peoples, or religious communities, questions also arise about their self-image and their self-determination as a group" (Kadelbach and Günther 2011, p. 36). Subsequently, the two authors differentiate whether legitimation is based on democratic decision-making or on a tradition in a merely sociological sense. Finally, they prefer a weak legal pluralism in which the state, as the largest unit, can intervene when necessary, if subsystems contradict indispensable principles (Cf. Kadelbach and Günther 2011, p. 37).

Religious law must not be lumped together with, for example, internet law, because it is not about the "temporal order" but about the "eternal vocation"[4] of the human being, as is very well seen by Schuppert. All other manifestations of law relate to the secular sphere and can, therefore, legitimately be more closely interwoven and placed above or below each other. Rather, their basis of legitimacy can instead be measured by the standards of state law. If differentiations are necessary within a plurality of laws, then this is especially true for the dividing line between religious and secular, because this dividing line is of a more fundamental nature. Only when this is considered do the new approaches help to better understand and justify the existence of religious law alongside other manifestations of law.

Discussion of the results

In the preliminary remarks, different notions of legal pluralism were distinguished. The analysis of the various scholars shows that they represent – in Ferrari's words – a weak rather than a strong legal pluralism. Legal pluralism in the sense of several partial legal systems existing side by side would be unthinkable in Germany, as in most European states.

In conclusion, a paradox can be stated: Religions often advocate an essentialist and value-oriented concept of law, which is closely linked, for example, to the idea of justice, to a particular revelation, or to the cosmic order. In contrast, legal pluralist approaches either do without a concept of law at all or use a very broad and vague concept that is defined more in formal and functional terms. The paradox now is that it is precisely the pluralistic concept of law that is open to religious law, although the latter itself rejects a concept of law that is relativistic and arbitrary in content. Thus, it ultimately benefits from a legal concept that it itself does not adopt (Cf. Berkmann 2020b, p. 100).

4 Second Vatican Council. 1965. Pastoral Constitution on the Church in the Modern World. Gaudium Et Spes. In Actae Apostolicae Sedis 58, pp. 1025–1120, Art 76.

Religious law benefits from a pluralistic conception of law insofar as its recognition is easier and the need for justification is less than in a monistic conception. One advantage of legal pluralism is precisely that it promotes collective autonomy or self-legislation of special units and, thus, ultimately freedom (Cf. Gailhofer 2016, pp. 18 and 21; Kadelbach and Günther 2011, p. 39). Turner even sees "legal pluralism as the natural companion of political liberalism, allowing peoples and their institutions some protection from centralized authoritarian rule" (Turner 2016, p. 61). On the other hand, the vagueness of the legal concept entails the risk of mixing up different things and not taking the specific nature of religious law seriously. Indeed, there is a danger that the law of religious communities will be given too little respect in its specific nature as religious law, if it is placed on the same level as other extra-state forms of law such as the lex mercatoria or the lex sportiva, which are frequently viewed critically and rejected in terms of discrimination and power control (Cf. Kadelbach and Günther 2011, p. 39). Thus, it is not foreseeable whether the growing awareness of legal pluralism will bring more freedom or stronger restrictions for religious law. In Germany, religious communities already enjoy a comparatively far-reaching right to self-determination (Cf. Berkmann 2020b, p. 100).

Apart from indigenous laws, religious laws are the oldest non-state laws being discussed today in the context of legal pluralism. Now that there is renewed interest in religious laws, it would be desirable for experts on these laws to become involved in the current discourse on religious pluralism. The study of religious pluralism and the study of legal pluralism will benefit from mutual cooperation.

References

Augsberg, Ino. 2009. Noli me tangere. Funktionale Aspekte der Religionsfreiheit. *Der Staat* 48, pp. 239–258.

Augsberg, Ino. 2012. Taking Religion Seriously: On the Legal Relevance of Religious Self-Concepts. *Journal of Law, Religion and State* 1, pp. 291–308.

Augsberg, Ino. 2014. Religious Freedom as 'Reflexive Law'. In *Mapping the Legal Boundaries of Belonging. Religion and Multiculturalism from Israel to Canada.* Edited by Provost, René. Oxford: Oxford University Press, pp. 81–98.

Augsberg, Ino. 2015. Soziale Integration durch Religionsfreiheit? Zur Neubestimmung des Religionsverfassungsrechts im Verständnishorizont eines reflexiven Rechtspluralismus. In *Religionsverfassungsrechtliche Spannungsfelder.* Edited by Heinig, Hans Michael and Walter, Christian. Tübingen: Mohr Siebeck, pp. 113–128.

Augsberg, Ino and Ladeur, Karl-Heinz. 2007. Der Mythos vom neutralen Staat. *JuristenZeitung* 62, pp. 12–18.

Augsberg, Ino and Ladeur, Karl Heinz. 2009. 'Der Buchstaben tödtet, aber der Geist machet lebendig'? Zur Bedeutung des Gesetzesverständnisses der jüdischen Tradition für eine postmoderne Rechtstheorie. *Rechtstheorie* 40, Issue 4, pp. 431–471.

Benda-Beckmann, Franz von. 2009. Gefangen im Rechtspluralismus: Zum Umgang mit Normkollisionen in rechtlich pluralen sozialen Räumen. In *Normative Pluralität ordnen. Rechtsbegriffe, Normenkollisionen und Rule of Law in Kontexten dies- und jenseits des Staates.* Edited by Kötter, Matthias and Schuppert, Gunnar Folke. Baden-Baden: Nomos, pp. 169–190.

Berkmann, Burkhard J. 2018. *Internes Recht der Religionen. Einführung in eine vergleichende Disziplin.* Stuttgart: Kohlhammer.

Berkmann, Burkhard J. 2020a. *The Internal Law of Religions. Introduction to a Comparative Discipline.* Translated by Orton, David E. London, New York: Routledge.

Berkmann, Burkhard J. 2020b. Aktuelle rechtspluralistische Theorien in Deutschland und ihre Bedeutung für das Kirchenrecht. *Archiv für katholisches Kirchenrecht* 187, Issue 1, pp. 51–103.

Braun, Johann. 2001. *Rechtsphilosophie im 20. Jahrhundert. Die Rückkehr der Gerechtigkeit.* München: Beck.

Donlan, Seán Patrick and Heckendorn Urscheler, Lukas. 2014. Concepts of Law: An Introduction. In *Concepts of Law: Comparative, Jurisprudential, and Social Science Perspectives.* Edited by Donlan, Seán Patrick and Heckendorn Urscheler, Lukas. Farnham: Ashgate, pp. 1–17.

Duve, Thomas. 2011. Catholic Canon Law and Moral Theology in the 16th Century: Eine globale normative Ordnung im Schatten schwacher Staatlichkeit. In *Recht ohne Staat? Zur Normativität nichtstaatlicher Rechtsetzung.* Edited by Kadelbach, Stefan and Günther, Klaus. Frankfurt am Main: Campus, pp. 147–174.

Ferrari, Silvio. 2016. Religious Rules and Legal Pluralism: An Introduction. In *Religious Rules, State Law, and Normative Pluralism – A Comparative Overview.* Edited by Bottoni, Rossella, Cristofori, Rinaldo and Ferrari, Silvio. Zürich: Springer, pp. 1–25.

Fikentscher, Wolfgang. 1975. *Methoden des Rechts in vergleichender Darstellung*, vol. 1. Tübingen: J.C.B. Mohr.

Gailhofer, Peter. 2016. *Rechtspluralismus und Rechtsgeltung.* Baden-Baden: Nomos.

Günther, Klaus. 2001. Rechtspluralismus und universaler Code der Legalität: Globalisierung als rechtstheoretisches Problem. In *Die Öffentlichkeit der Vernunft und die Vernunft der Öffentlichkeit.* Edited by Wingert, Lutz and Günther, Klaus. Frankfurt am Main: Suhrkamp, pp. 539–567

Günther, Klaus. 2016. Normativer Rechtspluralismus – Eine Kritik. In *Das Recht im Blick der Anderen. Religion und Aufklärung*, vol. 26. Edited by Moos, Thorsten et al. Tübingen: Mohr Siebeck, pp. 43–62.

Hecker, Wolfgang. 2019. Integration islamischer Religionsgemeinschaften oder laizistische Reform der Religionsverfassung? *Zeitschrift für Rechtspolitik* 52, pp. 121–122.

Helms, Tobias. 2019. Familienrecht und Religion, Herausforderungen für das internationale Privatrecht. In *Familienrecht und Religion – Europäische Perspektiven.* Edited by Mayer, Claudia. Bielefeld: Gieseking, pp. 303–322.

Jestaedt, Matthias. 2012. Unverstandenes Staatskirchenrecht. Ein Zwischenruf zur 'pluralistischen' Überforderung des Religionsverfassungsrechts. *Kirche & Recht* 18, pp. 151–163.

Kadelbach, Stefan and Günther, Klaus. 2011. Recht ohne Staat? In *Recht ohne Staat? Zur Normativität nichtstaatlicher Rechtsetzung.* Edited by Kadelbach, Stefan and Günther, Klaus. Frankfurt am Main: Campus, pp. 9–48.

Lampe, Ernst-Joachim. 1995. Was ist 'Rechtspluralismus'? In *Rechtsgleichheit und Rechtspluralismus.* Edited by Lampe, Ernst-Joachim. Baden-Baden: Nomos, pp. 8–33.

Luhmann, Niklas. 1965. *Grundrechte als Institution: Ein Beitrag zur politischen Soziologie.* Berlin: Duncker & Humblot.

Lutz-Bachmann, Julia, 2015. *Mater rixarum? Verträge des Staates mit jüdischen und muslimischen Religionsgemeinschaften in Deutschland aus religionsverfassungsrechtlicher Sicht.* Tübingen: Mohr Siebeck.

Müller, Norbert. 2021. *Das Verhältnis zwischen Staat und islamischen Religionsgemeinschaften. Der Hamburger Staatsvertrag aus Praxisperspektive.* Frankfurt am Main: Akademie für Islam in Wissenschaft und Gesellschaft.

Pew Research Center. 2014. *Global Religious Diversity: Half of the Most Religiously Diverse Countries are in Asia-Pacific Region.* https://www.pewresearch.org/wp-content/uploads/sites/20/2014/04/Religious-Diversity-full-report.pdf.

Robbers, Gerhard. 2019. State and Church in Germany. In *State and Church in the European Union.* Edited by Robbers, Gerhard. Baden-Baden: Nomos, pp. 109–124.

Rohe, Mathias. 2014. Scharia und deutsches Recht. In *Handbuch Christentum und Islam in Deutschland. Erfahrungen, Grundlagen und Perspektiven im Zusammenleben.* Edited by Rohe, Mathias. Freiburg im Breisgau: Herder, pp. 377–418.

Scheffler, Gerhard. 2012. *Zum Islam-Vertrag in Hamburg.* Berlin: epubli.

Schott, Rüdiger. 1995. Rechtspluralismus und Rechtsgleichheit in den postkolonialen Staaten Afrikas. In *Rechtsgleichheit und Rechtspluralismus.* Edited by Lampe, Ernst-Joachim. Baden-Baden: Nomos, pp. 38–68.

Schuppert, Gunnar Folke. 2012. *When Governance Meets Religion: Governancestrukturen und Governanceakteure im Bereich des Religiösen.* Baden-Baden: Nomos.

Schuppert, Gunnar Folke. 2017. *Governance of Diversity: Dealing with Cultural and Religious Plurality in Secular Societies.* Frankfurt am Main, New York: Campus Verlag.

Seinecke, Ralf. 2015. *Das Recht des Rechtspluralismus. Grundlagen der Rechtswissenschaft*, vol. 29. Tübingen: Mohr Siebeck.

Shachar, Ayelet. 2001. *Multicultural Jurisdictions: Cultural Differences and Women's Rights.* Cambridge, New York: Cambridge University Press.

Shachar, Ayelet and Hirschl, Ran. 2018. Competing Orders? The Challenge of Religion to Modern Constitutionalism. In *The University of Chicago Law Review*, vol. 85. Chicago: The University of Chicago Law School, pp. 425–455.

Teubner, Gunther. 2012. *Verfassungsfragmente. Gesellschaftlicher Konstitutionalismus in der Globalisierung.* Berlin: Suhrkamp.

Teubner, Gunther and Korth, Peter. 2009. Zwei Arten des Rechtspluralismus: Normenkollisionen in der doppelten Fragmentierung der Weltgesellschaft. In *Normative Pluralität ordnen. Rechtsbegriffe, Normenkollisionen und Rule of Law in Kontexten dies- und jenseits des Staates.* Edited by Kötter, Matthias and Schuppert, Gunnar Folke. Baden-Baden: Nomos, pp. 137–168.

Turner, Bryan. 2016. Legal Pluralism: Freedom of Religion, Exemptions and the Equality of Citizens. In *Religious Rules, State Law, and Normative Pluralism – A Comparative Overview.* Edited by Bottoni, Rossella, Cristofori, Rinaldo and Ferrari, Silvio. Zürich: Springer, pp. 61–76.

Valcke, Catherine. 2014. Three Perils of Legal Pluralism. In *Concepts of Law: Comparative, Jurisprudential, and Social Science Perspectives.* Edited by Donlan, Seán Patrick and Heckendorn Urscheler, Lukas. Farnham: Ashgate, pp. 123–136.

Viellechner, Lars. 2012. Responsiver Rechtspluralismus. Zur Entwicklung eines transnationalen Kollisionsrechts. *Der Staat* 51, pp. 559–580.

Viellechner, Lars. 2013. *Transnationalisierung des Rechts.* Weilerswist: Velbrück Wissenschaft.

Weber, Max. 1980. *Wirtschaft und Gesellschaft: Grundriss der verstehenden Soziologie*, 5th ed. Tübingen: Mohr.

Wittreck, Fabian. 2016. Der gegenwärtige Konflikt zwischen Menschenrechten und religiösen Geboten – Vom Burkaverbot bis zur Zirkumzision. In *Menschenrechte und Religion – Kongruenz oder Konflikt?* Edited by Gunnarsson, Logi and Weiß, Norman. Berlin: BWV, pp. 93–132.

5 Reforming weddings law in England and Wales

Frank Cranmer[1]

Introduction

Although it has been heavily amended since its enactment, the Marriage Act 1949 remains the primary statute governing the formation of marriage in England and Wales. In December 2014, the Westminster Government asked the Commission to conduct a review of the law governing how and where people can marry in England and Wales. The Commission published a Scoping Paper in December 2015 in which it concluded that there was a need for a wholesale review of the law. The Government did not proceed further on that occasion, but after further consideration it announced at the time of the 2018 Budget that it would ask the Commission to undertake a full law reform project.

After agreeing on Terms of Reference for the project with the Government, the Commission began work in July 2019 and published its final recommendations in July 2022.[2] It should be noted that in its recommendations the Commission talks about "weddings law" or "wedding law" rather than "marriage law", on the basis that a wedding is a discrete event that constitutes the marriage, while the marriage itself is a continuing process or state of being.

What follows is principally, though not exclusively, about religious weddings conducted by faith communities (as opposed to civil weddings conducted by civil registrars) and about religious weddings conducted in England and Wales. But weddings law is a devolved matter and, as we shall see, the law on creating and recognising marriages in Scotland and Northern Ireland is very different from that of England and Wales.

1 Obliging as always, Russell Sandberg commented on a very early draft of this chapter, and my ideas were further developed when I presented at the conference in Córdoba and by subsequent discussions in Cardiff with the current cohort of LLM (Canon Law) students and the Revd Dr Helen Hall. My thanks to all those who engaged with me so helpfully.

2 Law Commission of England and Wales, *Celebrating Marriage: A New Weddings Law* (HC 557, Law Com no. 408, 19 July 2022).

DOI: 10.4324/9781003502845-5

Weddings law in England and Wales

How we got here

As Diarmaid MacCulloch has pointed out, in Western Christendom weddings in church were a much later development that one might have imagined:

> [T]he Early Church . . . never associated marriage with any ceremony celebrated in church. There was no such thing as a church wedding in the Western Church until the tenth or eleventh centuries. It took a twelfth-century revolution in ecclesiastical reorganisation from Rome before it became the norm for folk to get married in church.[3]

Under the mediaeval canon law, most marriages in Western Christendom were what a Scots lawyer would call "irregular marriages".[4] Early mediaeval canon law operated on the basis that two people were married when they exchanged mutual consent to marry one another, always providing they were free to marry and that their consent was voluntary and was given in the present tense. Alternatively, a couple might exchange consent in the future tense, in which case they became husband and wife next time they had sexual intercourse with one another.[5] However, the decree of the Council of Trent on the Reformation of Marriage in 1563 – *Tametsi*[6] – reformed the mediaeval practice by declaring that a marriage was canonically valid only if it had been witnessed by the parish priest or an authorised deputy.

In post-Reformation England and Wales, the legal requirements for a valid marriage had been governed by the canon law of the Church of England: banns had to be called or a marriage licence obtained before a wedding could take place, and the wedding had to be celebrated in the parish where at least one of the parties was resident. However, those requirements were not absolutely mandatory, and the absence of banns or a licence – or even the fact that the wedding had not taken place in a church – did not necessarily render the marriage void. The only indispensable requirement was that the wedding be celebrated by an Anglican clergyman. (In Scotland, because the Reformation of 1560 predated the Tridentine Decree of 1563, the Scots took no notice of it and simply carried on as before.)

3 D. MacCulloch, 'Living in Love and Faith', *Modern Church*, 16 November 2020. https://modernchurch.org.uk/prof-diarmaid-macculloch-living-in-love-and-faith.

4 For a brief history of which, see Anon, 'Irregular Marriage and the Kirk Session in Scotland', *Scotland's People*, 1 October 2021. www.scotlandspeople.gov.uk/article/irregular-marriage-and-kirk-session-scotland.

5 See J. A. Brundage, *Medieval Canon Law* (London: Longman, 1995), p. 73.

6 For an English translation, see H. J. Schroeder, 'Council of Trent, Decree *Tametsi* Concerning the Reform of Matrimony (1563)', in *The Decrees of the Council of Trent* (St Louis: Herder, 1941), pp. 183–190.

What changed the position in England and Wales was the Marriage Act 1753: "An Act for the Better Preventing of Clandestine Marriage", aka Lord Hardwicke's Act. It provided that for a marriage to be valid it had to be performed in a church – which in 1753 meant in the Church of England,[7] even if the parties were Roman Catholics or Dissenters – and either banns had to be published or a licence obtained. Those under 21 could only marry by licence with parental consent, though a marriage by banns was valid so long as the parent of a minor did not actually forbid the banns. Jews and Quakers were exempted from the provisions of the Act: I assume not so much out of respect for their beliefs, but rather to spare the consciences of Anglican clergy who would otherwise have been required to marry couples whom they knew did not share their religious views.

So why does the history matter?

Though the current law in England and Wales largely derives from the Marriage Act 1949 as subsequently amended, that Act was largely a consolidation of the earlier law. The result is that much of the current law goes back to the Marriage Act 1836 and even includes elements of Lord Hardwicke's Act of 1753.

There are currently two basic kinds of wedding ceremonies: civil and religious. And for historical reasons, there are four kinds of religious ceremonies:

- weddings solemnised in the Church of England and the Church in Wales;
- Jewish weddings;
- Quaker weddings; and
- "everyone else" weddings – from Ahmadi Muslims to Zoroastrians.

Furthermore, there is currently no special provision for "belief" weddings conducted by humanists or independent celebrants.

Under the 1949 Act, a religious wedding in England and Wales must take place in an authorised *building* (except for Quaker and Jewish weddings), though the Church of England and the Church in Wales are subject to slightly different rules. A temporary exception was made during the COVID-19 pandemic for *civil* weddings on approved premises, and that has since been made permanent. As we shall see, however, the law in Scotland and Northern Ireland is very different because, though weddings must be conducted by authorised *celebrants*, there is no requirement for weddings to be held in registered *buildings*.[8]

7 The Church of England in 1753 included the area that is now the Church in Wales.

8 My wife and I were married in Scotland in 2006 in a civil ceremony conducted by an assistant district registrar *in the open air*. That would have been impossible in England or Wales.

Civil partnership, same-sex marriage, and the "quadruple lock"

Civil partnership was introduced across the UK by the Civil Partnership Act 2004. The Marriage (Same Sex Couples) Act 2013 enabled same-sex couples in England and Wales to marry in a civil or religious ceremony and the Marriage and Civil Partnership (Scotland) Act 2014 did the same for Scotland. After something of a hiatus, the Westminster Parliament legislated to provide for same-sex marriage in Northern Ireland via Regulations[9] under section 8 of the Northern Ireland (Executive Formation etc.) Act 2019.

Part 1 of the 2013 Act (Marriage of same sex couples in England and Wales) included the famous (or perhaps infamous) "quadruple lock", under which:

1. religious organisations and individual ministers cannot be obliged to marry same-sex couples or to permit same-sex weddings to take place on their premises;
2. there is an opt-in system for religious organisations that wish to conduct same-sex weddings;
3. the Equality Act 2010 was amended to ensure that no discrimination claim may be brought against a religious organisation or an individual minister of religion for refusing to marry a same-sex couple; and, crucially,
4. *the legislation does not override the internal canon law of the Church of England or of the Church in Wales*, neither of which currently recognises same-sex marriage.

As a result of the last of these, for the Church of England to conduct same-sex weddings will require General Synod to pass an appropriate Measure and have it confirmed by both Houses of Parliament. The Church in Wales, however, has no such power to legislate for itself and can only be given the power to conduct same-sex weddings if the Westminster Parliament passes the necessary primary legislation to amend the 2013 Act.[10] So, currently, both Churches are effectively banned from conducting same-sex marriages unless and until they ask the UK Government to legislate.

Religious weddings: the problems

Even leaving aside the issue of same-sex religious marriage, there are various problems with the existing law on religious weddings in England and Wales. As the Law Commission explains, though the current law restricts how

9 Marriage (Same-sex Couples) and Civil Partnership (Opposite-sex Couples) (Northern Ireland) Regulations 2019.

10 Weddings law is not devolved to Wales, so it remains a matter for Westminster, not for the Welsh Senedd.

couples can celebrate their weddings, that is not because of current policy considerations but for historical reasons:

> Complexity and inconsistency mean that different couples are bound by different rules. Because of unnecessary restrictions, many couples cannot have a legally recognised wedding in a place that is meaningful to them. Many couples also cannot have a ceremony which contains the vows, rituals and music that best reflect their beliefs and preferences. Unnecessary regulation and bureaucracy contribute to some couples having to spend more on the legal aspects of their wedding than other couples.[11]

The Commission believes that the current law requires reform for various reasons.

First, *the religious composition of society has changed.* The basic law goes back to the nineteenth century, when the religious makeup of society was very different and Christianity was the religion of the overwhelming majority, even if only nominally so. The latest figures from the 2021 Census in England and Wales, released in November 2022, show that for those who answered the voluntary question about their religious affiliation, 27.5 million claimed to be Christians, 3.9 million Muslims, 1 million Hindus, 524,000 Sikhs, 273,000 Buddhists, and 271,000 Jews. 348,000 respondents said that they professed "other religions".[12] For comparison, in 2020 there were about 20,000 Quakers.[13]

Secondly, *the requirement for "approved buildings" may be seen as discriminatory.* Most groups of Christians tend to have church buildings, whereas some groups of non-Christians, such as Pagans and Parsees, may not have any convenient building in which to hold a wedding ceremony, or it may be their custom to hold wedding ceremonies elsewhere: for example, in a hotel or in the open air.

Thirdly, *the current law is excessively complicated* and may give rise to innocent mistakes. Perhaps an extreme example of this was *MA v JA*,[14] in which a Muslim couple believed that they had been validly married but found that they were not when the wife applied for a marriage certificate. There had been a technical misunderstanding by the mosque where their wedding had taken place and the imam who had married them had not been an "authorised person" under the 1949 Act. They had to go to the High Court to seek a declaration that they were in fact married; what saved the day was the fact that the chairman of the mosque had been one of their witnesses and since 1998 *he*

11 Law Commission of England and Wales (n 2), p. 1.

12 Office of National Statistics, *Religion, England and Wales: Census 2021* (London, 29 November 2022). www.ons.gov.uk/peoplepopulationandcommunity/culturalidentity/religion/bulletins/religionenglandandwales/census2021#religion-in-england-and-wales.

13 Britain Yearly Meeting of the Religious Society of Friends (Quakers), *Patterns of Membership Including the 2020 Tabular Statement* (London, 2021), p. 2. www.quaker.org.uk/documents/tabular-statement-2021.

14 *MA v JA and the Attorney General*, [2012] EWHC 2219 (Fam).

had been an "authorised person". Moylan J granted the couple the declaration sought – but it was highly unfortunate, to say the least, that they should have found themselves in that situation in the first place.

More generally, *the absence of provision for humanist weddings appears to be in breach of Article 9 ECHR* (which, it should not be forgotten, protects thought and conscience as well as religion). In *R (Harrison & Ors)*[15] it was held that Article 9 was engaged by that absence of provision and that the claimants, a group of humanists, had been discriminated against; however, Eady J concluded that the Law Commission's ongoing review of weddings law meant that "a fair balance has been struck between the individual rights of the Claimants and wider community interests".[16] But that was in July 2020, the Law Commission reported in 2022, and at the time of writing, the Government had still not announced its policy on humanist weddings.

There is also *a rigid distinction between civil and religious weddings*. So, for example, a couple may not have a reading or piece of music at a civil ceremony that the officiating registrar regards as "religious" – and what is "religious" is sometimes a matter of opinion. For example, Mendelssohn's *Wedding March* is from his incidental music to *A Midsummer Night's Dream* and Wagner's *Bridal March* is from his opera *Lohengrin*: so, might they be considered "religious" just because they tend to get played at church weddings?[17]

Weddings law and devolution

Weddings law is devolved to Scotland and Northern Ireland. In Scotland, the basic legislation is the Marriage (Scotland) Act 1977, while the Marriage (Scotland) Act 2002 extended the availability of civil weddings to "approved places" in addition to local authority register offices and to any other place used in exceptional circumstances. Weddings can either be conducted by "authorised celebrants" (often but not always a minister of religion – there are many humanist celebrants who conduct a considerable number of ceremonies) or by an "authorised registrar". Both parties must submit a marriage notice to the registrar of the district in which the marriage is to take place, and for a religious marriage the registrar will then issue a marriage schedule. The marriage schedule must then be produced to the person performing the wedding ceremony; otherwise it cannot take place. The parties complete the schedule after the ceremony. It is signed by the couple, their witnesses and the person performing the marriage, then submitted to the local registry office so that

15 *R (Harrison & Ors) v Secretary of State for Justice*, [2020] EWHC 2096 (Admin).

16 *R (Harrison & Ors)* (n 15) at [129].

17 Conversely, Mendelssohn wrote the opening of what became his A-major Organ Sonata specifically as a bridal processional for his sister Fanny's Lutheran wedding – but it is not especially associated with weddings in British culture and I doubt if any registrar would object to its use in a civil wedding unless s/he happened to be an organist and knew about the circumstances in which it was composed.

the marriage can be registered. For civil weddings, the schedule is kept by the officiating registrar and signed after the ceremony.

The law in Northern Ireland is very like that in Scotland. When Mo Mowlam was Secretary of State for Northern Ireland between May 1997 and October 1999, she decided that the existing law, which largely dated back to the nineteenth century, was antiquated and referred the matter to Northern Ireland's Law Reform Advisory Committee.[18] The Committee decided in favour of wholesale reform on the Scottish model rather than the English, and the Marriage (Northern Ireland) Order 2003 was passed by the Westminster Parliament after the Northern Ireland Assembly was suspended on 14 October 2002 and an Assembly Bill to reform the law fell.

In brief, the critical difference between the law in England and Wales and the law in Scotland and Northern Ireland is that, in England and Wales, under the Marriage Act 1949 as amended, ***authorised persons*** are registered to conduct religious marriages in ***approved buildings*** – which categories include by default all licensed clergy and all churches of the Church of England and the Church in Wales. In Scotland and Northern Ireland, however, the emphasis is on ***registered celebrants***, without reference to the buildings in which weddings are conducted. So, for example, Louisa Hodkin had to go all the way to the UK Supreme Court to gain the right to be married in a chapel of the Church of Scientology in England because the Registrar-General had refused to register the building for weddings,[19] while her brother David had earlier been married in a Scientology ceremony in Scotland.

Age of marriage and civil partnership

UNICEF – the United Nations Children's Fund – defines child marriage as any formal marriage or informal union between a child under the age of 18 and an adult or another child, and the UN Sustainable Development Goals call for global action to end child marriage by 2030.[20] In 2016, in its consideration of the fifth periodic report of the UK on its implementation of the Convention on the Rights of the Child, the UN Committee on the Rights of the Child recommended to the UK that it raise the minimum age of marriage to eighteen.[21]

Because weddings law is a devolved responsibility, the situation is different in each of the three jurisdictions. In February 2023, the minimum age

18 The predecessor of the Northern Ireland Law Commission.

19 See *R (Hodkin & Anor) v Registrar-General of Births, Deaths and Marriages*, [2013] UKSC 77 and Ian Johnston, 'Couple Get Married in Britain's First Scientology Wedding', *The Independent (London)*, 23 February 2014. The strapline to the piece should have read '*England's* first Scientology wedding'.

20 UNICEF, 'Child Marriage'. www.unicef.org/protection/child-marriage accessed 29 November 2022.

21 UN Media Center, 'Committee on the Rights of the Child Reviews the Report of the United Kingdom', 24 May 2016. www.ohchr.org/en/press-releases/2016/05/committee-rights-child-reviews-report-united-kingdom accessed 29 November 2022.

in England and Wales was raised to eighteen when the Marriage and Civil Partnership (Minimum Age) Act 2022 came into effect. In July 2022, the Northern Ireland Executive announced plans to raise the minimum age for marriage to eighteen,[22] though currently the Northern Ireland Assembly is for all practical purposes in suspension and, at the time of writing, the minimum age for marriage remains sixteen in Northern Ireland with parental consent (or, if appropriate, via a court order) and otherwise eighteen.[23]

The position in Scotland is different again. Prior to 1929, Scots law simply followed Roman law: girls could marry at twelve and boys at fourteen, without any requirement for parental consent. The Age of Marriage Act 1929 (which applied to Scotland, England, and Wales but not to Northern Ireland) made void any marriage between persons either of whom was under the age of sixteen. The minimum age for marriage in Scotland remains sixteen *but parental consent to the marriage is not required.* So far as I am aware, there is no current proposal from the Scottish Government to raise the minimum age for marriage or civil partnership in Scots law – though under section 4 of the Marriage and Civil Partnership (Minimum Age) Act 2022, a wedding or civil partnership which is entered into in Scotland or Northern Ireland and which involves an under-eighteen where one of the parties is domiciled in England and Wales will not be legally recognised in England and Wales.

Reforming the law: the commission's main recommendations

The principal recommendations of the Law Commission for the reform of the law in England and Wales are as follows:

- There would be a shift away from regulating *buildings* to regulating *officiants* responsible for conducting wedding ceremonies. This is by far the biggest change proposed by the Commission, and it would bring the law in England and Wales largely into line with the law in Scotland and Northern Ireland.
- Universal laws would be introduced for *all* weddings, whether civil or religious, with only very few exceptions.
- There would be a greater appreciation of different beliefs and more flexibility about the ceremony itself. There would be a greater choice of *content* for the ceremony, to allow individuals to have a wedding that reflects their

22 Conor Murphy MLA, *Marriage Law Written Ministerial Statement* (Northern Ireland Assembly, 1 July 2022). www.finance-ni.gov.uk/sites/default/files/publications/dfp/Marriage%20Law%20Consultation%20-%20Ministerial%20Statement.pdf. All URLs cited in the footnotes were last accessed on 17 July 2023.

23 The Northern Ireland Executive's website states that 'If you are aged over 16 and under 18 years old you can marry in Northern Ireland, but you should note that your marriage will not be legally recognised in the Republic of Ireland. The minimum age for marriage in the Republic of Ireland is 18 years of age and this remains the case even if you marry in Northern Ireland' www.nidirect.gov.uk/articles/guidance-marriage-procedures-northern-ireland.

values and beliefs – and that would be achieved by having stricter rules about the *formalities*.

- Ceremonies would no longer have to include "prescribed words", and couples who opted for a civil ceremony would be able to have religious songs, readings, and hymns, always provided that the ceremony was still identifiable as a civil ceremony rather than a religious one.
- There would be a greater choice of wedding venues, including the possibility of holding ceremonies in outdoor venues that were not connected with a building.
- There would be increased clarity about the consequences of not complying with the required formalities. New offences would be introduced criminalising an officiant who misled anyone to think that he or she was legally married when that was not the case.
- There would be a facility for couples to give notice of their forthcoming wedding online.

In brief, the Commission's proposals, if implemented, would reform weddings law in England and Wales along the lines of the current law in Scotland and Northern Ireland.

The response of the Church of England

At the July 2023 meeting of the General Synod of the Church of England, a written question urged the Church to lobby the Government "to take actions to support marriage according to the doctrine of the Church", to which the Bishop of Durham replied on behalf of the House of Bishops as follows:

> Our active engagement with HMG about marriage is currently focused upon the recent Law Commission report on Weddings. At the consultation stage, I responded to the draft proposals, severely criticizing the Law Commission's approach. The fundamental problem is that they focused on the law surrounding weddings whilst explicitly refusing to engage with the meaning of marriage. Consequently, their report was seriously deficient, suggesting, for example, that a wedding must be "dignified" without any notion of what that would mean or how it could be enforced.
>
> The fundamental shift they called for was to move from a premises-based to a celebrant-based system. Whilst that approach works adequately in Scotland, the recommendations were clearly intended to open the "weddings market" more widely to commercial celebrants operating for profit.[24]

24 Church of England General Synod, 'Questions of Which Notice has been Given under Standing Orders 112–116', July 2023, p. 55. www.churchofengland.org/sites/default/files/2023-07/questions-notice-paper-july-2023.pdf.

Apart from the fact that the answer has more than a whiff of "good enough for Scotland but not good enough for England", it appears to be based on a misunderstanding of the nature of the Law Commission's project: the Terms of Reference agreed between the Commission and the Government specifically excluded "The rights or responsibilities which marriage creates, such as the financial entitlements of surviving spouses or the consequences of divorce".[25] And as I have already suggested, a wedding is a discrete event, while a marriage is a continuing process.

Some outstanding issues

Humanist and "belief" weddings

The terms of reference that the Law Commission agreed with the Government included the issue of how marriage by humanist and other non-religious belief organisations could be incorporated into a revised or new scheme and how provision could be made for the use of independent celebrants, ***but only if the Government so decided.*** The terms of reference stated that "the Law Commission will not make recommendations as to whether the groups who can solemnize marriages should be expanded".[26]

In Scotland, humanists have been able to register as wedding celebrants since 2005 – and by 2019 there were more humanist weddings in Scotland than Christian ones. Given that the High Court has already ruled in *R (Harrison)* that the current lack of provision for legal humanist weddings in England and Wales is in breach of Article 9 ECHR, it remains to be seen what the Westminster Government will do next.

Unregistered religious weddings

The Commission's proposals do not address the problem of unregistered religious weddings, where the couple – whether intentionally or unknowingly – purport to marry in a religious ceremony that does not create a valid marriage under the 1949 Act. The Commission's proposal to criminalise officiants who ***intentionally mislead*** such couples goes part of the way, as does the shift from authorising buildings to authorising officiants, but it does not appear to cover the situation where an officiant makes an honest mistake or simply does not understand the law, as in *MA v JA* noted earlier.

There is also the situation where the couple ***themselves*** do not want a legally-valid ceremony – for example, devout Muslims who have an unregistered ***nikah*** wedding simply so that they can be together unchaperoned. Opinions are divided on this: the first recommendation of the Government

25 HM Government and Law Commission of England and Wales, 'Terms of Reference – Weddings Project', 29 July 2019, 1.5(3).
26 Law Commission of England and Wales (n 2), p. 450.

review of *sharia* chaired by Mona Siddiqi was that the Marriage Act 1949 and the Matrimonial Causes Act 1973 should be amended to make it an offence for the celebrant of *any* marriage, including Islamic marriages, to fail to ensure that the marriage was also civilly registered.[27]

There is obviously an issue about consent and the possibility of improper family pressure to marry, and discussions about unregistered religious marriages are often framed in terms of mature adult males marrying immature young females. Equally, however, it is perfectly possible that a devout unmarried Muslim couple in their twenties or thirties might desire a *nikah* ceremony simply because they do not wish to overstep the bounds of what is considered *halal*. And if it is a couple's unfettered, free choice is to have an unregistered religious marriage – what the Siddiqi review called "couples wishing to cohabit who see Islamic marriage as a way of appeasing family but are not 'ready' to marry legally" – should that be a matter for the secular law at all? What should certainly not be possible, however, is for a couple who fully intend to create a valid marriage to fail to do so because of a technical flaw in the proceedings for which they are not responsible.

Cohabitation and the decline of marriage in England and Wales

Historically, Scotland recognised various kinds of "irregular marriage"; but the last of them, "marriage by cohabitation with habit and repute", was abolished by the Family Law (Scotland) Act 2006. Though the idea that there was ever such a thing as "common law marriage" *in England and Wales* – that people somehow acquired legal rights just by living together – has been comprehensively debunked by Rebecca Probert,[28] it persists nevertheless, and cohabiting couples often discover their lack of legal married status and legal protection only when their relationship ends on death or by separation. The suspicion is also that the less well-educated and less articulate probably suffer disproportionately in such circumstances because they will be less likely to have made proper testamentary provision for their partners.

What the Law Commission's proposals do *not* do (because the matter was not included in the terms of reference: how could it have been?) is to make any proposals for proper legal protection for the interests of cohabitants, though in July 2007 the Commission had published a report in which it had accepted that reform was needed to address inadequacies in the current law and had recommended a new statutory scheme for cohabitants on separation.[29]

27 *The Independent Review into the Application of Sharia Law in England and Wales* (Cm 9560 February 2018), p. 5.

28 R. Probert, 'Common-Law Marriage: Myths and Misunderstandings', *Child and Family Law Quarterly* 20, no 1 (2008).

29 Law Commission of England and Wales, *Cohabitation: The Financial Consequences of Relationship Breakdown* (Cm 7182, Law Com no. 307, July 2007).

Recently, the House of Commons Women and Equalities Committee published a report[30] urging the Government to "reform family law to better protect cohabiting couples and their children from financial hardship in the event of separation" and to implement the opt-out cohabitation scheme that had been proposed by the Law Commission in its 2007 report. The Government accepted in part the Committee's recommendation that it "should conduct a public awareness campaign to highlight the legal distinctions between getting married, forming a civil partnership, or choosing to live together as cohabiting partners",[31] agreed with the Committee's views on the "common law marriage" myth[32] and agreed in part with the Committee's recommendation for "a targeted information campaign aimed at women in religious communities where religious-only marriages are commonplace", highlighting the risks of not having a ceremony which meets legal formalities.[33]

But that was about as far as the Government was prepared to go. Overall, it rejected the Committee's core proposals on several grounds:

- that the existing work on the law of marriage and divorce needed to be concluded first;
- that the Government was currently working on the framework for a review of the law of financial provision on divorce;
- that cohabitation needed to be considered in the context of the Law Commission's recommendations on reforming weddings law generally;
- that the Law Commission's recommendations were in any case fifteen years old and would need reviewing and a fresh round of consultations; and
- that any future review of the 2007 proposals or fresh consultation would have to take account of subsequent changes in the law.

The latest estimate by the Office for National Statistics is that in 2020 there were more than three million cohabiting couples in England and Wales:[34] six million people – ***about one-tenth of the total population.*** In my view, that statistic alone should prompt Government action.

30 House of Commons Women and Equalities Committee, *The Rights of Cohabiting Partners* (Second Report of Session 2022–23 HC 92, August 2022).

31 Paragraph 24.

32 *Ibid.*

33 Paragraph 32.

34 Office for National Statistics, *Population estimates by marital status and living arrangements, England and Wales*, 16 December 2021: Table 4: Living arrangements by age group and sex for all persons, England and Wales, 2002 to 2020. For a summary of the current law, see C. Fairbairn, '*Common Law Marriage' and Cohabitation* (London: House of Commons Research Briefing, November 2022). https://researchbriefings.files.parliament.uk/documents/SN03372/SN03372.pdf.

In conclusion

The first issue to bear in mind is that the Law Commission's proposals for reform are exactly what they say they are: *proposals*, not law. Whether the Government will introduce the necessary bill to implement them remains to be seen; the next General Election must be held by January 2024, so there is little parliamentary time left for legislation. We have been here before – and nothing was done on the previous occasion.

The other is this. In 2021, before the Commission's final proposals had been announced, Russell Sandberg published an interesting critique[35] of the Commission's thinking on reform, in which he concluded that its proposals were important steps forward that would go a long way to improving the current law, but that they were certainly not a magic bullet for all its problems. I largely agree with Russell's overall conclusions, but a major hurdle to comprehensive reform is that reforming the law on weddings cannot of itself either resolve the issue of unregistered religious ceremonies where the parties make a deliberate, intentional choice not to register them or address the problem of the lack of legal rights for cohabitants. The problem is that "weddings" are, by definition, *precisely what those things are not.*

In my view, both those issues require much more radical – and subtle – approaches. But I cannot begin to guess what those approaches might be.

35 R. Sandberg, *Religion and Marriage Law: The Need for Reform* (Bristol: Bristol University Press, 2021). For his initial reaction to the Commission's final proposals, see R. Sandberg, *Déjà I Do: Some Initial Thoughts on the Law Commission's 'Celebrating Marriage'* Report (Law & Religion UK, 23 July 2022). https://lawandreligionuk.com/2022/07/23/deja-i-do-some-initial-thoughts-on-the-law-commissions-celebrating-marriage-report/.

6 Challenging the right to change religion or belief

Interpreting Article 18 of the International Covenant on Civil and Political Rights

Mirjam van Schaik and Jasper Doomen

Introduction

It is no longer a serious matter of debate that the freedom of religion or belief is important, and the number of treaties including it gives the impression that it is well protected. However, studies demonstrate that implementing the freedom to change religion or belief, as an aspect of this overall freedom, meets difficulties in state practises. Doctrinal and historical research is conducted regarding the UN legal documents and the drafting history to demonstrate that the phrasing of the provisions has been gradually altered since the legal establishment of the freedom to change religion or belief in 1948. The central question of this chapter is to what extent the explicit right to apostasy is recognized within the United Nations, and whether the concept of freedom to choose a religion as used by the United Nations provides sufficient protection to apostates.

Firstly, we analyse the current legal provisions, and inquire into a grammatical interpretation of the entrenched rights: we examine the (exact) wording of the legal contours of the provisions. This analysis in particular is significant as it demonstrates the scope of the freedom to change religion or belief. The views of some UN experts and the Human Rights Committee are also discussed. To properly understand and interpret the freedom to change religion, the drafting history of Article 18 ICCPR is studied. This is the second perspective from which the freedom to change religion or belief is researched.

The legislative history of Article 18 ICCPR is of particular interest, as the drafting parties had varying views about the scope and interpretations of several concepts of the provision. Due to the influence of a great range of states, it was a complicated process to reach consensus on the various concepts and terminology; it took nearly two decades. It is imperative to understand this legal historical analysis and to assess the current academic debates on the freedom to change religion or belief, which will be the third perspective from which this topic is discussed. The stances of several renowned authors in academia about the freedom to change religion or belief are discussed, and we will demonstrate that these conceptions seem to diverge.

DOI: 10.4324/9781003502845-6

The analyses from these three perspectives lead to the argument that within the UN, member states have managed to alter the provisions, resulting in conceptual ambiguity regarding the right to change religion or belief. We will argue that it is a matter of concern that within the UN and in academia, there is little recognition that the explicit right to apostasy has been disregarded, diminishing the normative force of this essential element of the religious freedom provision.

In conclusion, we will argue that conceptual clarity is needed. In order for the freedom of religion or belief to have a scope broad enough to include the freedom to change religion or belief, it must be explicitly included in the formulation so as to minimize the risk of misinterpretation. This would mean that Article 18 ICCPR has to be reconceptualized.

Legal provisions

In- or excluding apostasy in the legal framework

The controversial issue of the right to change religion or belief, and whether this should be recognized in international standards, was extensively discussed during the drafting of the Universal Declaration of Human Rights (UDHR) (1948), the ICCPR (1966), and the 1981 Declaration on the Elimination of All Forms of Intolerance and of Discrimination Based on Religion or Belief.

The right to change belief or religion adds to the general right of freedom of religion or belief: (1) the right to adopt another religion or belief than the one which one has acquired from the parents or guardians; (2) the right to adopt another religion or belief than the one initially chosen by the believer him- or herself; (3) the right to relinquish all religion. The last option means that the right to change religion or belief implies the option of *apostasy*.

Although there is no clear definition of apostasy, and various definitions are used within religions,[1] in general terms it includes the (total) desertion of, or departure from, one's religion, principles, community, and cause.[2] The Oxford Dictionary adds to this "the act of rejecting your former religious or political belief".[3] It is the act of refusing to continue to follow, obey, or recognize any religious faith or belief whatsoever.[4] For this reason, it is highly controversial. It is even more controversial when referred to as an actual right, which is the topic of this chapter.

1 See for the usage of these various definitions David G. Bromley, *The Politics of Religious Apostasy: The Role of Apostates in the Transformation of Religious Movements*, ed. D. G. Bromley (Westport: Praeger Publishers, 1998).

2 'Apostasy', *Encyclopædia Britannica*. britannica.com accessed 25 May 2020.

3 'Apostasy', *Oxford Advanced Learner's Dictionary*, 2020. oxfordlearnersdictionaries.com accessed 22 October 2020.

4 'Apostasy', *Merriam-Webster*. merriam-webster.com accessed 25 May 2020.

While this inquiry, given its focus on conceptual clarity, is primarily theoretical, it is useful to mention some examples of relevant Human Rights Committee cases, in which pertinent rights are invoked under the banner of apostasy. An appeal to (inter alia) Article 18 ICCPR is at issue in a case where an objection is raised against deportation (to Afghanistan) by an individual who has converted to Christianity, which is, he claims, " considered as a breach of a fundamental rule of Islam, and apostasy is a crime and punishable by death".[5] The Convention against Torture and Other Cruel, Inhuman or Degrading Treatment or Punishment (CAT) is appealed to in this respect.[6] Apostasy insofar as the right to relinquish all religion is concerned is also appealed to.[7]

The legal framework that was established regarding the freedom to change religion or belief in the UN is the following:

Article 18 UDHR

Everyone has the right to freedom of thought, conscience and religion; this right includes *freedom to change his religion or belief*, and freedom, either alone or in community with others and in public or private, to manifest his religion or belief in teaching, practice, worship and observance.

Article 18 ICCPR

1. Everyone shall have the right to freedom of thought, conscience and religion. This right shall include *freedom to have or to adopt a religion or belief of his choice*, and freedom, either individually or in community with others and in public or private, to manifest his religion or belief in worship, observance, practice and teaching.

5 *Decision Adopted by the Committee under the Optional Protocol, Concerning Communication no. 2338/2014* (CCPR/C/119/D/2338/2014), para 3.1; cf. the similar case in *Views Adopted by the Committee under Article 5 (4) of the Optional Protocol, Concerning Communication no. 2594/2015* (CCPR/C/121/D/2594/2015), para 3.2.

6 'In assessing the risk of torture in the present case, the Committee notes the complainant's allegations that as a Christian convert, he risks being subjected to torture and possibly to death . . . if returned to Afghanistan, where conversion is considered as apostasy in Islamic law and shameful in society'. *Decision Adopted by the Committee under Article 22 of the Convention, Concerning Communication no. 908/2019* (CAT/C/71/D/908/2019), para 8.6. Cf. *Decision Adopted by the Committee under Article 22 of the Convention, Concerning Communication no. 1016/2020* (CAT/C/77/D/1016/2020), para 2.3, and *Decision Adopted by the Committee under Article 22 of the Convention, Concerning Communication no. 662/2015* (CAT/C/60/D/662/2015), para 3.2.

7 See, for example, *Decision Adopted by the Committee under Article 22 of the Convention, Concerning Communication no. 918/2019* (CAT/C/72/D/918/2019), para 5.6, and *Communication no. 470/2011: Decision Adopted by the Committee at Its Fifty-Third Session (3–28 November 2014)* (CAT/C/53/D/470/2011), para 5.8.

Article 1 1981 Declaration

> 1. Everyone shall have the right to freedom of thought, conscience and religion. This right shall include *freedom to have a religion or whatever belief of his choice*, and freedom, either individually or in community with others and in public or private, to manifest his religion or belief in worship, observance, practice and teaching.

On a *textual level*, the articles differ in several respects. Over the years textual changes have been implemented: Article 18 ICCPR differs from Article 18 UDHR and the 1981 Declaration in at least three respects.

Firstly, in Article 18 ICCPR a second paragraph was adopted that states: "no one shall be subject to coercion which would impair his freedom to have or to adopt a religion or belief of his choice". In addition, a third paragraph was added in which a limitation clause was adopted. This limitation clause was repeated fifteen years later in Article 1 of the 1981 Declaration. The aforementioned paragraph and limitation clause were, however, absent from the Universal Declaration. Instead, in the Universal Declaration a more general provision was attributed in Article 29 paragraph 2. Secondly, in Article 18 ICCPR, a new paragraph was inserted that grants parents or legal guardians the freedom to ensure the religious and moral education of their children in conformity with their own convictions. This paragraph was also adopted in the following 1981 Declaration in an even more substantive manner in Article 5.

Thirdly, and as the focus of this chapter, the alterations in phrasing in the legal framework with regard to the freedom to change religion or belief must be addressed. In Article 18 UDHR, the phrase "this right includes freedom to change his religion or belief" was included, whereas in Article 18 ICCPR, the words "the freedom to have or to adopt a religion or belief of his choice" were adopted, and in Article 1 of the 1981 Declaration the clause "freedom to have a religion or whatever belief of his choice" were used.

These various *textual alterations* demonstrate that there is a change in phrasing from "to change religion or belief" to "have or to adopt a religion or belief of choice" to "religion or whatever belief of choice". The textual changes indicate that the 1948 formula was not repeated in 1966 and 1981. As our following analysis will demonstrate, during the ICCPR drafting process, all references to the wording "to change religion or belief", which were used in the Universal Declaration, were in the end deleted. A similar situation occurred during the preparations for the 1981 declaration; the language of its predecessor, the 1966 Covenant, was only partially adopted since the phrasing "to adopt a religion", which was used in the ICCPR, remained absent. In Article 6 of the 1981 Declaration, the freedoms included in the general freedom of religion or belief, are summed up; no references are made to the 1948 or 1966 formula. To accommodate the states that opposed this approach, Article 8 was introduced, which states that "[n]othing in the present Declaration shall be construed as restricting or derogating from any right defined in the

Universal Declaration of Human Rights and the International Covenants on Human Rights."

If these phrases were grammatically interpreted, the interpretation would be based exclusively on the literal meaning of the words themselves. The usage of a different formulation would then suggest a change in meaning.[8] The interesting question now arises whether the difference in wording implicates a difference in rights, or rather indicates a change in the *de jure* situation prevailing in the international legal order. If so, does the variety in phrases have *de facto* consequences for implementing the right? In other words, do these gradual textual changes have any legal or normative implications for the freedom of religion and belief and, more specifically, for the right to apostasy? In order to answer these questions, the views of some UN experts are discussed in the following sections.

Pertinent UN reports

In 1960, Arcot Krishnaswami, Special Rapporteur of the Sub-Commission on Prevention of Discrimination and Protection of Minorities, with the authorization of the UN Commission on Human Rights and the UNECOSOC, was responsible for *The Study of Discrimination in the Matter of Religious Rights and Practices.* In this study, Krishnaswami addresses, inter alia, the topic of changing religion or belief and writes that "any instance of compelling an individual to join or of preventing him from leaving the organization of a religion or a belief in which he has no faith must be considered to be an infringement of the right to freedom of thought, conscience and religion."[9]

Krishnaswami furthermore notes that "it must none the less be pointed out that the consensus of world opinion, as expressed in the Universal Declaration of Human Rights, is unequivocally in favour of permitting an individual not only to maintain but also to change his religion or belief in accordance with his convictions."[10] Moreover, Krishnaswami argues that "[t]he same idea is also brought out succinctly in Article 18 of the draft covenant on civil and political rights."[11]

In 1987 Elizabeth Odio Benito, the former Special Rapporteur on the Elimination of All Forms of Intolerance and Discrimination Based on Religion or Belief, wrote the annual report *Study on the current dimensions of the problems of intolerance and discrimination on grounds of religion or belief.* Odio Benito elaborates on Article 18 UDHR, Article 18 ICCPR, and the 1981 Declaration in this study. One of the conclusions Odio Benito draws concerning the

8 A. J. Kwak (ed.), *Holy Writ: Interpretation in Law and Religion* (Farnham: Ashgate, 2009); A. Scalia and B. A. Garner, *Reading Law: The Interpretation of Legal Texts* (St. Paul: Thomson/West, 2012).

9 A. Krishnaswami, *Study of Discrimination in the Matter of Religious Rights and Practices* (New York: United Nations, 1960), p. 16.

10 *Ibid.*, 25.

11 *Ibid.*, 26.

freedom to change religion or belief in the provisions is that "although they varied slightly in wording, all meant precisely the same thing, that everyone has the right to leave one religion or belief and to adopt another, or to remain without any at all."[12] She writes, "it is implicit in the concept of the right to freedom of thought, conscience, religion and belief, regardless of how that concept is presented."[13]

Regarding Article 6 of the 1981 Declaration, Odio Benito elaborates on this view by pointing out that although it does not explicitly mention the freedom to change religion or belief, the "1981 Declaration, without repeating the Universal Declaration or the International Covenant word for word, encompasses the right to change one's religion or belief and to adopt another or to have none at all."[14]

In 1993, the Human Rights Committee addressed the issue of freedom of religion or belief and elaborated on Article 18 ICCPR in General Comment 22 in eleven paragraphs.[15] Concerning this subject, the Committee states that Article 18 ICCPR protects theistic, non-theistic, and atheistic beliefs as well as the freedom not to profess any religion or belief.[16] It explicates that "[i]t does not permit any limitations whatsoever on the freedom of thought and conscience or on the freedom to have or adopt a religion or belief of one's choice."[17]

Paragraph 5 engages this topic explicitly: "the freedom to "have or to adopt" a religion or belief necessarily entails the freedom to choose a religion or belief, including the right to replace one's current religion or belief with another or to adopt atheistic views, as well as the right to retain one's religion or belief."[18] Additionally, it elucidates that Article 18 paragraph 2 "bars coercion that would impair the right to have or adopt a religion or belief, including the use of threat of physical force or penal sanctions to compel believers or non-believers to adhere to their religious beliefs and congregations, to recant their religion or belief or to convert."[19]

An analysis of General Comment 22 demonstrates that there are some noticeable aspects concerning this topic. Firstly, it is indicated clearly that the right to apostasy is protected since it includes the right to replace one's current religion or belief with another or to adopt atheistic views. It is, however,

12 E. Odio Benito, *Study on the Current Dimensions of the Problems of Intolerance and Discrimination on Grounds of Religion or Belief* (1987), p. 4. (E/CN.4/Sub. 2/1987/2 6 31 August 1986).

13 *Ibid.*

14 *Ibid.*, 50.

15 Human Rights Committee, General Comment 22 (48), Article 18, ICCPR/C/21/Rev.1/Add.4 (30 July 1993).

16 *Ibid.*, para 2.

17 UNHRC, ICCPR *General Comment no. 22: Article 18 (Freedom of Thought, Conscience or Religion)*, 30 July 1993, ICCPR/C/21/Rev.1/Add.4, para 3.

18 UNHRC, ICCPR *General Comment no. 22: Article 18 (Freedom of Thought, Conscience or Religion)*, 30 July 1993, ICCPR/C/21/Rev.1/Add.4, para. 5.

19 *Ibid.*

remarkable that in the overall text, the concept of 'change' is not even used once; the wording of the Universal Declaration is thus set aside. The second point is that the wording of the ICCPR is used rather than the language of the later drafted 1981 Declaration. Instead of "this right shall include freedom to have a religion or whatever belief of his choice", the phrase "the freedom to have or adopt a religion or belief of one's choice" is used, meaning that there is a *reintroduction* of the concept of 'adopt', which was essentially absent in the 1981 Declaration.

Based on textual analysis, it is clear that there was a textual change, i.e., a grammatical difference in defining the right to change religion or belief, apparent from the alteration of the words in "to have and adopt" and the use of the concept of 'choice'.

Considering the adjustment of these phrasings, it may be said that there is a decline from an *explicit* recognition of the right to a sort of *implicit* recognition. However, according to the two rapporteurs, the Universal Declaration, the ICCPR and the 1981 Declaration all attribute the freedom to change religion or belief, even though the language of the Universal Declaration is not repeated. Does this mean that the legal concepts do not have to be repeated to be legally valid? Does interpretation suffice? Here we seem to arrive at a general reflection on "What is the law?" The text as it has been formulated by the lawgiver? Or the text drafted by the lawgiver *and* the interpretation by the legal experts?

Within UN circles, the prevailing view is still that Article 18 ICCPR includes the right to apostasy, but, as we will demonstrate in the subsequent sections, it may be argued that the evidence for this stance is not completely convincing. Agreement as to the meaning of the clauses "to have or adopt a religion or belief of choice" and "to change religion and belief" is imperative to understand and assess this assumption. Therefore, the legislative history is studied and discussed in the following sections. This is useful in clarifying the motivations of the drafters of the ICCPR for changing the concepts. Perhaps they intentionally changed the wording in the provisions in order to assert different normative contours. This is the second perspective from which we will examine the freedom to change religion or belief.

Legislative history

The contents of Article 18 ICCPR

The debate on Article 18 ICCPR in the Commission on Human Rights seemed to focus on three main issues: the nature or concept of "freedom of thought, conscience and religion", the right "to change or maintain" one's religion or belief, and the scope of legitimate limitations of "freedom to manifest one's religion or belief".[20] The Commission had decided that the "freedom of

20 A/2929, chapter VI, 136–143.

thought, conscience and religion was frequently characterized as 'absolute', 'sacred' and 'inviolable'. The first clause of the article accordingly declared in clear and simple terms, and without qualifications, that 'everyone shall have the right to freedom of thought, conscience and religion'. No restrictions of a legal character, it was generally agreed, could be imposed upon man's inner thought or moral consciousness, or his attitude towards the universe or its creator; only external manifestations of religion or belief might be subject to legitimate limitations."[21]

The Commission on Human Rights adopted three changes regarding draft Article 18 ICCPR that had consequences for the Third Committee's subsequent debate. The first change was made within the context of the debate on proselytism and apostasy and specifically concerned the possible coercion of an individual to change religion. Pressured by the Egyptian and Lebanese delegations, a compromise was made, which consisted of the insertion of the words "to maintain" besides the words "to change" in Article 18 ICCPR.[22] The suggested change was adopted unanimously.[23] The second change consisted of adding a second paragraph to the provision stating that "no one shall be subject to coercion which would impair his freedom to maintain or to change his religion or belief". The concept of "coercion" was interpreted not to include "moral or intellectual persuasion" or "any other legitimate limitation of freedom to manifest one's religion or belief".[24] The third change was the introduction of the limitation clause in the third paragraph of the provision.[25] The Commission on Human Rights adopted Article 18 paragraph 1 unanimously, paragraph 2 unanimously, and, finally, the article as a whole unanimously.[26]

The Third Committee discussed the draft Article 18 ICCPR at various successive meetings.[27] The article gave again rise to debate, and several amendments

21 *Ibid.*, para 106.
22 E/CN.4/L.187, E/CN.4/SR.319, 3.
23 E/CN.4/SR.319, 13.
24 A/2929, chapter VI, para 110.
25 *Ibid.*, paras 112–114.
26 E/2573, annex B. The draft of Article 18 that was at the end introduced to the Third Committee stated:

1. Everyone shall have the right to freedom of thought, conscience and religion. This right shall include freedom to maintain or to change his religion, or belief, and freedom, either individually or in community with others and in public or private, to manifest his religion or belief in worship, observance, practice and teaching.
2. No one shall be subject to coercion which would impair his freedom to maintain or to change his religion or belief.
3. Freedom to manifest one's religion or beliefs may be subject only to such limitations as are prescribed by law and are necessary to protect safety, order, health, or morals or the fundamental rights and freedoms of others. E/2573, annex I B.

27 From its 1021st to its 1027th meeting. See A/4625, fifteenth session, agenda item 34, U.N. Doc. A/4625, para 43.

were submitted by, inter alia, Greece,[28] Saudi Arabia,[29] Brazil, and the Philippines.[30] The last two amendments are relevant for present purposes.

The proposal to delete the salient elements

In the Third Committee, the Saudi Arabian delegation addressed the subject of the freedom to change and maintain religion and strongly contested the suggestions of the Commission on Human Rights. The Saudi Arabian delegate proposed to delete the words "to maintain or to change his religion or belief" from both paragraphs 1 and 2 in the provision.[31] With this alteration, the explicit right of the individual to change religion or belief was deleted in both paragraphs of the provision.[32]

Jamil M. Baroody, the Saudi Arabian representative introduced and substantiated the suggestion.[33] This was the same delegate who had dominated the discussions regarding this topic during the drafting process of the Universal Declaration more than a decade earlier. The adoption of the words "to change religion" was one of the reasons for the Saudi Arabian delegation to abstain from the final vote regarding the adoption of the Universal Declaration.[34] Baroody was aware that the insertion of the words "to maintain" besides the words "to change religion or belief" in the draft covenant was intended to accommodate the Saudi Arabian's stance; he was, however, still not content with the phrasing of the provision.[35]

Baroody repeated the words of the Commission on Human Rights, which had qualified the freedom of thought, conscience, and religion as absolute, sacred, and inviolable.[36] He found it "important to note that those terms had been used in connexion with all three elements, and not with religion alone. His delegation felt that the article should not be regarded, as there had been a tendency to do, as pertaining exclusively to religion; as the article's first sentence indicated, the three freedoms mentioned were of equal value."[37] As a result, Baroody focussed in his preliminary statement on the supposedly

28 A/C.3/L.875.
29 A/C.3/L.876.
30 A/C.3/L.877.
31 A/C.3/L.876; A/C.3/SR.1021, para 15, See Official Records of the General Assembly, Tenth Session, Annexes, agenda item 28 (part 1); A/C.3/L.460, 11; A/2808, para 45. Report of the Third Committee, Ninth Session Agenda item 58, 29 November 1954. The amendment was first introduced with A/C.3/L.422. A/C.3/SR.1023, para 11. During this meeting Baroody formally introduced his suggestions by introducing amendment A/C.3/L.876.
32 A/4625, para 48, E/2573, annex I B.
33 'Jamil the Irrepressible', *Time* 98, no. 24 (1971), 32–34; Wolfgang Saxon, 'Jamil M. Baroody, Saudi Arabia's U.N. Delegate, Dies', *The New York Times*, 5 March 1979.
34 A/PV.183, Plenary Meeting 10 December 1948, 933–934.
35 A/C.3/SR.1021, para 7.
36 *Ibid.*, para 8.
37 A/C.3/SR.1021, para 8. In a later session Baroody expressed in this regard that '[i]n mentioning only the two possibilities of maintaining or changing one's religion, the present

unequal emphasis in the article. Baroody continued that "[t]here could be no compulsion to believe, and religion was an entirely personal matter. It was wrong, therefore, to do any more than enunciate the right to freedom of religion; the emphasis laid on the right to change one's religion was totally unjustified."[38]

Baroody proceeded to underline that there was no such thing as a right to proselytize and warned the Third Committee not to "lend itself to such practices".[39] Importantly, this discussion must be placed against the background of the age of Christian colonialism. There was a worldwide resentment of Christian proselytizing practises, and the mere act of proselytism was considered a threat. Interestingly, Muslims were at that time by far not as well organized in this respect as Christians. In the last decades, there have been various developments that have changed this balance, and presently there are various organizations who strive to be the "collective voice of the Muslim world".[40]

In his formal amendments, Baroody explained in more detail his motivations and held the "firm conviction" that a reference to the freedom to maintain or change religion was "superfluous".[41] He said that "[t]he new text, while detracting nothing from the statement of the freedom, would allow for every possibility – the right to maintain or change one's religion, the right to doubt, question, return to one's former religion, and so on. All those were emotional states which were not covered by the words "to maintain or to change"."[42]

This last remark is interesting, for it can be interpreted as Baroody implying that an *explicit* reference does not have to be made to the freedom to maintain or change religion because it is already *implicitly* included in the first part of the sentence. Although this view was shared by several delegates, some delegations adopted a different stance. For conceptual clarity, we have distinguished this view into an implicit and explicit right to apostasy in the freedom of religion or belief provision.

Referring implicitly or explicitly to apostasy

The arguments of the representatives that adopted the first line of reasoning, *viz.*, that no *explicit* reference to the individual's freedom to maintain

---

article also contained an incomplete enumeration, which his amendments sought to remedy'. A/C.3/SR.1023, para 12.

38 A/C.3/SR.1021, para 11.

39 *Ibid.*

40 B. M. van Schaik, 'Religious Freedom and Blasphemy Law in a Global Context: The Concept of Religious Defamation', in P. B. Cliteur and T. Herrenberg (eds.), *The Fall and Rise of Blasphemy Law* (Leiden: Leiden University Press, 2016); B. M. van Schaik, 'Blasphemy: In the Eye of the Beholder? Religious Freedom And Blasphemy Law in a Global Context: The Concept of Religious Defamation', *Free Inquiry* 37, no. 4 (2017).

41 A/C.3/SR.1023, para 12.

42 *Ibid.*

or change religion should be made, varied. There were representatives who agreed with Baroody's line of reasoning, such as the Ghanaian representative Dadzie, who thought "the article could do more justice to the multifarious shades of religions and beliefs represented in the world by protecting freedom of religion in general terms."[43] Mantzoulinos, who represented Greece, adopted a similar stance and expressed that "[t]he right proclaimed in that first sentence, in a categoric, definite and positive formulation, was obviously bound to imply the right to maintain or change one's religion or one's belief. That last clarification was superfluous and could only weaken the strength of the preceding statement."[44] The Canadian representative, Steen, argued that " her delegation held that freedom of religion involved the right to maintain or to change one's religion whether the right was spelled out or not."[45]

These responses seem to imply that the representatives who did not favour an explicit mention of the rights to maintain or change religion were not actually against the rationale or the existence of the right to apostasy but held the view that the right was implicitly included in the first sentence. An enumeration of it was more or less deemed a ***redundant*** addition.

There were also delegations who opposed Baroody's amendment with various arguments. Representative Lopez from the Philippines argued that if the phrasing was deleted the "freedom of thought and of conscience would no longer be safeguarded for non-conformists."[46] The Dutch representative, Boersma, expressed that "Article 18 also contained a legal check against excessive manifestations of religious proselytism, in that all attempts on the part of believers and churches alike to promulgate certain religious beliefs were subject to the limitation that they must not encroach upon freedom of thought in any manner contrary to the spirit of the article."[47]

The representative of Liberia, Dennis, pointed out that "a man who could not change his religion in fact had a religion imposed on him."[48] He furthermore explained that "[t]he essential point was not the religion a man chose, but his freedom to choose any religion he wished. That freedom automatically supposed another, the freedom to change his religion, even if the tenets of his original religion forbade such a change. That very important right was spelled out in the second sentence of paragraph 1, which could not, therefore, be considered redundant."[49] The representative of Yugoslavia, Karapandza, argued that if the delegations thought the right was implicit in the first part of the provision, there was no actual reason for it not to appear in the provision.

43 A/C.3/SR.1025, para 17.
44 A/C.3/SR.1022, para 1.
45 A/C.3/SR.1024, para 2.
46 A/C.3/SR.1022, para 11.
47 A/C.3/SR.1025, para 41.
48 A/C.3/SR.1024, para 7.
49 A/C.3/SR.1023, para 8.

He also emphasized that all representatives had stated that their "respective religions allowed for such change".[50]

The Pakistani delegate, Begum Aziz Ahmed, perceptively stated: "Nothing could be lost by elaboration, but something could be lost by failure to elaborate."[51] The French representative, Bouquin, indicated that the adoption of the amendments would result in "rendering a very important article meaningless".[52] He furthermore emphasized the importance of Article 18 UDHR and underlined the similarities between the two articles. He stated that "the arguments adduced were not sufficient to justify any drastic change in the wording adopted in the [Universal Declaration]".[53] Ceylon's representative, Perera, shared this view and stated that the explicit mention in Article 18 of the Declaration "made it necessary to consider very carefully before accepting an amendment to delete it".[54]

More arguments were brought forward. The United States representative, Lamey, noted, "it was sometimes advisable to spell out such a right in language which could not be misunderstood, rather than to leave its consequences to be inferred."[55] The Israeli delegate, Eshel, offered an argument of similar nature and commented that "brevity was not a desirable aim, unless it made for clarity. The draft Covenant, as a legally binding instrument, should be both clear and explicit."[56] The delegate of Cuba, Griñan, drafted an argument more of a social nature and expressed that "[i]n view of the social evolution in the overwhelming majority of countries, it was proper to give explicit recognition to everyone's right to maintain or to change his religion."[57]

The Brazilian and Philippine amendment: religious choice

The analyses in the previous sections indicate that it was unlikely, with the current formulation in place, that draft Article 18 ICCPR would be endorsed by a vast majority of the members of the Third Committee. The Philippine delegate, Lopez, came up with a suggestion. He said that "[i]n supporting the principle that an individual had the right to maintain or change his religion or to have no religion at all, he had merely been emphasizing one major principle,

50 A/C.3/SR.1027, para 23. The Philippian representative, Lopez, made a similar argument.
51 A/C.3/SR.1024, para 23.
52 A/C.3/SR.1026, para 6.
53 *Ibid.*
54 A/C.3/SR.1022, paras 4–5, 19.
55 A/C.3/SR.1027, para 19.
56 A/C.3/SR.1025, para 45.
57 A/C.3/SR.1026, para 9.

the right of an individual to have freedom of choice."[58] Lopez, therefore, proposed to alter the second sentence in the provision into:

> This right shall include freedom to have a religion of his choice and freedom, either individually or in community with others, to manifest his religion or belief in worship, observance, practice and teaching.[59]

Lopez expected that this "neutral wording" would be satisfactory to all the members of the Third Committee.[60] He furthermore said that "[h]e was not insensitive to the Saudi Arabian representative's argument that the wording of the article should in no way give direct or positive encouragement to the practice of proselytizing but at the same time it would be wrong to think that the article could ever be interpreted as prohibiting the activities of missionaries."[61]

During the following meeting, the Philippine and Brazilian delegations (representative Lima, who had supported Baroody's amendment) collaborated and drafted a suggestion which they hoped would be satisfactory to many states.[62] They introduced two formal amendments, consisting of the proposal introduced by Lopez during the previous meeting.[63]

Lopez motivated their amendment by arguing "that the basic purpose of Article 18 of the draft Covenant, and the corresponding article of the Universal Declaration of Human Rights, was to ensure to everyone the untrammelled right to exercise freedom of choice in the matter of religion or belief"."[64] He continued by explaining that "[h]is objection to the Saudi Arabian proposal to delete part of the sentence . . . had been that it might lead to misinterpretations of the scope of the right in question. It was not sufficient to say that the right to change one's religion or belief was implicit in the right to freedom of religion."[65] Lopez wanted to emphasize that "the two delegations were not proposing anything which would affect the underlying freedoms concerned or which would in any way alter the scope of the article as it had been drafted by the [Commission on Human Rights] . . . . The amendments fully implied the right of individuals to maintain or change their religion or belief, inasmuch as that would constitute the exercise of their freedom of choice."[66] It seems that these delegates had sincere intentions but, as will be demonstrated, the introduction of this amendment would alter the course and scope of Article 18 ICCPR indefinitely.

58 A/C.3/SR.1024, para 8.
59 *Ibid.*
60 *Ibid.*
61 A/C.3/SR.1024, para 8.
62 A/C.3/SR.1025, para 1.
63 A/C.3/L.877.
64 A/C.3/SR.1025, para 2.
65 *Ibid.*
66 *Ibid.*

Baroody, reacting to the proposal, stated that he did not find it "satisfactory".[67] The delegates who were sympathetic to his cause, however, disagreed. In previous meetings, Amadeo, the Argentinian representative, had expressed that he favoured a simple text and had therefore been supportive of the Saudi Arabian proposal. With regard to the Brazilian and Philippine amendments, he was positive, for they brought out the "essential point, which was the individual's freedom of choice in religious matters."[68] Malyali, the representative from Cyprus, expressed that he had similar thoughts as the Brazilian and Philippine delegate and would, therefore, endorse the amendment.[69] The Spanish representative, De Las Barcenas, expressed that the amendment "improved the text".[70]

The United Arab Republic, represented by EL-Erian, was also positive and stated that the amendments offered an "excellent basis for agreement".[71] Perera thought that the amendment "offered a very satisfactory solution."[72] Even Afghan delegate Farhadi, who stood fiercely by Baroody during his amendment, thought that the suggestion was "clear and very general in scope; it should be acceptable to all delegations which favoured the principle set forth in Article 18 . . . . In essence, it was only a matter of wording that separated the various members of the Committee."[73]

A meeting later, it seemed that Baroody had changed his mind. He again emphasized "that the right of everyone to change, maintain and even renounce his religion or belief was implicitly recognized in the first sentence of Article 18. Nevertheless, as certain representatives were anxious to have the right expressly proclaimed his delegation was prepared to withdraw its amendments . . . in favour of the compromise text submitted by Brazil and the Philippines".[74] He continued that the amended "text of Article 18 would not be entirely satisfactory to his delegation but it would no longer be liable to convey the impression that the Committee unwittingly sanctioned interference with beliefs that some people regarded as sacred".[75] For these reasons, the Saudi Arabian delegation withdrew its amendment, giving way to the amendment drafted by Brazil and the Philippines.[76]

However, not all representatives were so easily persuaded by the amendment with its suggested *compromise text*. For instance, Venezuelan representative Rey argued that the suggestions "were judicious and well phrased", but rightly remarked that the newly formulated freedom did not explicitly

67 A/C.3/SR.1025, para 13.
68 *Ibid.*, para 25.
69 *Ibid.*, para 30.
70 A/C.3/SR.1026, para 3.
71 *Ibid.*, para 13.
72 *Ibid.*, para 20.
73 *Ibid.*, para 1.
74 *Ibid.*, para 26.
75 *Ibid.*, para 27.
76 A/4625, para 46.

proclaim the right of the individual to change religion.[77] He preferred the text as it was introduced by the Commission on Human Rights.[78] Representative Dobson from Australia shared this opinion.[79] Eshel, the Israeli delegate, had a similar view and said that she would not support the Philippine and Brazilian amendment as it "did not spell out the rights in question clearly and unambiguously".[80] Boersma from the Netherlands also wished to continue with the text of the Commission on Human Rights, for he found it clearer.[81] These delegates rightly stressed that the concept of 'choice' embodied an *ambiguity*.

What sort of freedom is at issue?

In the 1027th meeting, the last meeting in which this subject was discussed, the UK's representative, Hoare, drafted a suggestion that would indefinitely alter the explicit mention of the freedom to change religion or belief.

Hoare argued that the discussions in the Third Committee had made it clear that there was no discrepancy in the understanding of the actual scope of the article, or that the right to maintain and change religion was implicitly included. He continued that the discussion was now merely about the article's phrasing, especially since Saudi Arabia had withdrawn its amendment. He stated that it was unwise of the representatives to imply that they differed on the substance of the provision,[82] since the provision "dealt with a very delicate and sensitive subject, it should be adopted unanimously".[83] To accommodate the state delegates who preferred the text of the Commission on Human Rights, he suggested inserting the words "or to adopt" after the words "to have" in the second sentence of paragraph 1.[84] This means that the text would be changed into:

> This right shall include freedom to *have or to adopt* (emphasis added) a religion of his choice and freedom, either individually or in community with others, to manifest his religion or belief in worship, observance, practice and teaching.

This was thus the addition of the concept of 'adopt' to the Brazilian and Philippine amendment.

77 A/C.3/SR.1026, para 14.
78 *Ibid.*
79 *Ibid.*, para 16.
80 A/C.3/SR.1025, para 46.
81 *Ibid.*, para 43.
82 A/C.3/SR.1027, para 1.
83 *Ibid.*
84 *Ibid.*, para 2.

The Brazilian and Philippine delegations welcomed the British suggestions and said that the "words not only made no change in the substance, they even strengthened its formulation. The expression 'to have a religion or belief' was somewhat neutral, whereas the idea of adopting a religion or belief was more active and was a better reflection of the underlying idea of the right to change one's religion."[85]

The first delegate who accepted this revised text was the Italian delegate, Capotorti. He thought that the freedom to change religion or belief was guaranteed by the altered text.[86] The delegate from Indonesia, Djohan, had initially endorsed the text of the Commission on Human Rights, but after the UK complemented the Brazilian and Philippine amendment, he also voted in favour of it.[87] As the final vote would demonstrate, this was to be the general opinion.

Karpadanza was one of the few delegates who were not a proponent of the new suggestions. He argued that it still derived from the actual wording of Article 18 UDHR. However, he accepted the amendments "in a spirit of compromise", as they had been drafted in a "conciliatory spirit".[88] The representative of the Dominican Republic, Cappa, had a similar opinion.[89] Rey said that he still preferred the text of the Commission on Human Rights, for it explicitly addressed the freedom to maintain and change religion, and suggested to combine it with the UK, Brazilian, and Philippine amendment.[90] However, his idea did not find any support.

The debates regarding Article 18 ICCPR eventually ended, and it came to the voting procedure. It would soon become clear that the combination of amendments introduced by Brazil, the Philippines, and the UK was decisive in the debate regarding the freedom to change or maintain religion or belief, or the freedom to have or adopt a religion of choice.

Separate votes were conducted on the amendments and paragraphs.[91] The most impressive but baffling conclusion was that Article 18 ICCPR as a whole was adopted unanimously. This meant that all opponents of the text, including Baroody, and the delegates who still preferred the text as was drafted by the Commission on Human Rights, voted in favour.[92]

85 A/C.3/SR.1027, para 3.
86 *Ibid.*, para 11.
87 *Ibid.*, paras 14–15.
88 *Ibid.*, para 25.
89 *Ibid.*, para 32.
90 A/C.3/SR.1026, para 14.
91 The Brazilian and Philippine amendment, which included the words 'freedom to have a religion of his choice' was adopted by 67 votes to none, with 4 abstentions. The UK amendment which introduced the words 'or to adopt' was adopted by 54 votes to none, with 15 abstentions. The amended paragraph 1 of Article 18 ICCPR was adopted by 70 votes to none, with 2 abstentions. Paragraph 2 of Article 18 ICCPR, as amended, was adopted by 72 votes to none, with 2 abstentions. Paragraph 3 of Article 18 ICCPR was adopted unanimously.
92 A/C.3/SR.1027, para 36. A/4625, para 57.

A spirit of compromise

An analysis of the debates indicates that there was a vast resistance against the phrasing of the text regarding the freedom to change religion or belief. Various delegates had expressed that they were striving for a text that could be adopted unanimously and were therefore willing to discuss and revise the wording of the article. Accordingly, in a conciliatory spirit, efforts were made to reach a consensus. In a *spirit of compromise*, amendments were introduced and accepted.

Evidently, this is what a legislator does: make compromises to reach consensus. This introduces some interesting questions, like: did this conciliatory spirit *strengthen* or *weaken* the text of Article 18 ICCPR? Or rather, did the spirit of compromise and objective for consensus have an impact on realizing the normative aspirations that were set out in Article 18 UDHR in 1948? From the previous analysis, it seems that with the exceptions of some, the delegates thought this not to be the case. However, as the analyses have also demonstrated, this may actually depend on how the concept of 'choice' is interpreted. It seems that an ambiguity is introduced in the phrasing of the text, which leads to the risk of misinterpretation, misuse, or arbitrary application. This assumption requires clarification, but first, we will examine, in the subsequent sections, how the textual alteration of the freedom to change religion or belief was received and interpreted within academic circles. This will be the third perspective.

The inclusive and the exclusive stance

The inclusive stance

Within academia, there are various views regarding the interpretation of Article 18 ICCPR, which generally can be distinguished into two perspectives. On the one hand, there is the view that the freedom to change religion is clearly anchored within the phrasing 'the freedom to have and adopt a religion of choice' in Article 18 ICCPR, which we will refer to as the *inclusive stance*. On the other hand, there is the view that it is not self-evident that the adopted phrase includes this freedom, which we identify as the *exclusive stance*. Both stances will be discussed. We will start with the former.

One of the scholars who adopts an inclusive stance is Derek H. Davis. Davis examined the three primary international documents regarding religious freedom and addressed the topic of changing and maintaining religion. Davis correctly recognizes that throughout the drafting process of the Universal Declaration and the ICCPR the right to change religion was a "controversial issue".[93] He furthermore writes that "[i]n drafting the 1981 Declaration,

93 D. H. Davis, 'The Evolution of Religious Freedom as a Universal Human Right: Examining the Role of the 1981 United Nations Declaration on the Elimination of All Forms of

references to the right to change one's religion were deleted from the text in both the preamble and Article 1, departing, therefore, from the language used in the Universal Declaration and the 1966 Covenant. Consequently, the text of the 1981 Declaration was weakened, but to satisfy those who objected to the deletion, a new Article 8 was added, which states that the 1981 Declaration does not in any way derogate or restrict the freedoms as adopted in the Universal Declaration or the ICCPR."[94] This matter was also addressed in the previous section. What is relevant in this regard is that Davis recognizes the fact that the text was weakened, but overlooks the fact that the phrase "to change religion or belief" was already deleted from the text of the ICCPR. This negation can also be inferred from the fact that he writes that "Article 18 ICCPR guarantees the same rights listed in Article 18 of the Universal Declaration, then adds more".[95]

Some scholars seem to disregard the possible legal implications of textual changes altogether and assume that the freedom to change religion was ensured in both the Universal Declaration and the ICCPR, like legal scholar Paul Taylor, who has made an extensive study of the systematic treatment of both international and European practices regarding religious freedom. Taylor takes a somewhat similar stance to Davis concerning the ICCPR and claims that "[t]here is little doubt that in spite of the immense struggle over the drafting of Article 18(1) of the ICCPR, it embraces freedom on the part of the individual at all times either to change or to maintain religious belief or adherence."[96] He concludes his paragraph regarding this topic with the words "the right to change one's religion seems firmly established in both the United Nations and European systems."[97] According to Taylor, the fact that there was a difference in phrasing does not lead to any consequences.

Theo van Boven comes to a similar view in his dissertation after examining the *travaux préparatoires*. In contrast to Davis and Taylor, Van Boven does address the phrasing of the provision in the ICCPR. He emphasizes that editorial adjustments were made to the text of the Universal Declaration in the ICCPR. He claims that the only notable difference was the modification of the words "freedom to change his religion or belief" into – then still in drafting – "freedom to have or adopt a religion or belief of his choice".[98] According to Van Boven, however, the modification is more of a "psychological than

Intolerance and of Discrimination Based on Religion or Belief', *Brigham Young University Law Review* 2002, no. 2 (2002), 229.

94 *Ibid.*

95 *Ibid.*, pp. 225–226. This stance can also be derived from other passages, for example on page 229.

96 Paul M. Taylor, *Freedom of Religion. UN and European Human Rights Law and Practices* (Cambridge: Cambridge University Press, 2005), p. 31.

97 *Ibid.*, p. 42.

98 Th. C. van Boven, *De volkenrechtelijke bescherming van de godsdienstvrijheid* (Assen: Van Gorcum, 1967), p. 160.

substantial nature".[99] He writes that it "[o]bviously . . . gives the Muslim countries satisfaction that the words 'to change', at which they have resisted in a most emotional way, no longer appear in Article 18 of the draft convention. On the other hand, the replaced formula guarantees the freedom of every person to come to a new decision of faith and to draw the consequences."[100]

Karl Josef Partsch comes to a similar conclusion, claiming that "[i]n a spirit of compromise . . . the language was changed to make explicit the right to maintain one's religion as well to change it. The final wording recognizes the individual's right 'to have or to adopt a religion or belief of his choice'. That clearly implies the right to abandon a religion to which one adhered previously as well as the right to adopt a different religion."[101] This is in line with Richard B. Lillich, according to whom "the gist of Article 18 [Universal Declaration] finds expression in Article 18(1) of the Political Covenant, although the freedom 'to change' has been replaced by the freedom 'to have or to adopt a religion or belief', a shift which appears to be one more of verbiage than of substance."[102] He elucidates this point in a footnote, stating that "[i]ts omission from the Political Covenant appears insignificant, however, in view of statements by representatives of such states that this freedom was implicit in the guarantee of religious freedom."[103]

John P. Humphrey, in his capacity as a professor at McGill University and no longer the leader of the UN Secretariat, observes that the right to change religion or belief "is not mentioned in Article 18 of the Political Covenant, an omission that can be attributed to the persuasive powers of the active representative of Saudi Arabia. But the language of the Political Covenant as adopted certainly included the right to change one's religion or belief."[104]

For these authors (Davis, Taylor, Van Boven, Lillich, Partsch, and Humphrey) it seems that the textual changes, from "the right to change religion" in accordance with the text in the Universal Declaration, to "the right to have or adopt a religion of choice", were merely a matter of semantic adjustment or a shift in verbiage, which did not affect the substance of the legal provision. They adopt the *inclusive stance*, which means that the adopted formulations in 1948, 1966, and 1981 seem to imply the same right: the freedom to change religion or belief.

99 *Ibid.*

100 *Ibid.* The original text is in Dutch.

101 K. J. Partsch, 'Freedom of Conscience and Expression, Political Freedoms in The international Bill of Rights', in L. Henkin (ed.), *The Covenant on Civil and Political Rights* (New York: Columbia University Press, 1981), p. 211.

102 R. B. Lillich, 'Civil Rights', in Th. Meron (ed.), *Human Rights in International Law: Legal and Policy Issue* (Oxford: Clarendon Press, [1984] 2012), p. 159.

103 *Ibid.*

104 J. P. Humphrey, 'Political and Related Rights', in Th. Meron (ed.), *Human Rights in International Law. Legal and Policy Issues* (Oxford: Clarendon Press, [1984] 2012), p. 179. Humphrey retired from the UN in 1966.

To what does a 'choice' amount?

On a semantic level this inclusive stance can be adopted. Still, considering what the attitude is of countries where a firm state religion (especially Islam) is established towards the freedom to change religion, the omission of these words seems more significant and substantial than assumed by these scholars – and UN experts, since they also take this view. It fails to recognize the precarious position of apostasy and apostates in Islamic countries. In a broader sense, it can be argued that the freedom of religious choice is a sensitive issue for all religions.[105] But, as various scholars have argued and research has demonstrated, the conversion to another religion or the renunciation of Islam may have far-reaching consequences in various Islamic states, from the dissolution of marriage to blasphemy and the death penalty.[106]

What is relevant in this regard is that it must be questioned whether the concept of 'choice' implies the same consequences, or rather rights, as the concept of 'change'. Or does 'choice' mean choosing a religion and conforming to it, and does choice then mean choosing once and for all, the choice necessarily being a definitive one? More pertinently: what if the choice is already made by simply being born in a particular religious family? By being born in an Islamic family, the choice to be Muslim is already made by the parents. In Islam, it is generally presumed that every child is born a Muslim, especially if it is born from an Islamic mother. This view stems from the views on creation within Islam.[107] However, from a non-Islamic or an outsider's perspective, the parents

105 The reaction to apostasy may differ within the various religious communities, varying from disappointment and ex-communication to stoning.

106 A. E. Mayer, 'Universal versus Islamic Human Rights: A Clash of Cultures or a Clash with a Construct?', *Michigan Journal of International Law* 15, no. 2, 308–404; A. E. Mayer, *Islam and Human Rights: Tradition and Politics* (Boulder: Westview, 2007); R. Koopmans, *Het vervallen huis van de islam. Over de crisis van de islamitische wereld* (Amsterdam: Prometheus, 2019); C. Schirrmacher, *Let there be no Compulsion in Religion (Surah 2:256). Apostasy from Islam as Judged by Contemporary Islamic Theologians* (Eugene (Oregon): Wipf and Stock, 2016); C. Schirrmacher, 'Apostasy. What do Contemporary Muslim Theologians Teach about Religious Freedom?', *International Journal for Religious Freedom* 6, no. 1 (2013), 189–201; P. Marshall and N. Shea, *Silenced: How Apostasy and Blasphemy Codes are Choking Freedom Worldwide* (Oxford: Oxford University Press, 2011); P. Sookhdeo, *Freedom to Believe: Challenging Islam's Apostasy Law* (Three Rivers (Michigan): Isaac Publishing, 2009); 'Which Countries Still Outlaw Apostasy and Blasphemy', *Pew Research Center*, 2016. pewforum.org updated 29 July 2016; S. M. Zwemer, *The Law of Apostasy in Islam: Answering the Question Why there are so Few Moslem Converts, and Giving Examples of Their Moral Courage and Martyrdom* (London, Edinburgh and New York: Marshall Brothers, 1924). P. B. Cliteur, *The Secular Outlook: In Defense of Moral and Political Secularism* (Chicester: Wiley-Blackwell, 2010).Global Legal Research Center, *Laws Criminalizing Apostasy in Selected Jurisdictions* (Washington, DC: The Law Library of Congress, 2014); 'Trends in Global Restrictions on Religion', *Pew Research Center*, 2016. pewforum.org updated 23 June 2016; P. B. Cliteur, *The Secular Outlook: In Defense of Moral and Political Secularism* (Chicester: Wiley-Blackwell, 2010).

107 This is generally called 'Fitra'. See 'Fitra', *The Oxford Dictionary of Islam*, accessed 5 March 2021.

choose to raise their child in an Islamic way. Is this then automatically the sole choice that is 'allowed', and is it definitive? In this view, freedom of choice does not explain that additional choices to the original may be made.

By diverting to the concept of 'choice', it can be argued that an ambiguity was introduced in the text. It seems that the states played into the hands of the delegations who opposed the right to apostasy, for the reason that with the freedom of choice, there seems to be more room to interpret the provision according to national law in which, for instance, the right to apostasy is not guaranteed. It provides the possibility for states to interpret the freedom of religious choice as the freedom for the individual to make a choice in what religion to adhere to, and that is a permanent decision. It does not (explicitly) clarify that the individual has the right to change their mind in religious matters at any time the individual likes. The provision now lacks ***conceptual clarity***.

The question of how there can be a 'free choice' without the right to change is vital. The interpretation that the right to free choice implies difficulties for the right to apostasy seems at first glance unsubstantiated; it seems like an interpretation that renders the right meaningless because it is logically inconsistent. One might even say that this is neither a matter of interpretation nor a matter of semantic adjustment but a matter of logic. However, this argument does not consider that the concept of 'choice' may be interpreted differently and that various conceptions are thus possible.

Considering these remarks, the freedom of religious choice does not necessarily seem to imply the right to apostasy, since it does not unequivocally imply freedom to change religion, from which is certain that it implies multiple 'changes'. For this reason, not using the concept of change seems to be more than mere window dressing, as was suggested by the UN experts and the scholars who adopt the inclusive stance.

To this stance, a critical side note must be made. We do not argue that enacting the right to adopt the religion of one's choice is worse than having no provision on the freedom of religion (adopted unanimously) at all. In addition, with this observation, we do not mean to say that granting the right to adopt a religion of one's choice as such is counterproductive in Islamic countries. We argue that it *can* be counterproductive. What is emphasized here is that the current wording of the text is rather ambivalent and was (perhaps) unwittingly enabled by the other states, who were seeking consensus for political reasons. On the surface, the text may appear to be the same, but the implementation may vary. We will elaborate on this issue, though, once we have discussed the exclusive stance.

The exclusive stance

The exclusive stance, so the position which does not uncritically adopt the view that Article 18 ICCPR encompasses the freedom to apostasy, is, inter alia, supported by legal scholar Malcolm D. Evans, who perceptively states that "[t]he wording finally adopted might seem to anchor the article within comfortable proximity of the right to change one's religion. Yet precise wording to this effect was expressly excluded from the text; it is open to the interpretation that it allows an individual to continue in a faith, to adopt a faith, but not abandon a faith already held. It has, however, become generally accepted that Article 18 does embrace the right to change religion, although the evidence advanced in support of this is not wholly convincing."[108] Evans thus points out that it might be possible to interpret the covenant such that the right to apostasy is absent from it.

Bahiyyih G. Tahzib continues this line of reasoning. She writes that a difference is notable between Article 18 Universal Declaration and Article 18 ICCPR and points out that "[u]nlike Article 18 of the UDHR, Article 18, paragraph 1, of the ICCPR no longer explicitly enumerates freedom to change one's religion or belief as an indispensable component of the right to freedom of thought, conscience and religion. It is hence left to the discretion of individual States Parties to determine whether the freedom to change one's religion or belief falls within the scope of the right to freedom of thought."[109]

In this regard, the stance of Belgium human rights activist Willy Laes is relevant. Laes argues that the eight abstentions from the final vote of the Universal Declaration were covered with the "cloak of love" by the consenting states. Laes devotes a chapter in his book to what he calls the "vanishing act of Articles 18 and 16 of the Universal Declaration". He argues that Islamic states, in this case, Afghanistan, Egypt, Saudi Arabia, and Yemen, failed in their endeavour to delete the freedom to change religion or belief from the Universal Declaration but eventually succeeded in it when the phrasing in Article 18 ICCPR was altered.[110]

Compromising the normative force

Evans, Tahzib and Laes share their views regarding the textual changes of Article 18 ICCPR and its possible consequences: the conception that the freedom to change one's religion does not (have to) naturally stem from the currently chosen wording. Moreover, from their perspectives, it can be inferred that the difference in phrasing is not merely a matter of semantic adjustment. The argument made by Tahzib that the actual attribution of the right to change religion can now come down to the discretion of the individual state is essential.

In line with this argument, it may be argued that the consequences may be more severe: The text is now open to various interpretations, which could result in legal inequality between the individual states. This seems to undermine the

108 M. D. Evans, *Religious Liberty and International Law in Europe* (Cambridge: Cambridge University Press, 1997), pp. 201–202.

109 B. G. Tahzib, *Freedom of Religion or Belief. Ensuring Effective International Legal Protection* (The Hague: Martinus Nijhoff Publishers, 1996), p. 87.

110 W. Laes, *Mensenrechten in de Verenigde Naties. Een verhaal over manipulatie, censuur en hypocrisie* (Antwerpen: Garant, 2011), p. 122.

direct legal obligations for states, which were supposed to be imposed with the adoption of the Covenant. By altering the concepts and offering room for various interpretations, it allows states to use a *restrictive interpretation* of the freedom of religion and belief, resulting in a narrow conception of the right.

This is undesirable, since the availability of the right to apostasy could be the mere result of interpretation. It can come down to the *willingness* of the state to attribute the right. Obviously, with the implementation of legal provisions, interpretation is a continual issue, which is merely the act of understanding or giving a particular meaning to a legal concept. In this case, however, when fundamental rights are concerned, it should be made explicit in the formulation. For an individual to have the right to apostasy as a mere result of interpretation seems to be in contrast with the principle of equality before the law and the principle of *legal certainty*. As is often advocated in the human rights discourse, in order to protect fundamental rights from misinterpretation, misuse, or arbitrary application, the state must formulate the freedoms in such a way, preferably explicitly, that the individual knows exactly what his rights are in the legal order. If this is not the case, the state and its judiciary will be able to *disregard* the right to apostasy and state that the right in question is not a protected dimension of the freedom of religion or belief. Individuals trying to leave religion may be left empty-handed (legally).

The ICCPR should have been a continuing substantiation of the right established in 1948, but this formulation may be interpreted as a deviation from the original intent of the delegates of the world community to protect the right to apostasy. It can be considered a weakening of the moral persuasiveness of the Universal Declaration. Evidently, the enshrinement of the freedom of religion or belief in an international treaty was a significant advance towards the realization of an international legal order, and it is important that this be recognized; however, it has come at the expense of conceptual clarity, putting the right to apostasy at stake, resulting in diminishing the *normative force* of an essential element of the religious freedom provision.

In a certain sense, it is a matter of concern that within the UN and in academia there is little recognition of the fact that the last decennia have seen an implicit diminishing of the normative force of an essential element of the religious freedom provision. With the (present) religious freedom violations it should be realized that the implementation or, rather, an actual appeal to the freedom to change religion or belief by an individual, is not a simple given. With the current phrasing, the right to apostasy can be construed on the basis of Article 18 ICCPR, but we need text and original intent to come to this conclusion. The text of the Universal Declaration is therefore preferable to the text in the Covenant.

The plea for actually reasserting this right in states where it is under pressure by, for example, UN experts or state representatives when discussing international relations and policy will be more persuasive if there is a well-defined, conceptually clear, and distinctive normative fundament which is directly binding. A reconceptualization of the freedom to change religion or belief as a part of the general right of freedom of religion or belief would for this reason not only be welcome but seems necessary for a (re)establishment of the normative contours of this right. However, given the (legal) development of the freedom of religion or belief and the current political environment this suggestion seems unfortunately unrealistic.

Conclusion

In this chapter, we have addressed the issue of the freedom to change religion or belief. This subject has been examined from three perspectives. We have argued that the various textual alterations demonstrate that there is a change in phrasing from "to change religion or belief" to "have or to adopt a religion or belief of choice" to "religion or whatever belief of choice". These textual changes indicate that the 1948 formula was not repeated in 1966 and 1981. These textual alterations amount to a decline from an explicit recognition of the right to change religion or belief to an implicit recognition.

The second analysis has demonstrated the motivations of the drafters of the ICCPR for changing concepts. This legal historical analysis has proved imperative to understand and assess the complex debate regarding the right to apostasy. The drafters had difficulty reaching consensus on the phrasing of the freedom to change religion or belief. The debates were fierce, and the Saudi Arabian delegation continually objected to the chosen language of "to change religion or belief". It was clear that Baroody wanted to make the text more palatable for his constituency and utilized his persuasive powers to dominate the discussions. Although his stance triggered fierce responses from the other delegates, in a conciliatory spirit and willing to reach consensus the representatives continued to alter the phrasing of the text.

In the end, Brazil and the Philippines suggested a new approach, and with an addendum of the United Kingdom, the 'solution' was in sight. The explicit right to change religion was replaced by the ambiguous phrase to "have or to adopt a religion or belief of choice". Predominant treaty consensus-seeking is unquestionably a complicated exercise, but the result was a deviation from the Universal Declaration language since no references are made anymore to an explicit right to apostasy. The results of the compromises seem therefore somewhat paradoxical in that they amount to keeping control at the price of losing it. One may even say that Saudi Arabia gained what it "lost" in 1948.

The third analysis contained the views regarding this topic within academia. We have argued that several renowned authors have adopted the view that the freedom to change religion or belief is anchored within the current phrasing of the provision: the inclusive stance. These scholars did not consider the omission of the explicit freedom to change religion or belief substantial. To them, it is merely a shift in verbiage. Fortunately, in academia, there are scholars who have adopted the exclusive stance: the freedom to change one's religion does not naturally follow from the currently chosen wording. It is not merely a matter of semantic adjustment. The argument that the actual attribution of the right to change religion can now come down to the discretion of the individual state is especially relevant.

In line with this stance, we have argued that the consequence of the various compromises was conceptual ambiguity: the text is open to various interpretations. By changing the wording in the provision, different normative contours have been asserted regarding the freedom of religion or belief, with the result that the explicit right to apostasy is disregarded. A reconceptualization of the right to apostasy as part of the general right of freedom of religion or belief would seem necessary for a (re)establishment of the normative contours of this right. However, this seems rather unrealistic, considering the development of the freedom of religion or belief and the current political climate.

7 Leaving or changing religion in the European Union Law

The impact of the European Data Protection Regulation (GDPR)

Fabio Balsamo

Article 9, para 2, lett. d) GDPR and the intra-confessional processing of former members' personal data

The introduction of the European Data Protection Regulation (GDPR) has amended the previous provision of Article 8, para 2, lett. d) of the Directive 95/46/EC of the European Parliament and of the Council.[1] That provision allowed religious organisations, with appropriate guarantees, to process for internal use the religious data and the other sensitive categories of data of members and persons who had regular contact with the organisations without their consent.[2]

Under the current Article 9, para 2, lett. d) GDPR, instead, the processing of religious and other special categories of personal data can be carried out by religious organisations without the legal basis of the data subject's consent, not only with regard to members and persons who have regular contact with the organisations but also with regard to former members.[3]

1 The Article 8, para 2, lett. d) of the Directive 95/46/EC of the European Parliament and of the Council provided an exception to the general prohibition to process personal data revealing "racial or ethnic origin, political opinions, religious or philosophical beliefs" when the processing was "carried out in the course of its legitimate activities with appropriate guarantees by a foundation, association or any other non-profit-seeking body with a political, philosophical, religious or trade-union aim and on condition that the processing relates solely to the members of the body or to persons who have regular contact with it in connection with its purposes and that the data are not disclosed to a third party without the consent of the data subjects".

2 For early comments on Law no. 675 of 1996 – transposing Directive 95/46/EC in Italian legal system – see A. Chizzoniti, 'Prime considerazioni sulla legge 675 del 1996 «Tutela delle persone e di altri soggetti rispetto al trattamento dei dati personali»', *Quaderni di diritto e politica ecclesiastica* 2 (1997), 379–384; V. Marano, 'Diritto alla riservatezza, trattamento dei dati personali e confessioni religiose. Note sull'applicabilità della legge n. 675/1996 alla Chiesa cattolica', *Quaderni di diritto e politica ecclesiastica* 1 (1998), 305–320; R. Botta, 'Trattamento di dati personali e confessioni religiose (Dalla L. 31 dicembre 1996, n. 675 al D.L.gs. 11 maggio 1999, n. 135)', *Il diritto ecclesiastico* 4 (1999), 882–927; D. Milani, 'Il trattamento dei dati sensibili di natura religiosa tra novità legislativa ed interventi giurisprudenziali', *Il Diritto Ecclesiastico* 1 (2001), 266–293.

3 On this theme, allow me to refer to F. Balsamo, *La protezione dei dati personali di natura religiosa* (Cosenza: Luigi Pellegrini, 2021), especially pp. 33–35.

DOI: 10.4324/9781003502845-7

This normative change has incorporated the numerous judicial pronouncements[4] and the national Data Protection authorities' decisions[5] about the cancellation from the baptismal register (‘*sbattezzo*’).[6] In its decision of 10 October 2002, for example, the Italian Data Protection Authority had also specified that the request of a baptized person to affix in the parish registers the annotation of his will to no longer belong to the Catholic Church is legitimate, since it is aimed at updating and integrating the personal data concerning him, with specific reference to the ‘sensitive data’ relating to religious affiliation.[7]

The affirmation of the legitimacy of intra-confessional processing of former members' personal data thus represented a definitive negative stance of the European Union Law towards the several requests submitted by former believers for obtaining the definitive removal of their names and data from the register of baptised persons, instead of a simple annotation.[8]‘*Sbattezzo*’ has

4 We refer to the well-known ruling of the Court of Padua (decree no. 3722, dated 29 May 2000), available in *Quaderni di diritto e politica ecclesiastica*, 3, 2000, 874–876. Cf. G. Dalla Torre, ‘Registro dei battesimi e tutela dei dati personali: luci e ombre di una decisione (nota a Trib. Padova, decr. 29 maggio 2000)’, *Giustizia civile* 1 (2001), 236–241.

5 With regard to the Italian legal system, we can refer to the Italian Data Protection Authority's decisions dated 9 September 1999 (available at the web address www.garanteprivacy.it/home/docweb/-/docweb-display/docweb/1044304) and 28 September 2006 (available at the web address www.olir.it/documenti/deliberazione-28-settembre-2006/).

For the first doctrinal considerations see, *ex plurimis*, S. Berlingò, ‘Si può essere più garantisti del Garante? A proposito delle pretese di «tutela» dai registri di battesimo’, *Quaderni di diritto e politica ecclesiastica* 1 (2000), 295–328; G. Boni, ‘Tutela rispetto al trattamento dei dati personali trattamento dei dati personali tra sovranità dello Stato e sovranità della Chiesa cattolica’, in *Il diritto di famiglia e delle persone* 4 (2001), 1687–1768.

6 About ‘*sbattezzo*’ see M. J. Arroba Conde, ‘L'atto formale di uscita dalla Chiesa nel diritto canonico’, *Diritto e Religioni* 2 (2012), 52–68; V. De Paolis, ‘Alcune annotazioni circa la formula “actu formali ab Ecclesia catholica deficere”’, *Periodica de re canonica* 4 (1995), 579–608; A. Perlasca, ‘L'abbandono della Chiesa cattolica e libertà religiosa. Implicazioni canoniche e di diritto ecclesiastico’, *Quaderni di diritto ecclesiale* 1 (2007), 60–81; C. Ventrella, ‘Diritto alle “identità” e profili interordinamentali: cambiamenti di status e certificazioni religiose’, *Diritto e religioni* 1 (2010), 249–278; M. C. Ruscazio, ‘Lo ‘sbattezzo’, tra libertà religiosa e norme implicite. Spunti di diritto comparato’, *Stato, Chiese e pluralismo confessionale, Online Journal* 3 (2018), 1–17. www.statoechiese.it.

7 The decision (*web* doc. no. 1066415) can be found at the following web address: www.garanteprivacy.it/home/docweb/-/docweb-display/docweb/1066415.

8 Article 2, § 9 of the General Decree of the Italian Bishops' Conference dated 20 October 1999, bearing ‘Dispositions for the protection of the right to good reputation and privacy’, stated that «*la richiesta di cancellazione di dati dai registri è inammissibile se concerne dati relativi all'avvenuta celebrazione di sacramenti o comunque attinenti allo stato delle persone. Tale richiesta deve essere annotata nel registro, e obbliga il responsabile dei registri a non utilizzare i dati relativi se non con l'autorizzazione dell'Ordinario diocesano*». Cf. Italian Bishops' Conference, ‘Decreto generale “Disposizioni per la tutela del diritto alla buona fama e alla riservatezza”’, *Notiziario della Conferenza Episcopale Italiana* 10 (20 October 1999), 376–397. For the first doctrinal comments see D. Mogavero, ‘Diritto alla buona fama e alla riservatezza e tutela dei dati personali’, *Ius Ecclesiae* 2 (2000), 589–610; A. Vitalone, ‘Buona fama e riservatezza in diritto canonico (il Civis-fidelis e la disciplina della privacy)’, *Ius Ecclesiae* 1 (2001), 261–280;

been also regulated by canonical normative interventions,[9] such as the *Actus formalis defectionis ab Ecclesia Catholica* dated 13 March 2006,[10] in which the *Pontifical Council for Legislative Texts* has established the constituent elements that the act of leaving the Catholic Church must present to be effective.

This chapter aims to verify the impact of *European Data Protection Regulation (GDPR)*, specifically the current Article 9, para 2, lett. d) GDPR, on the concrete exercise of the individual believer's right to freely leave or change religion within the European Union Law and in the multireligious societies of European Union State members, where the phenomena of deconversion or conversion to another religious faith are becoming increasingly common.[11]

In fact, the possibility for religious organisations to process former members' data without their consent may potentially hinder or interfere with the specific paths of changing or leaving religion,[12] especially because of the use of tracking and profiling techniques.

The impact of European Data Protection Regulation (GDPR) on religious propaganda activities and religious conversions

According to Article 10 of the Charter of Fundamental Rights of the European Union, "everyone has the right to freedom of thought, conscience and religion. This right includes freedom to change religion or belief".[13] The recognition of the right to change religious faith in the European Union Law

R. Terranova, 'Buona fama e riservatezza: il trattamento dei dati personali tra diritto canonico e diritto dello Stato', *Il Diritto Ecclesiastico* 1 (2001), 294–316; G. Boni, *Tutela rispetto al trattamento dei dati personali trattamento dei dati personali tra sovranità dello Stato e sovranità della Chiesa cattolica*, op. cit.

9 The procedure has been further detailed by the Italian Bishops' Conference through specific guidance disseminated to bishops and parish priests, as reported by A. Fuccillo (ed.), *Diritto, religioni, culture. Il fattore religioso nell'esperienza giuridica* (Turin: Giappichelli, 2022), pp. 326–332.

10 Cf. Pontifical Council for Legislative Texts, *Actus formalis defectionis ab Ecclesia Catholica,* 13 March 2006. The communication can be found at the following web address: www.vatican.va/roman_curia/pontifical_councils/intrptxt/documents/rc_pc_intrptxt_doc_20060313_actus-formalis_it.html.

11 See A. Maoz, 'Proselytism and the Right to Change Religion', in S. Ferrari and R. Cristofori (eds.), *Law and Religion in the 21st Century. Relations between States and Religious Communities* (London: Routledge, 2010), pp. 243–252.

12 For an examination of the rules provided for by the different religious laws about conversion or apostacy we can refer to S. Ferrari, *Problemi giuridici della conversione*; D. Francavilla, *La conversione nella tradizione giuridica hindu: salvezza e comunità*; M. Ricca, *Spazi di conversione. Una lettura corologica*; S. Ferlito, *Sulla conversione. Convertire chi? Convertire cosa?*; P. Stefani, *Conversione ed ebraismo*; E. Gozlan, *L'apostasie dans le judaïsme*: all published in *Quaderni di diritto e politica ecclesiastica* Special Issue (2016), respectively 3–18, 205–218, 91–144, 145–170, 191–204.

13 Article 10 of the Charter of Fundamental Rights of the European Union reproduces almost identically the wording of Article 9, para 1 of the European Convention on Human Rights.

necessarily postulates a correspondingly broad protection of the right to religious propaganda,[14] since conversion to another religious faith very often constitutes the result of a specific religious propaganda activity carried out by religious organisations. In addition to spreading the religious message, these may also take the form of religious proselytising activities.

The organisation of proselytising activities – which may take place using various techniques, not only door-to-door preaching – presupposes in most cases the prior acquisition of special categories of personal data of the person without his or her consent. For this reason, it is precisely with regard to the performance of religious proselytising activities that the main hypotheses of conflict between the right to religious freedom and the right to the protection of personal data[15] can abstractly be configured.[16] Hence the immediate impact of the European Data Protection Regulation (GDPR) on the performance of religious proselytising activities, in view of the general prohibition imposed by Article 9, para 1 GDPR on the processing of "special categories of personal data", including those personal data revealing religious belief.

The information used to establish a 'first contact' with the recipient of religious proselytising activities would appear to be represented in general by common personal data and other contact data contained in public registers. These are personal data for which the GDPR does not place any specific prohibition on processing. So, in these hypotheses, the legal basis of the data processing can be individuated in the legitimate interests of the organisation, as set out in Article 6, para 1, lett. f) GDPR.

In many other cases, and especially when the proselytising activity is directed towards a former member, the carrying out of an activity aimed at favouring the conversion (or reconversion) of the person is based on data revealing the recipient's different religious belonging or his/her non-religious affiliation. Similarly, the identification of the addressees of proselytising activities may be founded on the acquisition of information – such as data concerning the changed habits in religious matters – that can justify an attempt at conversion.[17] In all these circumstances, it is precisely the achievement of information concerning the individual's religious orientation that determines the religious organisation's choice of whether or not to direct religious proselytising activities towards that specific addressee.

That the European Union Law's rules on the protection of personal data and the related need to protect the individual's right to privacy may constitute

14 Cf. J. Pasquali Cerioli, *La propaganda religiosa: la libertà silente* (Turin: Giappichelli, 2018), p. 121.

15 Article 8 of the Charter of Fundamental Rights of the European Union states that everyone has the right to the protection of personal data concerning him or her and that data must be processed fairly for specified purposes and based on the consent of the person concerned or some other legitimate basis laid down by law.

16 Cf. F. Balsamo, *La protezione dei dati personali di natura religiosa*, op. cit., pp. 44–45.

17 *Ivi*, p. 46.

a significant limitation on the performance of religious propaganda activities also emerges from the European Court of Human Rights' and the Court of Justice of the European Union's case-law.

It's emblematic the ruling of the Court of Luxembourg concerning the incompatibility, as established by the Finnish National authorities, of the proselytising activities of the religious communities with data protection regulations regarding personal data collected in the context of door-to-door preaching without the explicit data subject's consent. With the ruling of the Grand Chamber dated 10 July 2018 in the case C25/17,[18] the Court of Justice of the European Union clearly affirmed the applicability of the European Union Law's data protection provisions[19] to the door-to-door preaching activity organised by Jehovah's Witnesses Community in Finland due to the non-domestic nature of this activity.

According to Considerandum no. 18, in fact, GDPR "does not apply to the processing of personal data by a natural person in the course of a purely personal or household activity and thus with no connection to a professional or commercial activity".[20] The Court underlined that such door-to-door preaching activities were aimed at spreading the creed to people outside the acolytes' families, with the effect of necessarily developing outside the individual sphere of the preachers. On this point, the Court of Luxembourg noted that the religious organisation planned the subsequent stages of this activity based on the data collected by the preachers, including sensitive data revealing the religious beliefs of the person and his or her desire to be contacted again in the future. More precisely, the Court underlined that "the data collected are more than informal notes in an address book, as the notes taken concern unknown persons and contain sensitive data relating to their religious beliefs".[21]

The preaching activity thus included the acquisition of sensitive data of interviewees in the absence of the legal basis of their consent, and it consequently

18 Cf. Court of Justice of the European Union, Grand Chamber, 10 July 2018 (case C25/17), available at *curia.europa.eu*. For a first comment of the judgment see R. Panetta and F. Sartore, 'Proselitismo religioso e protezione dei dati personali: tra esigenze di tutela e particolarità della fattispecie', *Responsabilità civile e previdenza. Rivista bimestrale di dottrina, giurisprudenza e legislazione* 1 (2019), 101 ff. See also S. Attollino, 'Le religioni nel mondo delle informazioni: tra privacy e accountability', *Diritto e Religioni* 1 (2021), 76–109, especially 100–103.

19 At the time of the case the Directive 95/46/EC of the European Parliament and of the Council was still in force, as transposed within the Member States' legal systems.

20 The Considerandum no. 18 has confirmed the principle already stated in the Considerandum no. 12 of the Directive 95/46/EC, according to which "the protection principles must apply to all processing of personal data by any person whose activities are governed by Community law; whereas there should be excluded the processing of data carried out by a natural person in the exercise of activities which are exclusively personal or domestic".

21 Cf. Court of Justice of the European Union, Grand Chamber, 10 July 2018 (case C25/17), op. cit., no. 19: "In that regard, account must be taken of the fact that, in the present case, the data collected are more than informal notes in an address book, as the notes taken concern unknown persons and contain sensitive data relating to their religious beliefs".

represented a violation of the European Union Law's provisions on personal data protection.

The Court of Justice of the European Union European also emphasised that the data collection activity carried out by the individual preacher was not extraneous to the general planning of proselytising activities prepared by the religious organisation,[22] in view of the importance assumed by the acquisition of the names entered in the so-called 'refusal register'. Hence the affirmation of the existence of the position of "co-processor" both with regard to the individual preachers and with regard to the Jehovah's Witnesses community itself, in accordance with the provisions of point no. 53 of the subsequent *Guidelines no. 7/2020 07/2020 on the concepts of controller and processor in the GDPR* of the European Data Protection Board.[23]

These principles have been further clarified in the recent ruling of the European Court of Human Rights (ECHR), dated 9 May 2023.[24] In this last case, the Court of Strasbourg was called upon to assess, *inter alia*, whether the *Data Protection Ombudsman*'s opinion of 2000 (89Ů/45/97) could constitute a possible violation of Article 9 of the European Convention on Human Rights, specifically of Article 9, para 2.[25] In the *Data Protection Ombudsman*'s opinion it was established, on the basis of the Finnish Personal Data Act,[26] that personal and sensitive data could be collected and processed in the course of door-to-door preaching by individual Jehovah's Witnesses only with the data subjects' consent.

In the religious denomination's appeal, the need to request explicit consent under the Finnish Personal Data Act before taking any personal 'notes' has been considered as producing a 'deterrent effect' on freedom of religion and expression because of its contrariety to what is guaranteed by Articles 9 and 10 of the European Convention on Human Rights.[27] Moreover, such a measure has been deemed as an excessive and disproportionate interference in the exercise of the right to religious propaganda "impeding the personal

22 *Ibid.*: "The fact that door-to-door preaching is an essential part of the Jehovah's Witnesses Community's activity, which is organised and coordinated by it and by its congregations, must also be taken into consideration".

23 The *Guidelines 07/2020 on the concepts of controller and processor in the GDPR* are available at https://edpb.europa.eu/our-work-tools/documents/public-consultations/2020/guidelines-072020-concepts-controller-and_it.

24 Cf. European Court of Human Rights, Second section, judgment 9 May 2023 (Application no. 31172/19), available at https://hudoc.echr.coe.int.

25 In the European Convention on Human Rights, the right to protection of personal data is guaranteed by the right to respect for private life under Article 8.

26 In the Finnish legal system, the Data Protection Act entered into force on 1 January 2019 and repealed, *inter alia*, the Personal Data Act (523/1999).

27 "Even when an occupant agreed to a follow-up visit, asking for consent would have a chilling effect, subjecting private religious conversations to suspicion and distrust, and creating an erroneous and stigmatising impression that the evangelism was a de facto marketing endeavour". Cf. European Court of Human Rights, Second section, judgment 9 May 2023 (Application no. 31172/19), no. 71.

expression of faith and dialogue integral to a free exchange of religious, atheistic, agnostic and philosophical ideas or views".[28] Moreover, the need to obtain the explicit data subject's consent, according to the Jehovah's Witnesses Community, would have prevented the storage of information collected during door-to-door preaching activities in the absence of the recipients.

The Court of Strasbourg, because of the incompatibility of the community's religious activities with the data protection regulations, has stated that such an interference, according to art. 9, para 2 of the European Convention on Human Rights, is "prescribed by law", has legitimate aims and is "necessary in a democratic society" to protect the right to privacy. In addition, the decision has been based on the circumstance – evidently of no small importance – that the Jehovah's Witnesses Community has not proved the prejudice caused to its right to religious propaganda.[29] The religious organisation, nevertheless, has not provided evidence – including by means of statistics showing the reduction in the conversion rate – that door-to-door preaching carried out on the basis of the explicit data subject's consent is less persuasive than the previous methods of carrying out the same activities conducted before the entry into force of the internal and European Union Law's provisions on personal data protection.

From the two judgments examined, it clearly emerges that the compliance of personal data processing with the GDPR can immediately condition the possibility of initiating and continuing religious proselytising activities. In fact, the performance of door-to-door preaching activities, although undertaken based on data contained in public registers or in the public domain, necessarily exposes a person outside the religious organisation to the risk of also providing, without his or her explicit consent, information concerning his or her religious identity or other 'special categories' of data, for which Article 9, para 1 GDPR imposes a general prohibition on processing.

It must be pointed out, however, that the need to acquire the legal basis of the explicit data subject's consent is required exclusively in the case of the processing of personal data belonging to the 'special categories' as contemplated by Article 9, para 1 GDPR. In other words, there is no necessity of acquiring the data subject's consent when only non-sensitive data are processed by the religious organisation in the "first contact" with the recipient of proselytising activities. The "first contact" initiated by a religious organisation for religious

28 *Ibid.*: "It was disproportionate to require, when taking a brief note containing personal data, that an individual Jehovah's Witness first establish a legal basis for doing so by obtaining the 'consent' of the interlocutor, then provide him or her with the identity of the 'controller', explain to him or her the purpose of the processing of the data, and then explain the right of access, rectification and erasure, in addition to complying with the many other requirements applicable to 'controllers'".

29 "The applicant community failed to present any supporting evidence of the alleged 'chilling effect' of the Board's order, notwithstanding the lapse of time since the decision of the Supreme Administrative Court". Cf. European Court of Human Rights, Second section, judgment 9 May 2023, op. cit., no. 95.

proselytising purposes must thus be considered always lawful if it is based exclusively on the use of personal data or telephone contacts contained in public registers or other data, also sensitive, manifestly made public by the data subject, according to Article 9, para 2, lett. e) GDPR.

In this sense, each prior prohibition imposed on religious organisations to establish a first contact with a person for propaganda purposes without a previous verification of the sensitive nature of the personal data processed must be considered an undue and disproportionate compression of the right to religious freedom of the organization. In fact, such a prohibition would obviously conflict with Article 6, para 1, lett. f) GDPR itself. Moreover, such a limitation to evangelisation activities would empty the fundamental right to religious freedom of its content, since, as recalled by the European Court of Human Rights itself in the judgment *Kokkinakis v Greece* dated 25 May 1993, the right to religious freedom includes "the right to try to convince one's neighbour, for example through "teaching", failing which, moreover, "freedom to change [one's] religion or belief" enshrined in Article 9, would be likely to remain a dead letter".[30]

The impact of new media in religious conversions

Another confirmation of the GDPR's impact on the conversion cases can be drawn on an empirical level, starting from the importance of the media and the new telematic tools of communication in the choice of leaving one's religious faith or maintaining the new status of apostate. In addition to this, propaganda activities can also be carried out using new communication tools within the telematic space; in this regard, it should be noted that in many cases, the new digital technologies also make it possible to reconstruct the religious orientations of users.[31]

In fact, nowadays the media and web provide the main interface for acquiring information on religion. Indeed, media are not only used to transmit information, but they can assume an active role in the framing of religious questions, ending up by conditioning even conversion choices, especially through the dissemination, increasingly targeted and profiled, of information concerning specific cases of religious conversion.[32] The trend of abandonments from the Finnish Evangelical-Lutheran Church that was recorded in 2010 in Finland is emblematic in this sense, following the dissemination in the media

30 Cf. European Court of Human Rights, judgment 25 May 1993, case of *Kokkinakis v Greece* (Application no. 14307/88), no. 31, available at https://hudoc.echr.coe.int.

31 On the theme cf. D. Durisotto, 'Diritti degli individui e diritti delle organizzazioni religiose nel Regolamento (UE) 2016/679. I "corpus completi di norme" e le "autorità di controllo indipendenti"', in *Federalismi.it*, 7 October 2020, especially p. 48.

32 In these terms T. Taira, 'Media and Communication Approaches to Leaving Religion', in D. Enstedt, G. Larsson and T. T. Mantsinen (eds.), *Handbook of Leaving Religion* (Leiden-Boston: Brill, 2020), pp. 335–348, especially p. 336, in which the impact of new media in conversion processes is expressly emphasised.

and on social networks of the first leavings because of the positions expressed by the Finnish Lutheran Church about homosexual rights.[33] Similarly, we can consider the different prominence given by the media to conversion cases from new religious movements or Islam, which generally receive greater echo-media coverage in Western countries than conversion experiences from Buddhism, Hinduism or Judaism. This is for example the case of Islamic asylum seekers converted to Christianity as a result of conversion processes that have matured especially in German evangelical circles, which are engaged at the forefront of actions to welcome migrants from Iran, Syria and Iraq.[34] And in this sense, the conversion, while genuine and firm,[35] is nonetheless part of a more overall effort to integrate the migrant within the destination societies.[36]

A final consideration is the use of the media by atheist organisations,[37] which proved particularly effective in the elaboration of the psychological processes of "secularisation of the institution", prodromal to leaving especially the new religious movements, that increasingly characterize contemporary multicultural European society.[38]

Processing of former and outgoing members' personal data in religious propaganda activities in current European Union Law

In light of these considerations, the significance that may be attached to the possibility for religious denominations to process the sensitive information of former or outgoing members without the legal basis of the data subject's

33 *Ivi*, p. 337, in which it's pointed out that the impact of withdrawal from the Finnish Evangelical-Lutheran Church have occurred despite the fact that the conservative press has explicitly encouraged believers not to leave the church, arguing for the need to contribute from within to its change.

34 Cfr. N. Stene, 'Leaving Islam for Christianity: Asylum Seeker Converts', in D. Enstedt, G. Larsson and T. T. Mantsinen (eds.), *Handbook of Leaving Religion*, op. cit., pp. 210–219, especially pp. 212–218, where it's underlined that «*conversion can be part of a migration and integration strategy*» (p. 225).

35 In relation to the role that religious conversion can play as a '*migration and integration strategy*' see specifically S. Akpacar, 'Conversion as a Migration Strategy in a Transit Country: Iranian Shiites Becoming Christians in Turkey', *International Migration Review* 4 (2006), 817–853; D. A. Miller and P. Johnstone, 'Believers in Christ from a Muslim Background: A Global Census', *Interdisciplinary Journal of Research on Religion* 11 (2015), 1–20.

36 Cf. N. Stene, *Leaving Islam for Christianity: Asylum Seeker Converts*, op. cit., p. 215. On the topic of social and economic integration of migrants within the destination contexts, see M. d'Arienzo, *Pluralismo religioso e dialogo interculturale. L'inclusione giuridica delle diversità* (Cosenza: Luigi Pellegrini, 2018), especially p. 95 ff.

37 See S. Baldassarre, 'Campagne pubblicitarie ateiste: un'applicazione asimmetrica del principio di laicità', in A. Cardone and M. Croce (eds.), *30 anni di laicità dello Stato: fu vera gloria?* (Roma: Nessun Dogma, 2021), pp. 367–382.

38 See M. Cardano and N. Pannofino, *Piccole apostasie. Il congedo dai nuovi movimenti religiosi* (Bologna: Il Mulino, 2015), *passim;* as well as G. Filoramo, 'Riflessioni in margine ai meccanismi di ingresso e di uscita da una religione', *Daimon. Annuario di diritto comparato delle religioni* 1 (2001), 149–161.

consent in order to carry out their institutional purposes in the current telematic and digital context is even more evident. Amongst the purposes, the calling back to the faith of the apostate or those who have formally manifested the intention to withdraw from the religious faith can certainly be included. In fact, religious organisations can now also use the power of media and new communication tools to process the former and outgoing members' data without their consent in the telematic space.

This possibility, which was precluded by the previous Directive 95/46/EC, seems instead to have been now admitted by GDPR. In this sense, the wording of the current Article 9, para 2, lett. d) GDPR, although it had the merit of incorporating the practice of the national Data Protection Authorities and the case law's pronouncements on '*sbattezzo*', has posed several application problems of no little importance.

The first concerns the difficulty, for some religious traditions, of distinguishing between the status of member or former member in the absence of a formal mechanism of abandonment from the religious faith.

This is the case of Judaism, where the eminently ethnic dimension of being Jew is dominant. In fact, membership of the Jewish faith, in Orthodox Judaism, is attributed from birth and regardless of the intention to convert or leave the religion.[39] Orthodox Judaism, based on the matrilineal principle prescribed by the *Halakha*, identifies the personal status of the mother as the determining criterion for the transmission of Jewish identity.[40] Moreover, in Judaism there are no records of 'registered' or officially 'active' members, apart from membership of a particular synagogue.[41]

Instead, the weakening of the ethnic criterion in favour of the affirmation of a cultural criterion of participation in Jewish social and religious life characterises Reform Judaism.[42] It follows that the choice of leaving Judaism can assume a tangible form only in cases of abandonment of Conservative Judaism, in which the choice to leave ultra-Orthodoxy in favour of an Orthodox or Reform Judaism is expressed in the breaking of the stringent forms of communal socialisation, together with the community's reaction aimed at preserving its integrity against any external influence.[43] It therefore seems evident that the distinction between members and former members introduced by GDPR with the current Article 9, para 2, lett. d), is of no use in terms of application with

39 Cf. D. Belfon, 'Leaving Orthodox Judaism', in D. Enstedt, G. Larsson and T. T. Mantsinen (eds.), *Handbook of Leaving Religion*, op. cit., pp. 142–153, especially p. 143 and S. Pasquetti, 'Ebreo per nascita, «apostata» per scelta', *Daimon. Annuario di diritto comparato delle religioni* 1 (2001), 12–51.

40 See S. Pasquetti, *Ebreo per nascita, «apostata» per scelta*, op. cit., p. 13.

41 See D. Belfon, 'Leaving Orthodox Judaism', in D. Enstedt, G. Larsson and T. T. Mantsinen (eds.), *Handbook of Leaving Religion*, op. cit., p. 143.

42 See S. Pasquetti, *Ebreo per nascita, «apostata» per scelta*, op. cit., specifically pp. 22–30, in which the author emphasises the adoption in Reform Judaism of a new criterion aimed at valuing the believer's participation in the cultural and social life of the Jewish community.

43 In these terms D. Belfon, *Leaving Orthodox Judaism*, op. cit., pp. 143–144.

respect to religious traditions that do not contemplate formal mechanisms of abandonment.

The second problematic aspect is of an interpretative nature and concerns the possible innovative character of Article 9, para 2, lett. d) GDPR with respect to religious propaganda activities.[44] In fact, under the previous Directive 95/46/EC, the doctrine excluded any possibility for religious organisations to process, for propaganda purposes, the former members' personal and sensitive data without their consent.[45] Under the previous regulation, the doctrine observed that the individual believer's right to informational self-determination and the right to reconstruct the religious identity after the change of religious faith[46] had always to prevail over the freedom of the religious organisation to spread its beliefs with propaganda activities directed to apostates. Consequently, about the individual's right to freely reconstruct the personal and religious identity at any time, the doctrine emphasised the need of the legal basis of the data subject's consent.[47]

Practice also confirmed this interpretation. In fact, as pointed out *supra*,[48] with the General Decree '*Dispositions for the protection of the right to good reputation and privacy*' of 1999, the Italian Bishops' Conference laid down in Article 2, § 9 that the request for "cancellation from baptismal registers" obliged the person in charge of the registers not to use the personal data except with the authorisation of the Diocesan Ordinary. Even more specifically, the indications dated 24 November 2006 on the formal separation of the Roman Catholic Apostolic Church stated that the annotation of this cancellation request implied a duty not to contact the person anymore for communications of an ecclesial nature.[49] Moreover, the Church of Jesus Christ of Latter-day Saints, in its defence submissions in the appeal decided by the Italian Data

44 For the freedom to proselytise in the European legal space see J. Martinez Torron, 'Libertad de proselitismo en Europa. A propósito de una reciente sentencia del Tribunal europeo de derechos humanos', *Quaderni di diritto e politica ecclesiastica* 1 (1994), 59–71.

45 As known, the Article 8, para 2, lett. d) of the Directive 95/46/EC did not mention the former members' category.

46 The right to religious freedom also includes, as known, the right to change one's denominational affiliation at any time. In these terms G. Catalano, *Il diritto di libertà religiosa* (Milan: Giuffrè, 1957), p. 68. Cf., *ex multis*, M. Tedeschi, 'Per uno studio del diritto di libertà religiosa', *Revista española de derecho canonico* 47 (1990), 169–187; M. d'Arienzo, 'Raffronti normativi in tema di libertà religiosa', *Il Diritto Ecclesiastico* 2 (2004), 502–520; M. Ricca, 'Art 19', in R. Bifulco, A. Celotto and M. Olivetti (eds.), *Commentario alla Costituzione*, vol. I (Turin: Utet, 2006), pp. 420–440.

47 Cf. J. Pasquali Cerioli, *La propaganda religiosa: la libertà silente* (Turin: Giappichelli, 2018), p. 151; as well as D. Milani, *Il trattamento dei dati sensibili di natura religiosa tra novità legislativa ed interventi giurisprudenziali*, op. cit., especially p. 283.

48 See *supra* the note no. 8.

49 Cf. Pontifical Council for Legislative Texts, *Actus formalis defectionis ab Ecclesia Catholica*, 13 March 2006, available at the following web address: www.vatican.va/roman_curia/pontifical_councils/intrptxt/documents/rc_pc_intrptxt_doc_20060313_actus-formalis_it.html.

Protection Authority on 16 July 2015, also moved in the same direction.[50] In fact, it confirmed that the believer who had requested to be removed from the Church's membership registers, should no longer be contacted for religious communications. Specifically, with the note dated 15 May 2015, the Church of Jesus Christ of Latter-day Saints reiterated that it was "not an organization of a commercial nature" and that it had never contacted the complainant for commercial purposes; further, it claimed that anyone can register on the '*lds.org*' website through their own account "regardless of Church membership" and that such registration can be automatically cancelled by the user; finally, the religious denomination assured that "none of the governing or institutional bodies of the Church itself will take action to make contact" with the complainant.[51]

So, it is on this well-established arrangement that the GDPR intervenes. And the current European Data Protection Regulation indeed seems to change the prevailing regulatory framework when it allows religious entities to use the former members' personal data for the performance of their own institutional activities without their consent and for internal use. Among the religious organizations' institutional activities, we can surely include religious propaganda,[52] often directed precisely towards apostates.

In fact, the religious propaganda is also frequently addressed to believers that have just manifested the intention to leave the religious faith. As underlined in doctrine, especially in the context of new religious movements, the process of abandonment of the religious faith hardly takes the form of a clear break, but rather unfolds through a prolonged and oscillating path characterised by repeated returns to the faith and new departures, interspersed with periods of personal crisis in which the pressure of the religious group can also manifest itself with considerable intensity.[53] Also for these reasons, the propaganda activities of the Church of Jesus Christ of Latter-day Saints,[54]

50 We can refer to the defensive deductions of in the proceedings settled by the Italian Data Protection Authority with the decision no. 430 dated 16 July 2015 (web doc. no. 4362736). The note is available at the web address: www.garanteprivacy.it/home/docweb/-/docweb-display/docweb/4362736.

51 *Ibid.*

52 See S. Ferrari, 'Diritto delle religioni e proselitismo', *Quaderni di diritto e politica ecclesiastica* 2 (2019), 217–224.

53 In these terms A. Hinderaker, 'Leaving Mormonism', in D. Enstedt, G. Larsson and T. T. Mantsinen (eds.), *Handbook of Leaving Religion*, op. cit., pp. 200–209, especially pp. 203–204. See also C. Luzzati, 'La non sempre garbata violenza del proselitismo e della propaganda', *Quaderni di diritto e politica ecclesiastica* 2 (2019), 229–240.

54 As underlined by C. Cianitto, 'Esiste un dovere di convertire nei diritti delle religioni?', *Quaderni di diritto e politica ecclesiastica* 2 (2019), 265–280, especially on p. 275: the Church of Jesus Christ of Latter-day Saints "manages thousands of young missionaries who, embedded in a widespread, quasi-military organization, are sent out to 'talk' to people to gain them to the new faith, never using them violence verbal or psychological in the deep conviction that everyone must be free to exercise his or her own free will (moral agency) in order to approach to salvation".

for example, "has not only, however, the function of expanding the ranks of believers, but also the purpose of refining and strengthening the faith and zeal of the church members themselves".[55]

The same can also be said about the expelled believers. In fact, in the Mormon context it is expressly recommended to "make every effort to show love to these people so that they may be encouraged to live in such a way as to deserve, once again, all the privileges granted by the Church".[56] It is no coincidence that the readmission baptism of the reinstated Mormons is expressly provided for.

Even in Islamic law, however, according to the major juridical schools, the apostate minor of age or woman is encouraged to reconvert to Islam before the punishment prescribed for the crime of apostasy can be imposed on them.[57]

The same propaganda activities, as anticipated, may also be directed by the religious organisations towards believers who have formally expressed the intention to withdraw or leave, even temporarily, the religious community to which they belong.[58]

The faculty for the religious denominations to process, under the current Article 9, para 2, lett. d) GDPR, the personal data, including sensitive data, of individuals who have expressed the intention to withdraw from their religious faith finds explicit confirmation in the Italian Protection Data Authority's decision no. 71 dated 25 February 2021.[59] In this decision, the Authority – called to jointly sift through a series of appeals brought by former believers against the Jehovah's Witnesses Christian congregation[60] – has expressly stated that

55 Cf. C. Cianitto, *Esiste un dovere di convertire nei diritti delle religioni?* op. cit., p. 275. See also F. M. Gedicks, 'Essere mormone', *Daimon. Annuario di diritto comparato delle religioni* 1 (2001), 71–89, especially pp. 83–84.

56 Cf. F. M. Gedicks, *Essere mormone*, op. cit., p. 82, note 61, in which it refers to J. A. Widtsoe, *Priesthood and Church Government in the Church of Jesus Christ of Latter-day Saints* (Salt Lake City: Deseret Book, 1962), p. 208.

57 Cf. S. Tellenbach, 'L'apostasia nel diritto islamico', *Daimon. Annuario di diritto comparato delle religioni* 1 (2001), 53–70, especially p. 59. About the punishment of the crime of apostacy (*hadd al-ridda*) in Islamic Law see D. Anselmo, *Shari'a e diritti umani* (Turin: Giappichelli, 2007), especially p. 94, in which it is underlined the vagueness and fluidity of the crime and the risks of its abuse for political and ideological purposes. See also R. Aluffi Beck Peccoz, 'Proselytism and the Right to Change Religion in Islam', in S. Ferrari and R. Cristofori (eds.), *Law and Religion in the 21st Century. Relations between States and Religious Communities,* op. cit., pp. 253–260.

58 C. Cianitto, *Esiste un dovere di convertire nei diritti delle religioni?* op. cit., pp. 265–280.

59 The Italian Data Protection Authority's decision no. 71 dated 25 February 2021 (web doc. no. 9574136) can be found at the website: www.garanteprivacy.it/home/docweb/-/docweb-display/docweb/9574136.

60 About the disfellowshipping of Jehovah's Witnesses Christian congregation's former member see also C. Cianitto, *Esiste un dovere di convertire nei diritti delle religioni?* op. cit., pp. 276–277.

It was precisely with respect to the possible discriminatory scope of ostracistic conduct that the Ghent Court of Appeal's decision dated 7 June 2022 has acquitted the Congregation of Jehovah's Witnesses for the charges of discrimination and incitement to hatred related to the

the activities aimed at recalling to faith those who have remained inactive and those who have manifested the intention to leave the religious community[61] are to be considered legitimate. The Italian Data Protection Authority has also stated that these activities can be carried out by religious organisations through public announcements and in accordance with religious precepts.

It seems evident that the possibility of addressing, without the data subject's consent, communications of an ecclesial nature even to persons who have already expressed the will to leave their faith, may influence the process of conversion of the individual believer to another religious faith or the deconversion process. Moreover, the space recognised for religious laws by Article 91 GDPR – to issue their own regulations about the intra-confessional personal data processing – could represent the opportunity to affirm the possibility of also addressing propaganda messages to former members or to members who have expressed the will to leave the faith. In fact, such a provision could hardly be considered in conflict with the European Union Law, specifically with Article 9, para 2, lett. d) GDPR.

Faced with these new issues, the Italian doctrine has reiterated the previous conclusions. In fact, the possibility that a former member can be reached, without his or her consent, by messages with religious content originating from the previous religious communities, can obstruct the fundamental constitutional right of the individual to freely leave the faith group. Nevertheless, this constitutional right, according to the doctrine, must be considered prevalent over the GDPR rules in any case.[62] Specifically, the right to privacy constitutes an essential element for the autonomous construction of the subject's identity, representing the expression of the freedom of self-determination, including religious freedom. The right to privacy can be counted among those inviolable rights or those fundamental freedoms of others hierarchically suited to demand satisfactorily balancing outcomes with the freedom to propagate one's beliefs.[63]

This assumption seems to be once again confirmed by the General Decree dated 24 May 2018 and drawn up by the Italian Bishops' Conference on the

disfellowshipping phenomenon. Cf. W. Fautre, 'BELGIUM: Jehovah's Witnesses Acquitted on Appeal for Alleged Discrimination and Incitement to Hatred', *The European Times*, 16 June 2022. https://europeantimes.news/2022/06/belgium-jehovahs-witnesses-acquitted-on-appeal-for-alleged-discrimination-and-incitement-to-hatred/.

61 For an examination of the Italian Data Protection Authority's decision and about the expulsion proceedings of the Jehovah's Witnesses Christian Congregation see D. Durisotto, 'Il trattamento dei dati personali da parte della Congregazione dei Testimoni di Geova e il provvedimento del Garante per la protezione dei dati personali n. 9574136 del 2021', *Quaderni di diritto e politica ecclesiastica* 3 (2021), 815–826.

62 See J. Pasquali Cerioli, *La propaganda religiosa: la libertà silente*, op. cit., p. 151.

63 *Ivi*, p. 147. Considerandum no. 4 of GDPR states that "the right to the protection of personal data is not an absolute right; it must be considered in relation to its function in society and be balanced against other fundamental rights, in accordance with the principle of proportionality".

base of Article 91 GDPR. Despite the innovation introduced by Article 9, para 2, lett. d) GDPR, the General Decree reiterates what was already provided for in the previous 1999 Decree, namely that the request of cancellation from register obliges the person in charge of the registers not to use the relevant personal data except with the authorisation of the Diocesan Ordinary.[64]

The balancing between religious propaganda and protection of individual's religious freedom in the Article 9, para 2, lett. d) GDPR. conclusive remarks

The Italian Data Protection Authority's decision dated 25 February 2021 and the confirmation of the possibility of processing the personal data of the apostate or those who have formally expressed the intention to leave the faith without their consent may prompt some reflections on the appropriateness of the wording of Article 9, para 2, lett. d) GDPR.

In fact, in our opinion, in order to ensure an effective protection of the individual's right to religious freedom, it could be useful to distinguish between the condition of the former member – removed from the registers or expelled from the organisation – and the different condition of the outgoing members who, although not formally removed from the registers, have merely manifested the intention of leaving the religious group, embarking on a path of deconversion or conversion to another religious faith.

Indeed, the current regulations regarding the position of those who are undergoing a process of exit from their religious faith still seem to be decidedly unbalanced in favour of the freedom of religious organisations, especially in those many cases in which there are no procedures to formalise the withdrawal from the religious denomination. In the absence of a definitive departure and even during a process of conversion or gradual exit from the religious group, the current European Union regulatory framework seems in fact to allow the processing of the subject's sensitive data without his or her consent for purposes internal to the organisation, without excluding the use of penetrating profiling techniques.[65] For these reasons the outgoing member can be subject to relevant forms of pressure exercised by the group to which he or she belongs, capable of decisively coercing his or her fundamental right to reconstruct the religious identity at any time.

64 Cfr. Italian Bishops' Conference, 'Decreto generale sulle Disposizioni per la tutela del diritto alla buona fama e alla riservatezza', *Notiziario della Conferenza Episcopale Italiana* 2 (31 May 2018), 94–133, available also online at the web address: www.chiesacattolica.it/wp-content/uploads/sites/31/2022/08/51507-2018_05_Decreto-generale-privacy_OK.pdf.

65 The *Considerandum* no. 71 GDPR defines profiling as a form of automated processing of personal data that evaluates personal aspects concerning a natural person, particularly for the purpose of analysing or predicting aspects concerning professional performance, economic situation, health, preferences or interests. On the use of profiling techniques in the processing of religious personal data allow me to refer to F. Balsamo, *La protezione dei dati personali di natura religiosa*, op. cit., especially pp. 81 ff.

Because of the invasiveness of the new automated methods of data processing, often entrusted to forms of artificial intelligence,[66] for a better balance between the organisational freedom of religious denominations and the religious freedom of the person it might be of some use to reaffirm, by amending the current wording of Article 9, para 2, lett. d) GDPR, the need of the legal basis of the data subject's consent for those personal data processing that are substantiated in the sending of religious communications or in propaganda activities addressed either to former members or to members who have formally manifested their intention to abandon or change religious faith, regardless of the definitive outcome of their conversion or deconversion path.[67]

This normative change could result in ensuring an effective protection of the individual's right to freely change his or her religious faith, and it could also limit those obstacles that challenge the exercise of this fundamental right, especially within new religious movements and within religious denominations without formal withdrawal mechanisms.[68]

In this sense, the regulatory solutions developed under Article 91 GDPR by religious organisations – the aforementioned provision in Article 8, § 8 of the General Decree of the Italian Bishops' Conference on the *'Dispositions for the protection of the right to good reputation and privacy'* dated 24 May 2018, and to the related prohibition to send religious communications to formers members – can serve as a stimulus for an adjustment of the current European Union Law's provisions on personal data protection.

66 Cf. *ex multis* F. Pizzetti (ed.), *Intelligenza artificiale, protezione dei dati personali e regolazione* (Turin: Giappichelli, 2018).

67 As underlined by C. Luzzati, *La non sempre garbata violenza del proselitismo e della propaganda,* op. cit., p. 234, the propaganda activities do not address itself only outside a group, to those who are not yet followers of certain beliefs, but also address the followers themselves, strengthening their associational ties and nurturing their identifications with common ideals.

68 Cf. M. Cardano and N. Pannofino, *Piccole apostasie. Il congedo dai nuovi movimenti religiosi,* op. cit., *passim.*

8 State law or religious precepts? The right to asylum

Stefano Testa Bappenheim

Introduction: *de qua agitur*

The current migratory flows in Europe are witnessing an increasing number of people who, after examination – by the authorities in charge – of the documentation submitted, are ruled to be lacking the legal requirements that would enable them to stay and should therefore, again in accordance with the law, be expelled from the EU country in which they are located.

In recent years, however, a widespread movement of opposition to the deportation of illegal immigrants has developed, particularly in the German Catholic and Protestant ecclesiastical world. This resistance is in fact perceived, based on the New Testament, as an essential duty for Christians, who go so far as choosing to follow their conscience by disobeying earthly law, the violation of which has nevertheless led to a large number of criminal trials for priests and religious personnel, men and women, accused of various offences from criminal conspiracy to aiding and abetting illegal immigration.[1]

Conscientious objection and the secular state

Can a non-denominational state today accept that some of its laws are openly violated by appealing to superior religious motives?

Can a citizen violate a law by appealing to his religious faith and invoking conscientious objection?

Would this be possible not (only) in the abstract and in principle, but in the concrete situations of the current legal system of a country like Germany?

Let us see.

Germany is a secular-neutral State, not a secularist State,[2] given that it contains an invocation to God in the Federal Constitution, and a reference

1 J. Martínez-Torrón, 'Las objeciones de conciencia de los católicos', *Revista General de Derecho Canónico y Derecho Eclesiástico del Estado* 3 (2005), 2 ff.; ID., 'Las objeciones de conciencia y los intereses generales del ordenamiento', *Revista de la Facultad de Derecho de la Universidad Complutense* 18 (1991–1992), 199 ff.

2 O. Fumagalli Carulli, 'L'antica idea di separazione', in AA.VV. (ed.), *Individuo, gruppi, confessioni religiose nello Stato democratico* (Milano: Giuffrè, 1973), pp. 975 ff.

DOI: 10.4324/9781003502845-8

thereto in those of almost all the Länder;[3] State neutrality, however, does not mean law without morality, but necessarily means a State that is built on certain moral values,[4] one that admits its incompetence to define the relationship between the faithful of any religion and their deities,[5] and also recognizes the ontological distinction between its own institutions and those of any religious creed, as well as the teleological diversity between its actions and those aimed at a relationship with the transcendent and metaphysical plane;[6] also, a State that does not require "any transcendent principle to justify its authority",[7] or one that ultimately is religiously neutral in the sense that it does not take a position between different religious beliefs or between faith and atheism[8].

Neutrality, in any case, does not appear to be synonymous with secularism,[9] since otherwise one would have "an 'ideological militancy' that would itself share in the eminent duty that is proper to 'religious testimony'"[10]. While it is true, therefore, that "the State is not the kingdom of God", at the same time "is it not licit for the State to transform itself into a religion; it must remain something profane, and thus differentiate itself from religion as such",[11] entrusting the facts of the spirit "totally to the irreplaceable management of

3 S. Testa Bappenheim, 'Cenni sulla costituzionalizzazione delle radici cristiane in Germania', *Ius Ecclesiae* 3 (2006), 755 ff.; ID., 'Il "Dio della fede" ed il "Dio dei filosofi" nel Codice penale tedesco', in G. Leziroli (ed.), *La Carta e la Corte. La tutela penale del fatto religioso fra normativa costituzionale e diritto vivente* (Cosenza: Pellegrini, 2009), pp. 277 ff.; ID., '"Veluti si Deus daretur": Dio nell'ordinamento costituzionale tedesco', in J. I. Arrieta (ed.), *Il ius divinum nella vita della Chiesa* (Venezia: Marcianum Press, 2010), pp. 253 ff.

4 P. A. D'Avack, 'La qualificazione dello Stato in materia religiosa e la sua applicazione allo Stato italiano', in AA.VV. (ed.), *Raccolta di scritti in onore di A.C. Jemolo* (Milano: Giuffrè, 1963), pp. 283 ff.; P. Bellini, 'Libertà dell'uomo e fattore religioso nei sistemi ideologici contemporanei', in AA.VV. (ed.), *Teoria e prassi delle libertà di religione* (Bologna: Il mulino, 1975), pp. 103 ff.

5 R. Baccari, 'La religione cattolica da religione dello Stato a patrimonio del popolo', *Il Diritto ecclesiastico* 98 (1987), 15 ff.

6 L. Arcidiacono, A. Carullo and G. Rizza, *Istituzioni di diritto pubblico* (Bologna: Monduzzi, 1997), pp. 33 ff.

7 F. Finocchiaro, 'Commento all'art. 7 Cost.', in G. Branca (ed.), *Commentario alla Costituzione. Artt. 1–12. Principi fondamentali* (Bologna-Roma: Zanichelli, 1975), pp. 377 ff.

8 V. P. Bellini, 'voce *Ateismo*', in *Digesto discipline pubblicistiche* (Torino: UTET, 1987).

9 La differenza consistendo nel fatto che 'uno Stato laico propriamente inteso non professa pertanto un'ideologia «laicistica» qualora si intenda per tale un'ideologia irreligiosa o antireligiosa', V. Zannone, 'voce *Laicismo*', in N. Bobbio and N. Matteucci (eds.), *Dizionario di politica* (Torino: UTET, 1972), pp. 511 ff. See also N. Bobbio, 'La polemica sulla cultura laica', *Nuova Antologia* 2168 (1988), 145 ff.

10 P. Bellini, 'Centralità della coscienza e condizionamenti dell'ambiente', in I. C. Ibán (ed.), *Libertad y derecho fundamental de libertad religiosa* (Madrid: Editoriales de Derecho Reunidas, 1989), pp. 90 ff.; G. Dalla Torre, *Il fattore religioso nella Costituzione* (Torino: Giappichelli, 2003), pp. 50 ff.

11 J. Ratzinger, *Svolta per l'Europa? Chiesa e modernità nell'Europa dei rivolgimenti* (Cinisello Balsamo: Edizioni Paoline, 1992), pp. 112 ff. V. M. Tedeschi, 'Quale laicità? Fattore religioso e principi costituzionali', *Il Diritto eccesiastico* 104 (1993), 548 ff.

individual consciences: the only ones capable of perceiving within themselves a movement of faith and of nourishing themselves with it".[12]

The State's obligatory commitment to neutrality in the religious sphere should not be understood as a categorical imperative in favour of indifference or secularism since civil law, "which oversees only the 'economy of politics' and is limited to the human reality of religious belief",[13] cannot but consider the latter as a "socially relevant consciential fact".[14]

The State's attitude remains one of absolute neutrality in the face of the different possible exemplars of the religious fact, which "lies at the foundation of every single social system (which is such and not a forced artificial aggregation of individuals) and determines and conditions its formal structures",[15] and, in general, in the pluralism of the values of conscience, following the guarantees of the GG to the fundamental freedoms of the individual.[16]

Reasons of conscience distinguish conscientious objection from arbitrary disobedience,[17] so that the "integrative instance of postulating the presence – at the formal apex of the system – of a supreme guaranteeing principle of 'personal self-determination with regard to the facts of the spirit'" is imposed. This principle is not simply inferable from the positive constitutional provisions but presupposed by them: as a normative greatness that transcends them all, surpassing their overall value. It is as if to say that the individual precepts of this or that democratic constitution that touch on moments of human promotion are just such . . . as if to imply (as a 'logically necessary premise', sharing the same degree of certainty) the existence of a more abstract publicist principle, which is responsible for presiding over the entire matter from above. They presuppose, in other words, a more general canon of protection for individual personal projects of human self-realization: which, just as it is reflected in the specific constitutional provisions, aimed at regulating one or another distinctly defined case, it also covers, with its superior normative scope, the forms of life commitment not explicitly contemplated. "Such is the

12 P. Bellini, 'voce *Ateismo*', op. cit. Cfr. anche M. G. Belgiorno de Stefano, 'Il diritto fondamentale all'obiezione di coscienza nell'esercizio della «libertas ecclesiae»', in AA.VV. (ed.), *Les droits fondamentaux du chretien dans l'Église et dans la société* (Fribourg: Herder, 1981), pp. 877 ff.

13 R. Bertolino, 'Assistenza religiosa, obiezione di coscienza e problemi morali e psicologici nel prisma della struttura ospedaliera', *Archivio giuridico Filippo Serafini* 209 (1989), 91 ff.

14 P. Bellini, 'Aspetti costituzionali con più specifico riferimento alla libertà religiosa', in AA.VV. (ed.), *Trattamenti sanitari fra libertà e doverosità* (Napoli: Jovene, 1988), pp. 74 ff.

15 P. Bellini, *Libertà dell'uomo e fattore religioso nei sistemi ideologici contemporanei*, op. cit., pp. 119 ff.; ID., 'voce *Ateismo*', op. cit.; M. G. Belgiorno de Stefano, *Il diritto universale alla libertà di coscienza* (Roma: Ianua, 2000), pp. 123 ff.; H. Küng, *Dio esiste? (Italian translation)* (Milano: Mondadori, 1979).

16 V. C. Mirabelli, *L'appartenenza confessionale* (Padova: Cedam, 1975), pp. 85 ff.; P. Bellini, 'Diritti inviolabili dell'uomo e formazioni sociali religiose', in AA.VV. (ed.), *Studi in onore di P.A. D'Avack*, vol. I (Milano: Giuffrè, 1976), pp. 230 ff.

17 G. Capograssi, 'Obbedienza e coscienza', *Foro italiano* 73 (1950), 48 ff.

logic that leads to the "normative hypostatization" of a general principle of protection of the "freedom of conscience", which does not merely preface the "religious freedom" of ordinary democratic constitutions but calls for a more articulate solution".[18]

Indeed, it is necessary to prevent 'human rights from bending and crumpling like soft surrealist clocks'.[19] Therefore, "it follows that – precisely because it is the '*regula et mensura*' of the relationships that are entertained between men -, the binding juridical law (insofar as it is incapable of penetrating into the interiority of the individual) can well assume this human reality as its own 'object of recognition and protection': as a singularly significant and delicate expression of each person's 'personality', deserving of special protective action. It is a matter – at the very least – of protecting it (that interiority of the individual) from the snares and abuses that may descend on it from the outside: due to the behaviour of other human beings who claim to press beyond the lawful limits on the conscience of the subject. On the contrary, the law must first of all concern itself with its own danger. So much so that the indefinable postulate of any democratic system cannot fail to rise to the ideal requirement that the law – in addressing subjects in an imperative key – takes charge, with the greatest possible care, of the ethical sensitivity (and susceptibility) of its addressees". In fact, "the meaning of conscientious objection as it is posed is intended to make us aware of the permanent tension and intimate connection between legality and morality . . . it shelters us from any totalizing conception of the State . . . This is the message that reaches us even from the non-integralist secular side, from a master such as Norberto Bobbio".[20]

It follows, therefore, that it is "incorrect to present the right to object solely or predominantly from the perspective of disintegration [of the very logic of the democratic state], because, on the contrary, it can become a constituent element of a citizenship pact that is more respectful of everyone's conscience and therefore an element of political social cohesion".[21]

The issues related to conscientious objection[22] have often manifested themselves on a practical level, in the refusal to carry out an activity that conflicts with the worker's religious convictions:[23] the conscientious objection of a Muslim who, while working in a slaughterhouse, also refuses to handle

18 P. Bellini, 'Centralità della coscienza e condizionamenti dell'ambiente', in I. C. Ibán (ed.), *Libertad y derecho fundamental de libertad religiosa*, op. cit., p. 83.

19 L. Lombardi Vallauri, 'La portée philosophique des droits de l'homme', *Nova et vetera* 57 (1982),17 ff.

20 P. Bellini, *Centralità della coscienza e condizionamenti dell'ambiente*, op. cit., pp. 85 ff.

21 S. Rodotà, 'Problemi dell'obiezione di coscienza', *quaderni di diritto e politica ecclesiastica* 10 (1993), 65 ff.

22 V. R. Botta, 'La libertà religiosa', in P. Cendon (ed.), *Trattato breve dei nuovi danni* (Padova: Cedam, 2001), pp. 747 ff.

23 V. ID., *Sentimento religioso e costituzione repubblicana* (Torino: Giappichelli, 1990), pp. 175 ff.

pork;[24] refusing to perform duties aimed at the production of weapons;[25] refusing to pay contributions to the national social security system; refusing to wear religious clothing accessories in a military environment; refusing to provide photographs for documents; refusing to use certain symbols on car number plates.[26]

"Fundamental and inviolable rights include, first and foremost, the right to life, in its complex meaning, both natural and connected to respect for moral and religious sentiments and ideological convictions, which, during human existence, allow everyone to implement and develop his own personality . . . [These principles] cannot be considered as mere theoretical propositions belonging to the 'pre-legal' sphere of legislative production. They are true and proper juridical norms, to be observed and put into effect, with the consequent identification of the addressees and the bodies that must implement them and the subjects that can claim their own subjective juridical positions".[27] In fact, "there are implicit constitutional recognitions that are no less valid and important than those explicitly formulated".[28]

The use of conscientious objection as a 'tactical tool' to express "with non-violent methods the voice of one's conscience against the dictates of state law [constitutes] a moment of confrontation and growth of society itself".[29] It takes on the role of a "valorisation of conscience in terms of a 'resource', communal and not only individual. In these cases, disobedience

24 R. Torfs, 'L'objection de conscience en Belgique', in European Consortium For Church-State Research (ed.), *Conscientious Objection in the EC Countries* (Milano: Giuffrè, 1992), pp. 239 ff. Cf. O. Fumagalli Carulli, 'La libertà religiosa in Europa', *Rivista internazionale dei diritti dell'uomo* 1 (1988), 7 ff.; P. Morozzo Della Rocca, 'Alterità nazionale e diritto alla differenza', *Rivista critica del diritto privato* 10 (1992), 69 ff.; S. Lariccia, 'L'obiezione di coscienza in Italia: vent'anni di legislazione e di giurisprudenza', *Il Diritto ecclesiastico* 103 (1992), 259 ff.

25 Pret. Milano, '5 Novembre 1977', *Rivista scientifica di diritto del lavoro e della previdenza sociale* 4 (1978), 140 ff.; Pret. Milano, '19 dicembre 1981', *Giustizia civile* 8 (1982), 1077 ff., with a note by A. Vitale, *Obiezione di coscienza e rapporto di lavoro, ivi*, 1081 ff.; Pret. Milano, '25 Febbraio 1982', *Orientamenti della giurisprudenza del lavoro* 31 (1982), 231 ff.; Trib. Milano, '12 Gennaio 1983', *ivi* 32 (1983), 25 ff. V. F. Onida, 'Prospettive di regolamentazione dell'obiezione di coscienza nelle prestazioni lavorative', *Questione giustizia* 6 (1987), 805 ff.; P. Moneta, 'Libertà religiosa e mondo del lavoro', in AA.VV. (ed.), *Scritti in onore di Dante Gaeta* (Milano: Giuffrè, 1984), pp. 195 ff.

26 V. R. Navarro Valls and J. Martinez Torron, *Le obiezioni di coscienza* (Torino: Giappichelli,1995), pp. 189 ff.

27 C. Mortati, *Istituzioni di diritto pubblico* (Padova: Cedam, 1975), pp. 155 ff.; M. G. Belgiorno de Stefano, 'L'obiezione di coscienza al servizio militare, diritto inviolabile dell'uomo e del cristiano', in AA.VV. (ed.), *Scritti in memoria di Pietro Gismondi*, vol. I (Milano: Giuffrè, 1988), pp. 36 ff.

28 G. Vassalli, 'Il diritto alla libertà morale (Contributo alla teoria dei diritti della personalità)', in AA.VV. (ed.), *Studi giuridici in memoria di Filippo Vassalli*, vol. II (Torino: UTET, 1960), pp. 1642 ff.; F. Bettinelli, 'Profili di diritto costituzionale della disciplina legislativa dell'obiezione di coscienza', *Giurisprudenza costituzionale* 17 (1972), 2923 ff.

29 M. G. Belgiorno de Stefano, 'Obiezione di coscienza selettiva e obiezione fiscale', *Il Diritto ecclesiastico* 98 (1987), 35 ff.

of the law does not nullify its underlying values, nay, it exalts them, and the principle of legality is not modified, but is instead pushed, beyond the form, towards the recovery of its substantive dimension of an adaptation to justice".[30]

If conscientious objection has found itself affecting a wealth of values and interests that are vital and primary for both the State and the Church (since "only the religions, at least until the threshold of modernity, upheld the rights of the individual conscience",[31] and "refusing out of loyalty to their faith to make sacrifices to the cult of the emperor, were not the first Christians the first martyrs, the first witnesses?",[32] so much so that the emergence of civil liberty seems to be due to them),[33] it then "moved on to protect also the ethical contents of conscience, not necessarily linked to religious beliefs":[34] these irreplaceable guarantees must certainly be ensured (in today's "ethically polytheistic" society)[35] for all citizens, whatever their religious or philosophical beliefs:[36] "the preceptive content of the law [must be such as to] put every person in a position to loyally fulfil the legal commandment addressed to him, without having to come into conflict with the dictates of his own moral code".[37]

"*Nulla lex satis commoda est*",[38] but "when one believes a certain law to be bad, he has the right, and may even have the duty, to seek to change it, but only in rare cases will he do the right thing by breaking it. I do not deny that there are situations in which breaking it becomes a duty: it is a duty when one deeply believes that it is a sin to obey it . . . Even if you are completely convinced that he is wrong, you cannot say that he should act differently from what his conscience dictates"[39] thus affirming, in the wake of Rousseau ("con-

30 S. Berlingò, 'Ordine etico e legge civile: complementarità e distinzione', *Iustitia* 49 (1996), 203 ff.

31 S. Lariccia, 'Laicità dello Stato e democrazia pluralista in Italia', *Il Diritto ecclesiastico* 106 (1995), 407 ff.

32 R. Remond, *Religion et société en Europe* (Paris: Seuil, 1998), pp. 236 ff.

33 A. Passerin D'entrèves, *Obbedienza e resistenza in una società democratica* (Milano: Edizioni di Comunità, 1970), pp. 210 ff. Cfr. anche L. Lombardi Vallauri and G. Dilcher (eds.), *Cristianesimo, secolarizzazione e diritto moderno* (Milano and Baden Baden: Giuffrè-Nomos Verlag, 1981); F. P. Casavola, 'Processi di secolarizzazione nella nascita del diritto moderno', *Iustitia* 41 (1988), 107 ff.

34 R. Navarro Valls and J. Martinez Torron, *Le obiezioni di coscienza*, op. cit., pp. 10 ff.

35 V. M. Weber, *Il lavoro intellettuale come professione* (tr. it., Torino: Einaudi, 1967); H. Jonas, *Le principe de responsabilité* (Paris: Les editions du Cerf, 1993), pp. 13 ff.

36 Cfr. C.Cost., 329/1997; C. Mirabelli, 'La libertà religiosa nella giurisprudenza costituzionale', in M. Tedeschi (ed.), *La libertà religiosa*, vol. I (Soveria Mannelli: Rubbettino, 2002), pp. 55 ff.

37 P. Bellini, *Centralità della coscienza e condizionamenti dell'ambiente*, op. cit., p. 86.

38 So Catone, defending *Lex Oppia*, in TITO LIVIO, XXXIV, 3.

39 B. Russel, *Autorità e individuo* (Milano: Longanesi, 1975), pp. 118 ff.

science is never wrong, it is man's true guide")[40] and Fichte ("conscience is the judge of all convictions, but it recognizes no judge above itself"),[41] the priority of conscience over law.[42]

Establishing that a citizen must submit to a norm that he considers profoundly immoral would be tantamount to sacrificing the value of the person, destined to conform the entire system[43] on the altar of the totalitarian state,[44] while a democratic society, on the other hand, must show that it has '*à la fois, un horizon et des racines*',[45] and tolerate in all cases the value of the person, and tolerate, in all scenarios involving religious or moral convictions, conscientious objection to the furthest possible limit. At the same time, the objector must also be willing to pay the price for his disobedience to the law[46] ("Antigone dies for wanting to throw a fistful of earth on Polynices' body, the Christian martyrs of the early centuries let themselves be killed for not burning a pinch of incense in front of the emperor's statue";[47] "from Socrates to Christ, the world has always moved forward thanks to men who accepted condemnations in order to put the law of their conscience before the contingent law of their city").[48]

40 J. J. Rousseau, 'Émile, IV', in *Oeuvres complètes*, vol. IV (Paris: Gallimard, 1969), pp. 594 ff.

41 J. G. Fichte, *La missione dell'uomo* (Roma-Bari: Laterza, 1970), pp. 170 ff.

42 F. D'agostino, 'L'obiezione di coscienza nella prospettiva di una società democratica avanzata', *Diritto ecclesiastico* 103 (1992), 75 ff.

43 D. Messinetti, 'voce Personalità (diritti della)', in *Enciclopedia del Diritto*, vol. XXXIII (Milano: Giuffrè, 1983), p. 378. Cf. L. Lombardi Vallauri, *Abortismo libertario e sadismo* (Milano: Scotti Camuzzi, 1976).

44 A. Passerin D'Entrèves, *Obbedienza e resistenza in una società democratica*, op. cit., pp. 225–229. Conforme G. Amato, 'Il dilemma del principio maggioritario', *Quaderni costituzionali* 14 (1994),171 ff.

45 A. Clavel, 'Avortement et clause de conscience', *Iustitia* 32 (1979), 244 ff.

46 A. Passerin D'Entrèves, *Obbedienza e resistenza in una società democratica*, op. cit., p. 231.

47 F. D'agostino, 'Obiezione di coscienza e verità del diritto tra moderno e postmoderno', *quaderni di diritto e politica ecclesiastica* 6 (1989), 4–5. Cfr. anche T. Ascarelli, 'Antigone e Porzia', in ID. (ed.), *Problemi giuridici*, vol. I (Milano: Giuffrè, 1959), pp. 6 ff.; P. Bellini, *Respublica sub Deo* (Firenze: Le Monnier, 1982).

48 A. C. Jemolo, 'Il diritto positivo e i diritti della coscienza', *Giurisprudenza italiana* 2 (1964), 93 ff. Cfr. R. Guardini, *La morte di Socrate. Interpretazione dei dialoghi platonici Eutifrone, Critone e Fedone* (Brescia: Morcelliana, 1984).

There are already numerous cases of conscientious objection cited in the Old Testament,[49] and, in an era closer to us, one thinks of Thomas More):[50] If the phenotype of the conflict between law and conscience, given the character of absoluteness of these two terms, is a radical and absolute irreconcilability, it follows that "objection *contra legem* is the only authentic form of objection, failing which there is only either the annulment of the norm in conscience, or, vice versa, the flattening of conscience in the norm".[51] Herein lies the 'juridical nature' of conscientious objection whereby, in the case of conflict between the internal norm (of conscience) and the external norm (set by law), the subject opts for the other possibility that the latter essentially offers him: disobeying

49 See the episodes of the midwives of Egypt, concerning the Pharaoh's command to kill all male Jewish newborns (Es., I, 17: '*Timuerunt autem obstetrices Deum et non fecerunt iuxta praeceptum regis Aegypti, sed conservabant mares*'); of the 'dissenting' Prophets vis-à-vis hegemonic powers, both royal and sacerdotal (1 Re, XVIII, 17: '*et, cum vidisset eum, ait: «Tune es, qui conturbas Israel?»*', 2 Sam, XII, 17: '*Steterunt autem seniores domus eius iuxta eum cogentes eum, ut surgeret de terra; qui noluit neque comedit cum eis cibum*'; Ger., XXXVII, 15: '*Et irati sunt principes contra Ieremiam, quem caesum miserunt in carcerem, qui erat in domo Ionathan scribae; eam enim in carcerem fecerant*'); of the disobedience of the Assyrian idolatrous system (Dn III, 16–18: '*[16] Respondentes Sedrac, Misac et Abdenago dixerunt regi Nabuchodonosor: «Non oportet nos de hac re respondere tibi: [17] Si enim Deus noster, quem colimus, potest eripere nos de camino ignis ardentis, et de manu tua, rex, liberabit. [18] Quod si noluerit, notum sit tibi, rex, quia deos tuos non colimus et statuam auream, quam erexisti, non adoramus»*'); of the objection to unjust norms (Tb I, 17–19: '*[17] Panes meos dabam esurientibus et vestimenta nudis et, si quem videbam mortuum et proiectum post murum Nineves ex natione mea, sepeliebam illum. [18] Et, si quem occidebat Sennacherib rex, ubi venit de Iudaea fugiens in diebus iudicii, quod fecit Rex caeli ex illo de blasphemiis, quibus blasphemaverat – multos enim filiorum Israel occidit in ira sua – ego autem corpora illorum involabam et sepeliebam; et quaesivit illa Sennacherib et non invenit illa. [19] Et abiit quidam ex Ninevitis et indicavit regi de me quoniam ego sepelio illos, et abscondi me et, ubi cognovi quod rex sciebat de me et quod inquiror, ut occidar, timui et refugi*'); of the seven Maccabean brothers (and their mother) who were slaughtered by King Antiochus for their refusal to partake of pork (2 Mac., VII: '*[1] Contigit autem et septem fra tres una cum matre apprehen sos compelli a rege attingere contra fas carnes porcinas, flagris et nervis cruciatos. [2] Unus autem ex illis exstans prior locutor sic ait: «Quid es quaesiturus, et quid vis discere a nobis? Parati sumus mori magis quam patrias leges praevaricari» . . . [30] Cum haec illa adhuc diceret, ait adulescens: «Quem sustinetis? Non oboedio praecepto regis, sed obtempero praecepto legis, quae data est patribus nostris per Moysen» . . . [37] «Ego autem, sicut et fratres mei, et corpus et animam trado pro patriis legibus, invocans Deum maturius genti nostrae propitium fieri, teque cum tormentis et verberibus confiteri quod ipse est Deus solus»*'): they all testify to the right-duty to conscientious objection and the axiological priority of conscience over laws that oppose its imperative: cf. C. M. Martini, 'La Chiesa opera a favore della interiorità', in AA.VV. (ed.), *Realtà e prospettive dell'obiezione di coscienza* (Milano: Giuffrè, 1992), pp. 445 ff.

50 V. V. Mathieu, 'Thomas More: ragioni d'una scelta', in ID. (ed.), *Luci ed ombre del giusnaturalismo ed altri scritti di filosofia giuridica e politica* (Torino: Giappichelli, 1989), pp. 217 ff. About 'superior feeling of dutifulness', or 'eminent dutifulness', see P. Bellini, *Libertà dell'uomo e fattore religioso nei sistemi ideologici contemporanei*, op. cit., p. 128.

51 V. F. De Gregorio, 'L'homo viator tra dovere etico e precettistica divina', *Rivista Internazionale di Filosofia del Diritto* 97 (2017), 635 ff.; P. Sassi, 'Confessioni religiose e "conflitti di lealtà", ovvero quando l'obbedienza non è più una virtù', *quaderni di diritto e politica ecclesiastica* 12 (1995), 448 ff.

the legislator's command, accepting the envisaged sanction . . . [here we grasp] the substantial difference between conscientious objection and other forms of resistance to the juridical norm: unlike the behaviour of other resisters, the conscientious objector does not give himself away by evading the sanction, just as he does not positively oppose the norm, that is, by seeking to avoid the sanction in some other way by resorting to the use of force (*vim vi repellere*)".[52]

"Through conscientious objection, the conflict is overcome without compromise, but with respect for and preservation of the different positions involved, without any one of them being attributed a condition of supremacy. It follows, therefore, that we are not only faced with an instrument that allows the question of conscience to be transferred from the internal to the external forum of a person, but with a form of social settlement that reduces, or eliminates altogether, the very possibility of conflict. Conscientious objection is thus configured as an indispensable technique for a pluralist society. Only it can allow the simultaneous permanence of values that would otherwise be destined to be in continuous conflict";[53] it is pragmatically pointed out, then, that "in a technologically advanced society, the specialization of activities ends up determining specific recipients of laws whose observance, however, is indispensable for the survival of society. If the criterion adopted [i.e. admitting conscientious objection] were to find further application, one would have to express many doubts about the capacity of a social system, so disarmed, to survive".[54]

Is an *interpositio legislatoris* therefore indispensable? "This is not always true, and even when it is true, it leaves open the problem of what the tone and type of legislative intervention should be".[55] Given that in any case the norm that recognized a given conscientious objection would not make it *secundum legem*, but would limit itself to ascertaining that it is already, in itself, *secundum ius*;[56] "it [indeed] appears by now inaccurate to appreciate it [= conscientious objection] juridically as an exceptional phenomenon and to have the normative discipline always subject to a restrictive interpretation".[57]

52 G. Dalla Torre, *Libertà della coscienza etica e limiti della norma giuridica*, op. cit., p. 1050. Sulla contiguità fra obiezione di coscienza e disobbedienza civile, see N. Bobbio, 'Item Disobbedienza civile', in N. Bobbio and N. Matteucci (eds.), *Dizionario di politica* (Torino: UTET, 1983), pp. 338 ff.

53 S. Rodotà, *Problemi dell'obiezione di coscienza,* op. cit., pp. 58 ff.

54 F. Onida, 'Prospettive di regolamentazione dell'obiezione di coscienza nelle prestazioni lavorative', *Questione giustizia* 6 (1987), 810 ff.

55 Magistratura Democratica, 'Obiettivo: legislazione e giurisdizione di fronte alle questioni bioetiche. Per una discussione su bioetica e diritti', *ivi* 18 (1999), 449 ff.

56 R. Bertolino, *L'obiezione di coscienza moderna. Per una fondazione costituzionale del diritto di obiezione* (Torino: Giappichelli, 1994), pp. 94 ff.

57 ID., 'voce Obiezione di coscienza. I) Profili teorici', in *Enciclopedia giuridica*; M. G. Belgiorno de Stefano, 'L'obiezione di coscienza e la Convenzione europea dei diritti dell'uomo', in R. Botta (ed.), *L'obiezione di coscienza tra tutela della libertà e disgregazione dello stato democratico* (Milano: Giuffrè, 1991), pp. 235 ff.; P. Consorti, *Obiezione, opzione di coscienza e motivi religiosi, ivi*, pp. 251 ff.; G. Dalla Torre, *Il primato della coscienza* (Roma: Studium,

Concrete phenotypes

The case law in this regard is quite substantial, and an analysis of it enables us to understand the orientation of German case law,[58] which was initially opposed to recognizing conscientious objection to laws regulating the deportation of illegal immigrants, sending the priests and religious personnel involved to trial. But then, at the end of 2014 in the case law, and subsequently in 2015 following an agreement between the BAMF and the Catholic and Evangelical Churches, a clear *revirement* of openness seems to have taken shape.[59]

In the first phase, in fact, the case law orientation is very strict: after a first and fleeting case in 1997,[60] in which conscientious objection against the deportation of illegal immigrants was not recognized as having any particular relevance, the case came up again in 2006, when a deportation order was executed against Turkish minors despite the fact that they had taken refuge in an evangelical parish, which had knowingly hidden them. According to the VG in Kassel, the deportation had to be carried out, so that no special consideration could be given to the conscientious objection invoked by the priests who had opposed the deportation.[61] Then, in 2009, there was a Protestant pastor condemned in the court of first instance for having hidden a Turkish citizen who had illegally entered Germany and who, unwilling to obey the deportation decree by which she had been caught, had gone into hiding: humanitarian reasons may exceptionally justify acts *praeter legem*, whereas conscientious objection endorsing acts *contra legem*, such as obstructing the execution of a deportation order for an illegal immigrant, would constitute a flagrant and unjustifiable violation of the law.[62]

In 2014, there was an initial rethink,[63] then in 2015 this open-minded attitude was consolidated and strengthened with a sort of de facto recognition of conscientious objection to expulsions by Catholic and Protestant priests and

1992), pp. 126 ff.; J.-P. Schouppe, 'Réflexions juridiques autour de la notion d'objection de conscience institutionnelle', in G. Boni (ed.), *Recta sapere. Studi in onore di Giuseppe Dalla Torre*, vol. II (Torino: Giappichelli, 2014), pp. 1205 ff.

58 J. Martínez-Torrón, 'Las objeciones de conciencia en el derecho internacional y comparado', *Estudios de derecho judicial* 11 (2006), 99 ff.; M. D'arienzo, 'Current and Historical Relevance of debate upon Relationship between Freedom and Institutions', in J. Naya Pérez and M. Hillar (eds.), *Michael Servetus, Heartfelt: Proceedings of the International Servetus Congress, Barcelona, 20–21 October 2006* (Lanham: University press of America, 2011), pp. 242 ff.

59 R. Nientied, 'Flüchdingshilfe in der Illegalität', *Herder Korrespondenz* 41 (1986), 216 ff.; ID., *Asylrecht: Beschränkung mit oder ohne Grundgesetzänderung, ivi*, 403 ff.; J. Müller, 'Politische Lösungsansätze des Flüchtlingsproblems und der Beitrag der Kirchen', in AA.VV. (ed.), *Flüchtlinge und Asyl. Politisch handeln aus christlicher Verantwortung* (Frankfurt a.M: Knecht, 1990), pp. 179 ff.

60 BayObLG, 19 mars 1997, n. 3z/br/73/97.

61 VwG Kassel, 13 April 2006.

62 OLG Hamm, I June 2010, no. III/3/RV/310/09; LG Osnabrück, 2 November 2001, no. 7/NS/131/01; OVG Saarland, 13 September 2006, no. 1/R/17/06; VG Cottbus, 3 November 2015, no. 5/L/727/15/a.

63 VG Stuttgart, 18 September 2014, no. A/2/k/3286/14.

religious personnel, thanks to an agreement between the Federal Office for Migration and Refugees (*Bundesamt für Migration und Flüchtlinge, BAMF*) and the Catholic and Evangelical Churches: In early 2015, in fact, the growing number of Catholic and Protestant priests and religious personnel hiding illegal immigrants who had received a deportation order gave rise to a moment of friction with the Federal Ministry of the Interior, which, in order to avoid a polemical escalation, recognized, together with the BAMF, a de facto legitimacy to conscientious objection to the deportation of illegal immigrants.[64]

This orientation is gradually confirmed by case law,[65] which begins to recognize conscientious objection to the reporting of illegal immigrants and cooperation in their deportation. Case law makes it clear that the German legal system does not recognize the existence of a specific conscientious objection to the deportation of illegal immigrants,[66] yet the federal government respects the humanitarian mission of the Church to help its neighbour.[67]

This agreement, further renewed in November 2022,[68] is the basis for the jurisprudence that followed: The judgment of 3 May 2018,[69] in the first instance, sees the asylum application of a Nigerian citizen being rejected and the subsequent decree of his deportation to Italy, but, his appeal against the deportation not having been upheld, he took refuge in a Protestant parish in July 2016. The pastor, pursuant to the 2015 agreement, informed the BAMF, which eschewed any raid. Despite that, however, the Landshut Public Prosecutor's Office initiated criminal proceedings against the persons involved for aiding and abetting the stay of illegal immigrants.

The Freising District Court acquitted the defendants[70] and the public prosecutor appealed, but the OLG upheld the acquittal: the BAMF, on the basis of the 2015 agreement, refrained from applying the law only by its own autonomous decision, and it was only for this reason that it did not raid the Protestant parish to retrieve the illegal immigrant; the church staff who cooperated in offering asylum, on the other hand, were not prosecuted for their aiding and abetting, because their conscientious objection fell within the fundamental right

64 V. J. I. Arrieta, 'La parrocchia come comunità di fedeli e soggetto canonicamente unitario', in AA.VV. (ed.), *La parrocchia. Atti delle riunioni culturali del 1996 dell'Arcisodalizio della Curia romana* (Città del Vaticano: LEV, 1997), pp. 21 ff.; M. G. Belgiorno, 'La parrocchia prima e dopo il Concilio Vaticano II', in AA.VV. (ed.), *Studî in onore di P.A. D'Avack*, vol. I (Milano: Giuffrè, 1976), pp. 206 ff.; F. Puig, 'Stabilità e continuità del titolare dell'ufficio parrocchiale', *Ius Ecclesiae* 27 (2015), 653 ff.

65 SG Stade, 17 Msrch 2016, no. S/19/ay/1/16/ER; LSG Bayern, 11 November 2016, no. l/8/aa/28/16/b/er.

66 VG Ansbach, 14 April 2016, no. 6/k/15.31132; VG Ansbach, 4 August 2016, no. 6/k/16.30155.

67 https://dserver.bundestag.de/btd/18/098/1809894.pdf.

68 www.bamf.de/SharedDocs/Anlagen/DE/AsylFluechtlingsschutz/merkblatt-kirchenasyl.pdf.

69 OLG München, 3 May 2018, no. 4/OLG/13/Ss/54/18.

70 AG Freising, 27 october 2017, no. 6/DS/506/JS/37436/16.

of religious freedom under Article 4 of the GG, i.e. out of religious conviction, based on the general love of one's neighbour that permeates the Gospels.[71]

We note, therefore, how in all the cases examined the judicial authorities have recognized – albeit always de facto – the profound historical juridical-canonical link of conscientious objection with membership of a Church,[72] a link that also has pre-juridical origins: suffice it to think of the examples cited in the Old Testament (Deut, XXIII, 16–17),[73] to which we should add the evangelical themes of love of neighbours, forgiveness, and mercy (Lk., VI, 36 ff.;[74] Jn., VIII, 1–11;[75] Mt., XII, 6–7).[76]

The idea of conscientious objection to expulsion measures is based on the notion that there is a sphere of religion unassailable by the State, which in the final analysis is also subtracted from human law, in this case State law; and therefore, conscientious objection would not constitute the claim of an enclave subtracted from the rule of State law but would be a constitutionally legitimate way of implementing religious freedom, that is, the application of the Gospel precept (Mt, XXV, 35), without calling into question the ultimate decision-making competence of the State order.[77]

71 V. S. Mückl, 'Herausforderungen der Migration für die Sendung der Kirche', in ID. (ed.), *Migration und Solidarität/Migration and Solidarity* (Berlin: Duncker & Humblot, 2020), pp. 227 ff.

72 See C. De Beaurepaire, 'Essai sur l'Asile religieux dans l'Empire Romain et la monarchie française', *Bibliothèque de l'Ecole des Chartes* 4 (1853–1854), 351 ff. www.persee.fr/doc/bec_0373-6237_1853_num_14_1_445135; S. Testa Bappenheim, 'Il diritto d'asilo fra radici storico-canonistiche e sua possibile ri-attualizzazione de lege lata e de lege ferenda: l'esempio tedesco', in AA.VV. (ed.), *Lex rationis ordinatio. Studi in onore di Patrick Valdrini* (Cosenza: Pellegrini, 2022), pp. 1350 ss.

73 '*[16] Non trades servum domino suo, qui ad te confugerit: [17] habitabit tecum in medio tui in loco, quem elegerit in una urbium tuarum, quae placuerit ei, nec contristes eum*'; all Biblical quotes are taken from www.vatican.va/archive/ITA0001/_INDEX.HTM.

74 '*[36] Estote misericordes, sicut et Pater vester misericors est. [37] Et nolite iudicare et non iudicabimini; et nolite condemnare et non condemnabimini. Dimittite et dimittemini; . . . [46] Quid autem vocatis me: «Domine, Domine», et non facitis, quae dico?*'

75 '*[1] Iesus autem perrexit in montem Oliveti. [2] Diluculo autem iterum venit in templum, et omnis populus veniebat ad eum, et sedens docebat eos. [3] Adducunt autem scribae et pharisaei mulierem in adulterio deprehensam et statuerunt eam in medio [4] et dicunt ei: «Magister, haec mulier manifesto deprehensa est in adulterio. [5] In lege autem Moyses mandavit nobis huiusmodi lapidare; tu ergo quid dicis?». [6] Hoc autem dicebant tentantes eum, ut possent accusare eum. Iesus autem inclinans se deorsum digito scribebat in terra. [7] Cum autem perseverarent interrogantes eum, erexit se et dixit eis: «Qui sine peccato est vestrum, primus in illam lapidem mittat»; [8] et iterum se inclinans scribebat in terra. [9] Audientes autem unus post unum exibant, incipientes a senioribus, et remansit solus, et mulier in medio stans. [10] Erigens autem se Iesus dixit ei: «Mulier, ubi sunt? Nemo te condemnavit?». [11] Quae dixit: «Nemo, Domine». Dixit autem Iesus: «Nec ego te condemno; vade et amplius iam noli peccare»*'.

76 '*[6] Dico autem vobis quia templo maior est hic. [7] Si autem sciretis quid est: «Misericordiam volo et non sacrificium*', *numquam condemnassetis innocentes».*

77 '*Esurivi enim, et dedistis mihi manducare; sitivi, et dedistis mihi bibere; hospes eram, et collegistis me*'.

From this point of view, therefore, ecclesiastical asylum would belong to the meta-legal sphere, and would be an *actio religiosa*, a specific form of charitable service, therefore falling within the sphere of constitutionally protected religious freedoms under Article 4 of the GG.

According to this interpretation, ecclesiastical asylum is also guaranteed by the jurisprudence of the Bundesverfassungsgericht, which, although not yet very extensive, has already dealt with ecclesiastical asylum,[78] emphasizing that Article 4, paragraph 2 of the GG covers not only acts of worship *stricto sensu*, but also other, unspecified "manifestations of religious faith or worldview".[79]

Ecclesiastical asylum would therefore appear to be admissible as a religiously motivated act, given the meaning of both Article 4 § 2 of the GG, which we have already seen, and Article § 3, on the basis of which ecclesiastical asylum can be justified by invoking protection for the freedom of the persons concerned to make individual decisions of conscience,[80] which are constitutionally protected under Article 4 § 3 of the GG as decisions sanctioned by supra-positential rules.[81]

Conclusions

The idea of ecclesiastical asylum, or rather asylum on religious grounds, is based on the notion that there is a sphere of religion unassailable by the State, which is ultimately also subtracted from human law, in this case state law; and therefore ecclesiastical asylum would not constitute the claim of an enclave removed from the reign of state law, but would be a constitutionally legitimate way of implementing religious freedom, i.e. the application of the evangelical precept, without questioning the ultimate decision-making competence of the state order.

From this point of view, therefore, ecclesiastical asylum would belong to the meta-legal sphere, and would be an *actio religiosa*, or a specific form of charitable service, thus falling within the scope of constitutionally protected religious freedom under Article 4 of the GG.

78 BVerfG, Ia Camera, II Senato, 24 January 2002, no. 2 BvR 957/99, in www.bverfg.de/e/rk20020124_2bvr095799.html; Ia Camera, II Senato, 4 October 2010, no. 2 BvR 1825/08, in www.bverfg.de/e/rk20101004_2bvr182508.html.

79 BVerfG, 16 October 1968, n. 1 BvR 241/66, in BVerfGE 24, 236–252.

80 V. P. Bellini, 'Libertà dell'uomo e fattore religioso nei sistemi ideologici contemporanei', in AA.VV. (ed.), *Teoria e prassi delle libertà di religione,* op. cit., pp. 128 ff.; ID., 'Centralità della coscienza e condizionamenti dell'ambiente', in I. C. Ibán (ed.), *Libertad y derecho fundamental de libertad religiosa,* op. cit., pp. 90 ff.; M. G. Belgiorno de Stefano, 'Il diritto fondamentale all'obiezione di coscienza nell'esercizio della «libertas ecclesiae»', in AA.VV. (ed.), *Les droits fondamentaux du chretien dans l'Église et dans la société, Actes du 4. Congrès international de droit canonique* (Milano: Giuffrè, 1981), pp. 877 ff.

81 BVerfG, 24 aprile 1985, nn. 2 BvF 2/83, 2 BvF 3/83, 2 BvF 4/83, 2 BvF 2/84, in BVerfGE 69, 1–92, 22 ff. V. M. Tedeschi, 'Quale laicità? Fattore religioso e principi costituzionali', *Diritto ecclesiastico* 104 (1993), 548 ff.

9 Refugee law, atheism and religious persecution

Silvia Baldassarre

Human dignity and freedom of religion and belief

The concept of "human dignity" is one of the most debated in all fields of knowledge, and it has been a topic of discussion in legal science since the second half of the last century. The reason is easily understandable. Despite the fact that humanity's history has been plagued by deep wounds, the first half of the twentieth century deserves to be designated as the age of material and moral catastrophe.[1] Human dignity was vaporised in the ashes of crematoria and in the shadows – still visible in Hiroshima – of people dissolved by the atomic bomb.[2]

The construction of the new national and international legal order started from the recognition of human dignity as an absolute and unconditional value, a legal principle put before the concept of freedom and its very foundation. Humanity had to recover its human dimension, its dignity, buried and annihilated by the perpetrators of inhuman events. In the book *If This is a Man*, Primo Levi wrote: "if I could enclose all the evil of our time in one image, I would choose this image which is familiar to me: an emaciated man, with head dropped and shoulders curved, on whose face and in whose eyes not a trace of a thought is to be seen".[3]

In this perspective, the Universal Declaration of Human Rights enshrines human dignity in its preamble, stating that the recognition of human dignity to all members of the human family and their equal and inalienable rights are the foundation of freedom, justice and peace throughout the world. The Declaration highlights that disregard and contempt for human rights have resulted in barbarous acts which have outraged the conscience of mankind, and the advent of a world in which human beings shall enjoy freedom of speech and belief and freedom from fear and want is the highest aspiration of the common people. After expressing the need for human rights "to be protected by legal norms if mankind is not to be forced to resort, as a last resort, to rebellion

1 E. J. Hobsbawm, *Il secolo breve 1914–1991* (Milano: BUR, 2000), p. 31.
2 In the Peace Museum (Heiwa Kinen Shiryōkan) in Hiroshima.
3 P. Levi, *Se questo è un uomo (If This is a Man)* (Torino: Einaudi, 1992), p. 82.

DOI: 10.4324/9781003502845-9

against tyranny and oppression", the Peoples of the United Nations reaffirm their "faith" in fundamental human rights, in the dignity and worth of the human being and in the equal rights of men and women. Article 1 further reaffirms that "All human beings are born free and equal in dignity and rights".

The ontological value of human dignity is reiterated in many legal texts. The *International Covenant on Civil and Political Rights* states that: "Everyone has the right to liberty and security of person" (art. 9, paragraph 1), and: "All persons deprived of their liberty shall be treated with humanity and with respect for the inherent dignity of the human person" (art. 10, paragraph 1).

Although the *European Convention on Human Rights* does not make any reference to dignity (with the exception of Protocol No. 13),[4] it is widely referred to in the case law of the Strasbourg Court, according to which the "essence" of the convention is respect for human dignity (see, among others, *Pretty v the United Kingdom*, 2002, § 65; *V.C. v Slovakia*, 2011, § 105; *Glass v the United Kingdom*, 2004, §§ 82–83; *Jehovah's Witnesses of Moscow v Russia*, 2010, § 135).

At the EU level, the *Treaty establishing a Constitution for Europe* (draft treaty signed in Rome on 29 October 2004 and then blocked by the negative outcome of referendums in France and the Netherlands and by obstacles to ratification in some countries), includes dignity among the indivisible and universal values on which the Union is founded (Art. 2). In Article 1 of Chapter I–entitled "Human Dignity"–the Treaty states that: "Human dignity is inviolable. It must be respected and protected". The subsequent *Lisbon Treaty* (2009) reaffirms the value of human dignity as the foundation of the Union (Art. 1a) and of its action on the international stage (Art. 10 A).

Profound references to human dignity can also be found in the *Nice Charter* (2000), in which the terms "dignity" and the adjective "dignified" appear several times. In the *Charter*, "dignity" is qualified as an indivisible and universal value as the foundation of the European Union; Chapter I, entitled the latter, suggests that human dignity is specified in the rights and bans recognised in the Charter of Fundamental Rights of the European Union.[5]

The contribution of the Court of Justice is extremely relevant. In the *Omega Spielhallenund Automatenaufstellungs GmbH v Oberbürgermeisterin der Bundesstadt Bonn*, 2004, the Court counts dignity among the "common constitutional traditions" of the Member States and thus among the 'general principles' of Community law.

After the tragedies of the "short century", therefore, human dignity became the basic principle of rights and freedoms, and its widespread presence in legal

4 Protocol no. 13 to the Convention for the Protection of Human Rights and Fundamental Freedoms states that the abolition of the death penalty is essential for the protection of everyone's right to life, a basic right in a democratic society, and for the full recognition of the inherent dignity of all human beings.

5 R. Bifulco, 'Dignità umana e integrità genetica nella Carta dei diritti fondamentali dell'Unione europea', in AA.VV. (ed.), *Scritti in memoria di Livio Paladin*, vol. I (Napoli, 2004), p. 238.

texts constitutes a warning to remember and not to repeat the atrocities committed. In reality, the solemn theoretical enunciations still do not find full practical application today.[6] This is testified to by the persistence in many countries of the world, after centuries of wars and persecutions for religious reasons,[7] of critical issues at different levels in the implementation of the fundamental right of religious freedom.

Discrimination, religious persecution and systems of control and/or restriction of religious freedom are still implemented today.[8] In this regard, the findings of the Pew Research Center give cause for concern:[9] "Globally, Social Hostilities[10] related to Religion decline in 2019, while Government Restrictions[11] remain at highest levels".[12] Moreover, in the current digital age, Pew Research Center experts point out how some countries are now using technology to monitor or restrict religious groups, citing (as in the case of Russia, China and Vietnam) security or anti-terrorism reasons as justifications. China's religious control policies constitute, in several cases, serious violations of the human rights of minorities, as in the case of the government's use of facial recognition technology to monitor and store the biometric data of Uyghur Muslims and other groups considered potential threats.[13]

Harassment does not only affect the religious, but also the "nones", a group that includes atheists, agnostics and people who do not identify with any

6 It should be noted that 'human dignity' presents definitional knots that are not easy to resolve, leading to jurisprudential outcomes, both national and supranational, that are profoundly different and sometimes irreconcilable. See P. G. Carozza, 'Human Dignity and Judicial Interpretation of Human Rights: A Reply', *The European Journal of International Law* 19, no. 5 (© EJIL 2008), 931–944. For more on human dignity in the Italian legal context see R. Bin, 'Quanto è laica la giurisprudenza della Corte costituzionale sulle questioni eticamente sensibili?', in A. Cardone and M. Croce (eds.), *30 anni di laicità dello Stato: fu vera gloria?* (Roma: Nessun Dogma-Iura, 2021), pp. 61–76.

7 See F. Ruffini, *La libertà religiosa. Storia dell'idea* (Milano: La Feltrinelli, 1991).

8 See A. Licastro, 'La persecuzione per ragioni di fede e il riconoscimento dello status di rifugiato', *Ordine Internazionale e Diritti Umani* 1 (2022), 38–70.

9 Twelfth Annual Report, 2019. www.pewresearch.org/religion/2021/09/30/globally-social-hostilities-related-to-religion-decline-in-2019-while-government-restrictions-remain-at-highest-levels/.

10 They are defined as «acts of religious hostility by private individuals, organizations or groups in society. This includes religion-related armed conflict or terrorism, mob or sectarian violence, harassment over attire for religious reasons and other forms of religion-related intimidation or abuse».

11 Government Restrictions are defined as «government laws, policies and actions that restrict religious beliefs and practices». They include «efforts by government to ban particular faiths, prohibit conversion, limit preaching or give preferential treatment to one or more religious groups».

12 See Pew Research Center, 'Globally, Social Hostilities Related to Religion Decline in 2019, While Government Restrictions Remain at Highest Levels'. www.pewresearch.org/religion/2021/09/30/globally-social-hostilities-related-to-religion-decline-in-2019-while-government-restrictions-remain-at-highest-levels/.

13 For more see P. Annicchino, 'La minoranza musulmana e lo stato nazionale di sorveglianza cinese', *Coscienza e Libertà* 63–64 (2022), 27–33.

religion. Again, the Pew Research Center has recorded a significant increase in harassment: in 2020, there were 27 countries in which people not affiliated with a religion experienced harassment by governments, private groups or both, five more countries than in the previous year.[14]

In the following paragraphs, the complex issue of granting refugee status to non-religious persons will be analysed. To this end, attention must first focus on the legal definition of "religion" to understand whether it also extends to non-religious persons.

The definition of "religion"

The semantic investigation of concepts relating to the multiform universe of "religion" runs the risk of being an operation destined to fail. The definition of religious feeling – one of the most debated topics in the human and social sciences and in the public law of religions – excludes assertive definitions. It encompasses a rich array of conceptual options, a heterogeneous plurality of experiential manifestations rooted in freedom of conscience and thought, rationality and irrationality, customs and cultural traditions.[15] Monotheists, polytheists, deists, agnostics, religious atheists, atheist-religious, humanist-atheists and humanist-religious, nones, freethinkers, atheists, non-religious, rationalists, sceptics, secularists, believers without affiliation,[16] affiliates without belief, practicing affiliates and non-practising affiliates are just some of the labels that denote the phenomenon of conscience.

The definition, prevalent until the last century in the West, which generally identified religion with reference to a personal god or a transcendent dimension, is now inadequate, or at least partial and reductive. Today, "what do we talk about when we talk about religion?"[17] If to religion we attribute the meaning of "binding" (from the Latin *religare*) to faith in a transcendent god, many religions, such as Buddhism,[18] the Hare Krishna movement, Confucianism, in

14 See Pew Research Center, 'Religiously Unaffiliated People Face Harassment in a Growing Number of Countries'. www.pewresearch.org/short-reads/2023/01/27/religiously-unaffiliated-people-face-harassment-in-a-growing-number-of-countries/.

15 «The word 'religion' to the ears of a North American may evoke a social phenomenon that to a South American is not to be considered as such. The same thing can happen in a dialogue between an Asian and a European. In fact, in contemporary multicultural society, the word 'religion' has many meanings, not always intelligible to all, sometimes hidden», M. L. Lo Giacco, 'Riflessioni sulla difficile interpretazione delle parole "Religione" e "Religioso" nel diritto delle società multiculturali', in *Annali del Dipartimento Jonico* (2015), pp. 267–283.

16 «Believing without belonging» is an expression coined by British sociologist Grace Davie to refer to the predominant religion in the West today, Cf. G. Davie, *Religion in Britain Since 1945: Believing without Belonging* (Hoboken: John Wiley & Sons, 1994).

17 J. Grondin, *Philosophie de la religion* (Paris: Puf, 2009), p. 25.

18 «Unlike Western religions, Buddhism has no doctrinal heritage to believe in . . . . With Buddhism we are at the antipodes of exclusivism, because it is a movement that tends to include or, at any rate, not exclude other religious experiences, in line with many Eastern religions, particularly those of Indian origin: the man strong in spirit, in fact, according to Hinduism,

which the postulation of the transcendent divinity is absent or not essential, could not be considered as such. The Buddha, in fact, is not a divinity, but an extraordinary "potential" present in the life of the world and in the life of every human being. If, on the other hand, we give "religion" a broader meaning, as the human being's tension towards the absolute that is in him/her, as well as outside him/her, the term becomes inclusive of several answers to the questions about the meaning of our brief permanence in time. As Introvigne points out: "There is . . . no essence, called Religion; there are only religious phenomena, more or less aggregated in systems called religions, which have a definite historical existence, in groups of men and in specific times".[19] Possible definitions of religion thus appear socially constructed, politically negotiated and oriented towards certain outcomes,[20] whereby socio-historical contextualisation, the acquisition of knowledge borrowed from other disciplinary fields and the adoption of a comparative method, become essential to bring out the cultural background, to understand the specificity, similarities and differences between different religious experiences.[21]

Internationally, since the Second World War, a legal paradigm of "religion" has become increasingly inclusive of heterogeneous semantic declinations: belief, non-belief, theism, non-theism, atheism, agnosticism, agnosticism. Although the right to non-belief was not explicitly mentioned in

---

finds God everywhere and especially in himself. Consequently, even Buddhism has no abstract truths to impose dogmatically, because it is not interested in concepts – including . . . that of God – but only in direct experience, it proposes a path to inner enlightenment that is necessarily free and, indeed, not incompatible with adherence to other faiths», N. Colaianni, *Diritto pubblico delle religioni. Eguaglianza e differenze nello Stato costituzionale* (Bologna: Il Mulino, 2012), pp. 129, 130.

19 M. Mauss, *Œuvres*, vol. 1 (Paris: Éditions de Minuit, [1904] 1968), p. 93.

20 Cfr. M. Introvigne, 'The Definition of Religion', in M. Introvigne and P. L. Zoccatelli (Dir.), *Religions in Italy*. https://cesnur.com/la-definizione-di-religione-2/.

Self-definition can also be instrumental in obtaining certain results; in China, where the communist regime views religions with suspicion, it is easier for many currents and schools to survive by qualifying themselves as non-religious; see M. Introvigne, 'Introduction to Chinese Religiosity'. https://cesnur.com/religioni-e-movimenti-di-origine-cinese-ed-estremo-orientale/introduzione-alla-religiosita-cinese/.

For specific insights on the legal and social condition of religious minorities in China, see M. Introvigne, 'Bitter Winter. A Magazine on Religious Liberty and Human Rights'. https://bitterwinter.org/?gclid=Cj0KCQjwl92XBhC7ARIsAHLl9akOdKuPD74cyqPdCOJ2Jmvqz32oTj67KaDdn1yBjEdFfTvt8qx4vlIaAtxqEALw_wcB. On China see also: All-Party Parliamentary Group for International Freedom of Religion or Belief, *Commentary on the Current State of International Freedom of Religion or Belief (2020)*, APPG for International Freedom of Religion or Belief February 2021, p. 25 ss., available in https://appgfreedomofreligionorbelief.org/media/2020-APPG-commentary-final.pdf.

21 On the relevance of an interdisciplinary approach and an intercultural perspective of law, see M. Ricca, *Culture interdette. Modernità, migrazioni, diritto interculturale* (Torino: Bollati Boringhieri, 2013). On models, technical tools and judicial solutions for the governance of differences in multicultural societies, see. P. Pannia, *La diversità rivendicata. Giudici, diritti e culture tra Italia e Regno Unito. Uno studio comparato* (Milano: Wolters Kluwer Cedam, 2021), pp. 83 ss.

the Universal Declaration of Human Rights, there is no doubt – as noted by Eleanor Roosevelt, Chair of the Drafting Committee – that the intention of the drafters was to consider religious freedom inclusive of theistic and atheistic conceptions.[22]

The Declaration announced a transition from the recognition of the rights of the citizen of a single state to the recognition of the rights of the citizen of the world, thus affirming what Kant called "cosmopolitan law" (*ius cosmopoliticum*).[23] Despite not being a legally binding instrument, the Declaration inspired the Constitutions and laws of many states.

Freedom of thought, conscience and religion has been reaffirmed in the *European Convention on Human Rights* (1950), the *International Covenant on Civil and Political Rights* (1966), the *Declaration on the Elimination of All Forms of Intolerance and of Discrimination based on Religion or Belief* (1981), becoming a *leitmotif* in international law, in Declarations of Principles, in short in every text whose provisions have contributed to the development of international standards of protection of freedom in religious matters.

Since the 1970s, the religion/belief binomial has been included in UN, EU, Council of Europe, OSCE/ODHIR texts and European jurisprudence.[24] The Concluding Document of the Vienna Meeting (1989)[25] affirmed for the first time the need for states to ensure "effective equality between believers and non-believers". Freedom of religion or belief, one of the founding principles of the OSCE, contained in Principle VII of the Helsinki Declaration of 1975, has been reaffirmed by the OSCE/ODHIR in a long series of documents in which the profound link between security and full respect for freedom of thought, conscience, religion or belief is stressed. Emphasis is also placed on the importance of promoting a climate of tolerance and mutual respect between believers of different communities and between believers and

22 Cfr. J. Morsink, *The Universal Declaration of Human Rights-Origins, Drafting and Intent* (Philadelphia: University of Pennsylvania Press, 1999), p. 261 ss. The failure to explicitly mention the right not to believe, however, astonished Haitian delegate Émile Saint-Lot, and French delegate René Cassin's proposal to replace the term 'croyance' with the more neutral term 'conviction' was not accepted, cfr. A. Verdoodt, *Naissance et signification de la Déclaration universelle des droits de l'homme (préface de R. Cassin)* (Louvain-La-Neuve: Nauwelaerts, 1964), p. 181.

23 I. Kant, *Scritti politici*, ed. N. Bobbio, L. Firpo and V. Mathieu (Torino: UTET, 2010), p. 543. On the universality of rights, Amartya Sen observed that there is « . . . something deeply seductive about the idea that every person everywhere in the world, regardless of his or her citizenship and the law of his or her country, is the holder of certain fundamental rights that others must respect», A. Sen, 'Elements of a Theory of Human Rights', *Philosophy & Public Affairs* 32, no. 4 (2004), 315.

24 J. Martínez-Torrón, 'Religious Liberty in European Jurisprudence', in AA.VV. (ed.), *Religious Liberty and Human Rights* (Cardiff: The University of Wales Press, 2002), pp. 99–127.

25 Concluding Document of the Vienna Meeting 1986 of representatives of the participating States of the Conference on Security and Co-operation in Europe, held on the basis of the provisions of the Final Act relating to the Follow-up to the Conference (Vienna 1989), § 16.1, available in www.osce.org/files/f/documents/a/7/40881.pdf.

non-believers,[26] especially in today's times, marked by new dynamics of radicalisation and religious (pseudo)conflicts.

The broad interpretation of religious freedom is clearly evident in international documents since the 1990s. In *General Comment No. 22* of 1993, which provides an official interpretation of the provisions of the *International Covenant on Civil and Political Rights*, the UN Human Rights Committee stated that the right to freedom of thought, conscience and religion (including the freedom to profess a belief other than a particular religion) enshrined in paragraph 1 of Article 18 has a wide scope. It includes freedom of thought in all spheres, personal belief and adherence to a conviction or belief, manifested individually or together with others. Point 2 of the *General Comment* specifies: "Article 18 protects theistic, non-theistic and atheistic beliefs, as well as the right not to profess any religion or belief. The terms "belief" and "religion" are to be broadly construed. Article 18 is not limited in its application to traditional religions or to religions and beliefs with institutional characteristics or practices analogous to those of traditional religions".[27]

In the last thirty years, after the fall of the Berlin Wall and the metamorphosis of societies due to the phenomenon of migration, a more substantive approach has become necessary to face the challenges of a rapidly growing and changing religious pluralism. The Charter of Fundamental Rights of the European Union states in Article 10 that everyone has the right to freedom of thought, conscience and religion, which right includes the freedom to manifest one's religion and the right to change it. Following the approval of the *Lisbon Treaty*, the *Nice Charter* has been given binding legal force equal to that of the treaties. Article 17 of the *Treaty on the Functioning of the European Union* is significant, as it places churches, religious associations or communities and philosophical and non-confessional organisations on an equal footing.[28] This article, by recognising the identity and specific contribution of

26 The formula 'non-believers' is not suitable for understanding the components of a heterogeneous universe of beliefs; it seems to reduce the complexity of the term 'believing' to a simple dichotomy between believing or not believing in transcendence, giving, in the second hypothesis, a negative meaning comparable to believing in nothingness. This leaves out the constructive and positive value universe of non-theistic beliefs. It also leaves out the increasingly obvious fact that the supernatural entity is a mere variable in the field of spirituality and human ideals. In Anglo-Saxon language, the expression 'non-religious people' is preferred; in French-speaking literature, the use of the term 'conviction', more neutral and inclusive than the term 'croyanc', has long been established.

In this work, the formulas 'believers' and 'non-believers' will be used for practical needs, since language, even legal language, is not yet able to fully grasp and express the wide variety of the religious phenomenon. The inadequacy of an 'all negative' language for non-belief was a topic of debate at the conference *Towards Substantive Understandings of Nonreligion and Secularity* (7–9 June 2023), organised by the University of Ottawa (Canada).

27 CCPR *General Comment no. 22*, 1993. www.refworld.org/docid/453883fb22.html.

28 However, some critical points should be highlighted in the wording of Article 17 TFEU. The equating of churches and philosophical and non-confessional organisations is less effective in light of the wording of the first two paragraphs of the same article, in which the Union

these actors, imposes for the first time a legal obligation on the EU to conduct an open, transparent, and regular dialogue with them.

Adopting the hermeneutic paradigm already found in international documents, in the *Kokkinakis v Greece* judgment (1993), the European Court of Human Rights observed that the freedom of thought, conscience and religion guaranteed by Article 9 of the Convention is a precious good not only for believers, but also for "atheists, agnostics, sceptics and the unconcerned".[29]

---

undertakes to respect and not to prejudice (this last statement refers exclusively to confessional organisations) the status enjoyed by philosophical confessions and associations in the member states. In most EU countries the status of philosophical associations is not comparable to that of religious denominations. See on this point: F. Margiotta Broglio, 'Confessioni e comunità religiose o "filosofiche" nel Trattato di Lisbona', in AA.VV. and L. De Gregorio (eds.), *Le confessioni religiose nel diritto dell'Unione europea* (Bologna: Il Mulino, 2012), pp. 33 ss.

Article 17 TFEU, basically, may favor a recognition at supranational level of national systems of regulating relations between the State and the religious phenomenon, often founded on a discriminatory basis. In this sense, it implicitly responds to the concern expressed by some confessions that «EU legislation may somehow undermine the many situations of 'privilege' (unilateral or alliance) of certain cults in the Member States or violate their autonomy and independence».

The structure of Art 17 also seems to testify the 'hybrid nature' of the European Union, resulting from the coexistence of the federalist orientation (participatory dialogue, Para. III) and the tendency of States to 'jealously preserve' their sovereignty (Para. I, II). A further critical profile of Art 17 TFEU is given by the evasive character of the provision that adopts the formula 'European Union' without specifying the institutional actors. In this sense, the gradual change of the institutional actors should be underlined: from the initial presidential level (Delors and the *Cellule de prospective*-CDP) there has been a shift to the Presidency's advisors (GOPA and BEPA) to arrive, during Jean-Claude Juncker's term of office (2014–2019), at the level of vice-presidency. Today, therefore, the Vice-Presidents of both the Commission and the European Parliament are in charge of the dialogue. The application of the provision in the third paragraph, concerning dialogue with churches and communities of thought, is also problematic. The officiality and legal obligation of the dialogue enshrined in the TFEU has not been followed by its structuring on the basis of defined criteria: neither the forms nor the contents of the dialogue have been established, and there is a lack of rules that objectively and not discretely identify the religious and philosophical collective actors involved.

Alongside the various critical aspects, it is necessary to emphasise the innovative scope of Article 17 TFEU, which, by equating theistic, non-theistic and atheistic conceptions also in their associative dimension, has taken a 'first step towards the construction of a European ecclesiastical law'; by taking further steps to overcome the critical aspects noted, Article 17 'will become the cornerstone of European Union ecclesiastical law and policy'. See I. C. Ibán, *È possibile una disciplina comune della libertà religiosa nei Paesi comunitari? Europa, diritto, religione* (Bologna: Il Mulino, 2010), pp. 133, 134; M. Ventura, 'L'articolo 17 TFUE come fondamento del diritto e della politica ecclesiastica dell'Unione europea', *Quaderni di diritto e politica ecclesiastica* 2 (2014), 293–304.

29 *Kokkinakis v Greece* (Application no. 14307/88), 25 May 1993, § 31: «As enshrined in Article 9 (Art 9), freedom of thought, conscience and religion is one of the foundations of a 'democratic society' within the meaning of the Convention. It is, in its religious dimension, one of the most vital elements that go to make up the identity of believers and their conception of life, but it is also a precious asset for atheists, agnostics, sceptics and the unconcerned. The pluralism indissociable from a democratic society, which has been dearly won over the centuries, depends on it».

Reiterating these general principles, in *Buscarini and Others v San Marino* (1999, § 34) the ECHR clarified that freedom of religion implies the freedom to have or not to have religious beliefs, to practise or not to practise a religion. As the United Nations High Commissioner for Refugees (UNHCR) noted, the *Buscarini* judgment have been further affirmed in national jurisprudence; for example, the *RT (Zimbabwe) and others (Respondents) v Secretary of State for the Home Department*, referred to this judgment, stating: "In Buscarini, the applicants were required, contrary to their wishes, to swear an oath on the Holy Gospels in order to take their seats in the San Marino Parliament. It was held that this requirement was not compatible with article 9. No part of the Grand Chamber's reasoning concerned the strength of the applicants' convictions that they should not be required to swear the oath. The essential point is that the court held that article 9 protects the right of the non-believer as well as that of the believer".[30] The concept of religious freedom as inclusive of theism and non-theism, related to the need to protect the rights of believers and non-believers equally, has subsequently been reiterated several times by the European Court of Human Rights.[31]

The Court has never defined the concept of "religion", noting that any definition should be "both flexible enough to embrace the whole range of religions worldwide (major and minor, old and new, theistic and nontheistic) . . . an extremely difficult, indeed impossible undertaking".[32]

30 Submission by the Office of the United Nations High Commissioner for Refugees in case numbers 202005668/1/V2 and 202102293/1/V2 before the Council of State, 2021, in www.refworld.org/docid/61925b574.html.

31 The binomial theism/atheism in the ECtHR jurisprudence, already affirmed in *Kokkinakis v Greece* (1993), has been reiterated since the 1990s until today in many judgments, including: *Buscarini and Others v San Marino*, GC, no. 24645/94, 18 February 1999, § 34; *Église Métropoltaine de Bessarabie and Others v Moldova*, 13 December 2001, § 114; *Refah Partisi (Parti de la prospérité) and Others v Turkey*, GC, 13 February 2003, § 90; *Leyla Şahín v Turkey*, GC, no. 44774/98, 10 November 2005, § 104; *Branche de Moscou de l'Armée du Salut v Russia*, 5 October 2006, § 57; *Hasan and Eylem Zengin v Turkey*, 9 October 2007, § 69; *Alexandridis v Greece*, 21 February 2008, § 31; *Miroļubovs and Others v Latvia*, 15 September 2009, § 80, a); *Sinan Işik v Turkey*, 2 February 2010, § 37; *Dimitras and Others v Greece*, 3 June 2010, § 76; *Wasmuth v Germany*, 17 February 2011, § 50; *Bayatyan v Armenia*, GC, 7 July 2011, § 118; *Dimitras and Others v Greece* (no. 2), 3 November 2011, § 27; *Erçep v Turkey*, 22 November 2011, § 54; *Feti Demirtaş v Turkey*, 17 January 2012 § 103; *Savda v Turkey*, 12 June 2012, § 90; *Tarhan v Turkey*, 17 July 2012, § 52; *Eweida and Others v the United Kingdom*, 15 January 2013, § 79; *S.A.S. v France*, GC, 1 July 2014, § 124; *Cumhuriyetçi Eğitim Ve Kültür Merkezi Vakfi v Turkey*, 2 December 2014, § 40; *Güler and Uğur v Turkey*, 2 December 2014, § 34; *Paroisse Gréco-Catholique Lupeni and Others v Romania*, 19 May 2015, § 131; *F.G. v Swiss*, GC, 23 March 2016; *İzzettin Doğan and Others v Turkey*, GC, 26 April 2016, § 103; *Osmanoğet Kocabas v Swiss*, 10 January 2017, § 82; *Hamidović v Bosnia Herzegovina*, 5 December 2017, § 36.

32 Guide on Article 9 of the European Convention on Human Rights Freedom of thought, conscience and religion Updated on 31 August 2022, *B. Convictions protected under Article 9*, § 14, available in www.echr.coe.int/documents/d/echr/guide_art_9_eng.

Concerning the term "convictions", the Court stated: "In its ordinary meaning the word "convictions", taken on its own, is not synonymous with the words 'opinions' and 'ideas', such as are utilised in Article 10 (art. 10) of the Convention, which guarantees freedom of expression; it is more akin to the term "beliefs" (in the French text: "convictions") appearing in Article 9 (art. 9) – which guarantees freedom of thought, conscience and religion – and denotes views that attain a certain level of cogency, seriousness, cohesion and importance.[33] Even more explicitly, the ECHR operates a "reductio ad unum" of the different *Weltanschauung* which, if deep and genuine, constitute convictions of sufficient cogency, seriousness, cohesion and importance guaranteed by Article 9 of the Convention.[34]

Even the definition of "religious minority" has uncertain semantic boundaries, but also in this case, the progressive inclusion of philosophical and non-denominational beliefs is visible; the consolidation of the use of the formula "belief" in UN documents is counterevidence of this. Moreover, as pointed out by the Recommendations *of the Forum on Minority Issues at its sixth session: Guaranteeing the rights of religious minorities, 26 and 27 November 2013*, no. 8: "The term "religious minorities" as used in the present document . . . encompasses a broad range of religious or belief communities, traditional and nontraditional, whether recognized by the State or not, including more recently established faith or belief groups, and large and small communities, that seek protection of their rights under minority rights standards. Non-believers, atheists or agnostics may also face challenges and discrimination and require protection of their rights".[35]

33 *Campbell and Cosans v United Kingdom*, 25 February 1982, § 36.

34 *Bayatyan v Armenia*, GC, no. 23459/03, 7 July 2011, § 110.

35 Faced with the deterioration of the human rights situation for many minorities in many countries around the world, Fernand de Varennes, United Nations Special Rapporteur on minority issues, with the contribution of many international experts (Silvio Ferrari for Italy), has drafted a Proposal for a Global Convention on the Rights of Minorities. An important point in the proposal is the reiteration of the formula 'religious or belief minority', which confirms the orientation, consolidated in international texts, to legally equalise theist and non-theist groups. The proposal states (Parte I, Art 1): «Every person belonging to a national or ethnic, religious or belief and linguistic minority . . . shall have the right to the full enjoyment, individually and collectively, of all human rights and fundamental freedoms as recognized in the Charter of the United Nations, the Universal Declaration of Human Rights and other international human rights law, including those specifically recognised for minorities in this convention». In Part II, Article 9 states: «Persons belonging to minorities shall not be subjected to coercion which would impair their freedom to adopt, maintain, change or renounce a religion or belief of their choice. Coercion includes any act or measure intended to compel believers or non-believers to adopt, maintain, change or renounce a religion or belief». The proposed draft convention and its protocols define the meaning of human rights of minorities and prepare a programme of action for their implementation, see F. de Varennes, 'Proposal for a Draft Global Convention on the Rights of Minorities', February 2023. www.ohchr.org/sites/default/files/2023-01/Annex1.-A-HRC-52-27_0.docx). For more on the definition of religious minority see G. Scala, *Diritto pubblico subiettivo e libertà religiosa. Profili di Diritto comparato* (Padova: Padova University Press, 2021), p. 14.

The *reductio ad unum* between theist and non-theist conceptions has a strictly legal value. "I am careful not to mistake an analogy for an identity":[36] according to Kelsen, the religion/transcendence link implies the impossibility and illegitimacy of interpreting modern philosophy, science and politics as "godless religions". According to the philosopher, if we consider what are merely analogies to be identities, we are unduly transferring concepts from one plane to another, denying the autonomy of the social sciences and bringing them back into the perspective of theology, recovering the ancient thesis of *ancilla theologiae*.[37] The historical evolution of the centuries-long debate on the relationship between faith and reason, which is impossible to summarise in a few short lines, has shown, particularly over the last two hundred years, a gradual divarication between the two concepts, therefore – as Colaianni remarks – at present the cultural debate does not support their *reductio ad unum*.[38] The protection of their differences is however a *point d'honneur* for constitutionalism, an essential element of pluralist secularism.[39] On a pragmatic level, it is not the jurist's role to enter into the merits of the matter, to assess similarities and differences between theistic and atheistic or philosophical conceptions, to try to reduce them to a homogeneous and monolithic whole; instead, it is his or her responsibility to ensure their substantive equal legal protection. The ideal matrix and prerequisite for equalisation is the extensive interpretation of religious freedom, also made necessary by the profound transformations taking place in an interconnected and multicultural world,[40] in which the physical and virtual encounter between people, who for

36 H. Kelsen, *Secular Religion: A Polemic Against the Misinterpretation of Modern Social Philosophy, Science and Politics as 'New Religions'* (Vienn: Verlag Osterreich GmbH-Hans Kelsen Institut, 2012).

37 For more on the debate on atheist religions, in particular the theses of Kelsen, Dworkin and Beck, see N. Colaianni, *La lotta per la laicità. Stato e Chiesa nell'età dei diritti* (Bari: Cacucci, 2017), pp. 100–106.

38 N. Colaianni, *La lotta per la laicità. Stato e Chiesa nell'età dei diritti*, op. cit., p. 106.

39 *Ibid.*, p. 106.

40 G. Davie, *Europe: The Exceptional Case. Parameters of Faith in the Modern World* (Londra: Darton, Longman and Todd, 2002); ID., *Religion in Modern Europe. A Memory Mutates* (Oxford: Oxford University Press, 2000); M. Ventura, *Creduli e credenti. Il declino di Stato e Chiesa come questione di fede* (Torino: Einaudi, 2014); R. Bichi and G. Rovati, 'La religiosità dopo la secolarizzazione', in F. Biolcati, G. Rovati and P. Segatti (eds.), *Come cambiano gli italiani. Valori e atteggiamenti dagli anni Ottanta a oggi* (Bologna: Il Mulino, 2020), p. 115 ss. In Italy, for example, the change in the religious landscape has been extremely rapid: Cesnur (Centre for the Study of New Religions) has recorded the passage from 658 religious and spiritual minorities present in an organised manner in Italy in 2001, to 866 today, an increase of about 30% in just 20 years; see M. Introvigne and P. Zoccatelli (eds.), 'Le religioni in Italia'. https://cesnur.com/dimensioni-del-pluralismo-religioso-in-italia/. For an overview of Italian and European religious demography and an analysis of the legal status of some religious minorities in EU countries see: *Atlas of European Values*. www.atlasofeuropeanvalues.eu/fr/maptool.html.

Franco Garelli's recent sociological survey revealed the apathy, religious illiteracy and disenchantment of the new Italian generations and their difficult relationship with faith; F. Garelli,

centuries remained distant and unknown to each other, generates innovative, hybrid, heterogeneous horizons of meaning.

The legal nature of the issue can be understood by considering the following observations: by unanimous acknowledgement there is no univocal legal definition of religion; every definition is historically and politically constructed and oriented; the boundary between religion and non-religion is not fixed, but uncertain, given the presence of "atheist religions", "religious atheisms"[41] and forms of immanent spirituality, new forms of religiosity – among which also the personal God, devoid of theology and dogma[42] – independent of the official Churches and linked to the life project and horizon of experience of the human person; in countries founded on the separation of the spiritual and temporal order, the state does not have the competence to value the content of religious

---

Gente di poca fede. Il sentimento religioso nell'Italia incerta di Dio (Bologna: Il Mulino, 2020). Garelli offers, through numbers, a picture of the religious change: compared to 25 years ago, the number of people who find in faith an answer to the questions of existence has decreased by about 15%. Moreover, whereas in the 1990s religious beliefs other than Catholicism involved 2% of the population, today the percentage is more than 8%. Followers of Islam and Orthodox Christianity account for 3 and 2.6% of Italian residents, respectively (pp. 36 and 47–49). In the same direction, see also F. Garelli, *Piccoli atei crescono. Davvero una generazione senza Dio?* (Bologna: Il Mulino, 2016); R. Cartocci, *Geografia dell'Italia cattolica* (Bologna: Il Mulino, 2011); A. Matteo, *La prima generazione incredula. Il difficile rapporto tra i giovani e la fede* (Soveria Mannelli: Rubbettino Editore, 2010); D. Di Sanzo and M. A. Maggio, 'La Geografia cattolica in un Paese in progress', in P. Naso and B. Salvarani (eds.), *Un cantiere senza progetto. Rapporto 2012 sull'Italia delle religioni* (Bologna: EMI, 2012), pp. 133 ss.

41 From a legal point of view, Dworkin states, atheists are to be assimilated to the religious: 'religious atheism' is not an oxymoron because religion does not coincide with theism; he theorises a general right to ethical independence, starting from the hypothesis that people share «a fundamental religious impulse that has manifested itself in various beliefs and emotions. For much of history», he states, «this impulse has generated two types of beliefs: a belief in a supernatural intelligent force – a god – and a set of deeply held ethical and moral convictions», R. Dworkin, *Religion Without God* (Harvard University Press, Cambridge, Ma, 2013), p. 17.

42 Ulrich Beck introduces the notion of 'personal God' starting from the dramatic experience of Etty Hillesum, a young victim of the Shoah. In her diary, written during her imprisonment in the Auschwitz concentration camp (1941-43), Etty Hillesum dialogues incessantly with her inner world, with her personal God, defending her human dignity in the midst of the barbarity of her daily life, convinced that only through love for one's fellow human beings could humanity be renewed. Beck observes that Etty removed the religious element from the public sphere, affirming her faith in a subjective, individual God, therefore not absolute, not omnipotent, not ascribable to historically established religious traditions: «The personal God is something one can put into practice, live, hope for, call to mind, only when God becomes 'one's own', . . . when the 'religious element' is removed from the public sphere and turned inwards. (Etty Hillesum) radicalised this separation, which marks the difference between religion and religiosity, she took God into her own hands. . . . The ego (in the sense of Fitchte and Sartre) in its complete, ruthless freedom and responsibility, and the personal God. From this union should result a small infinity, capable of guaranteeing, even when humanity breaks down, hope, love and life. This overturns the religious order . . . . The individual who decides and doubts becomes the Church, becomes the guardian of God and faith, while the Church turns into heresy», U. Beck, *Il Dio personale. La nascita della religiosità secolare* (Roma-Bari: Laterza, [2008] 2009), pp. 14, 15.

convictions; religious freedom includes the protection of theistic, non-theistic and atheistic conceptions. It is consequential, from a logical and legal point of view, to consider that the regulation of the non-theist phenomenon in its individual and associated dimensions must fall within the legal discipline of the religious phenomenon. The need to develop adequate legal instruments to face the challenges posed by a profoundly changed religious demography is becoming increasingly pressing. In this panorama, there is a significant fact: the massive growth of the non-theist phenomenon. It is difficult to quantify the number of non-believers because there is a lack of reliable and updated information. It is also necessary to distinguish between "nones" (not religiously affiliated: atheists, agnostics and people who do not identify with a particular religion in surveys and censuses) and those affiliated with philosophical and non-confessional organisations. The number of affiliate members varies greatly between associations, from a few hundred to several thousand; the "nones" are much more and they represent a large percentage of both the world population (16% according to *Pew Research Center*, 2015)[43] and the European population (20% according to the *Religions and Secularism Observatory*-ORELA, 2018). The gap between nones and affiliates is due to several reasons: some do not feel the need to affiliate themselves or believe that spirituality is something private and personal; some do not want to reveal their religious beliefs; some others fear a possible social stigma resulting from affiliation. But despite the difficulties of quantifying the number of non-religious people in the world, there is of course a strong presence of non-religious people in the West.[44]

Moving on to the specific issue of the protection of refugees on religious grounds, we do not find a definition of "religion" in the *Geneva Convention*; however, the *Guidelines on International Protection* of 28 April 2004[45] adopt a broad definition of this therm. The *Guidelines* note that no universally accepted definition of "religion" exists; its use in the 1951 Convention can therefore be taken to encompass freedom of thought, conscience or belief. The *Guidelines* also point out that, as the Human Rights Committee noted, "religion" is not limited to traditional religions or to religions and beliefs with institutional characteristics or practices analogous to those of traditional religions, but "[i]t also broadly covers acts of failing or refusing to observe a religion or to hold any particular religious belief".[46] In the context of international refugee law, "belief" should be interpreted in a way to include "theistic, nontheistic

43 Pew Research Center, 'Religious Composition by Country, 2010-2050', *Estimated Religious Composition of 198 Countries and Territories for 2010 to 2050*, 21 dicembre 2022. www.pewresearch.org/religion/interactives/religious-composition-by-country-2010-2050/.

44 For an overview of the spread of non-religiosity in the Member States of the European Union see *Atlas of religious or Belief Minority Rights*. https://atlasminorityrights.eu/index.php.

45 *Guidelines on International Protection: Religion-Based Refugee Claims under Article 1A (2) of the 1951 Convention and/or the 1967 Protocol relating to the Status of Refugees*. www.unhcr.org/media/guidelines-international-protection-no-6-religion-based-refugee-claims-under-article-1a-2.

46 *Guidelines on International Protection* (n 44), §§ 2.4, 2.5.

and atheistic beliefs".[47] As noted by the Human Rights Committee, "the freedom to 'have or to adopt' a religion or belief necessarily entails the freedom to choose a religion or belief, including the right to replace one's current religion or belief with another or to adopt atheistic views, as well as the right to retain one's religion or belief".[48]

EU refugee law has also adopted this inclusive approach, because it developed from the "cornerstones" of the international legal framework on refugee protection, namely the 1951 Convention and the Protocol of 31 January 1967. In this perspective, Article 10.1, b), of the Council Directive 2004/83/EC of 29 April 2004[49] specifies that "religion", as a ground of persecution, includes "theistic, non-theistic and atheistic beliefs". Directive 2011/95/EU (Art. 10.1, b) of the European Parliament and of the Council, which recast the 2004 Directive, adopted the same inclusive definition.

Looking back, as early as 1996, the Common Position of 4 March of that year, defined by the Council on the basis of Article K.3 of the Treaty on European Union and concerning the harmonised application of the definition of the term "refugee", extended the concept of religion to non-theistic or atheistic beliefs. The common position stated that religious persecution also occurs against those who: do not intend to profess any religion; refuse to embrace a particular religion; do not intend to submit to all or part of the rites and customs associated with a religion.

The framework of international refugee law thus admits/considers that religious persecution can also occur against non-religious *Weltanschauung*, whether professed individually or collectively.

The definition of "religious persecution"

With regard to the concept of "persecution", according to Article 1 of the Geneva Convention, a "religious refugee" is someone who has a well-founded fear of being persecuted in his/her Country of origin on account of his/her professed beliefs.

47 "Beliefs may take the form of convictions or values about the divine or ultimate reality or the spiritual destiny of humankind. Claimants may also be considered heretics, apostates, schismatic, pagans or superstitious, even by other adherents of their religious tradition and be persecuted for that reason», *Guidelines on International Protection*, § 2.6.

48 CCPR *General Comment no. 22*: Article 18 (Freedom of Thought, Conscience or Religion), §5.

49 *Council Directive 2004/83/EC of 29 April 2004 on Minimum Standards for the Qualification and Status of Third Country Nationals or Stateless Persons as Refugees or as Persons Who Otherwise Need International Protection and the Content of the Protection Granted*, Art 10.1, b): «the concept of religion shall in particular include the holding of theistic, non-theistic and atheistic beliefs, the participation in, or abstention from, formal worship in private or in public, either alone or in community with others, other religious acts or expressions of view, or forms of personal or communal conduct based on or mandated by any religious belief», www.refworld.org/docid/4157e75e4.html accessed 28 November 2022.

Persecution and discrimination are not the same thing. As specified in the 2004 *Guidelines*, asylum claims based on religion often imply discrimination. Although discrimination on the basis of religion is prohibited under international human rights law, not all discrimination necessarily reaches the level of severity that justifies the granting of refugee status. The existence of discriminatory laws, for example, does not itself constitute persecution, although these may be an important and even indicative factor that must be considered. In order to verify persecution, it is necessary to evaluate the actual implementation of the discriminatory laws and their concrete afflictive effect. Similarly, the existence of religious freedom legislation does not in itself mean that people are protected.

On a factual level, therefore, the assessment of whether one or more discriminatory treatments constitute persecution is an evaluation that is made on a concrete basis, case-by-case. Some indexes can support the evaluation. These include, for example: the importance of the sanctioned religious practice in the individual's life (in order to understand the risk that he/she runs in his Country of origin for observing that practice); other indexes are: the severity of penalties envisaged or the legitimacy of the limitations on freedom of religion and belief; these limitations in particular are legitimate, and not persecutory, only if "prescribed by law, objective, reasonable and due to reasons of public order, public security, and guarantee of the rights of others". According to Article 9(1) of Directive 2011/95, to be considered an "act of persecution", within the meaning of Article 1, Section A, of the Geneva Convention, an act must be sufficiently serious by reason of its nature or its repeated character to constitute a serious violation of fundamental human rights, in particular the rights from which no derogation is possible under Article 15, paragraph 2, of the ECHR, or be an accumulation of various measures, including human rights violations, which is serious enough to affect an individual in a comparable way. In accordance with Article 9(2)(b) and (c) of the directive, "acts of persecution", within the meaning of paragraph 1 of that article, may in particular take the form of legal, administrative or police and/or judicial authorities that are inherently discriminatory or implemented in a discriminatory manner and prosecutions or penalties that are disproportionate or discriminatory.

In the 2004 *Guidelines*, there is a non-exhaustive list of conduct that, considering their seriousness, may constitute cases of religious persecution, such as forced conversion or submission to or adherence to religious practices. The Court of Justice of the European Union, in the *Bahtiyar Fathi* judgment (2018), held that (§ 56) if legislation – in this case, the Apostasy Law – provides for the death penalty or imprisonment as a sanction, it may constitute in itself an "act of persecution" within the meaning of Article 9(1) of Directive 2011/95, provided that such a sanction is actually applied.[50]

50 CJEU, C-56/17, *Bahtiyar Fathi v Predsedatel na Darzhavna agentsia za bezhantsite*. https://eur-lex.europa.eu/legal-content/EN/TXT/?uri=CELEX%3A62017CN0056.

The inclusion of non-theist and atheist beliefs in the definition of religion as grounds for persecution is extremely relevant; as denounced by the 2021 *Freedom of Thought report* of Humanist International, the profession of atheism or, more generally, of non-religious *Weltanschauung*, can lead to the death penalty in 13 Countries of the world: Afghanistan, Iran, Yemen, United Arab Emirates, Maldives, Pakistan, Saudi Arabia, Malaysia and Qatar, Mauritania, Somalia, Sudan and Nigeria.[51] In other Countries, although there is no death penalty, non-religious people are subject to State-imposed forms of discrimination, systemic, legal or official forms of restriction of freedom of thought, belief and expression.

The report by Humanist International also notes that in 16 Countries it is difficult or illegal to run a humanist organisation and that in 2020, during the SARS-CoV-2 pandemic, there was an intensification of persecution against non-religious people, prevented by the lockdown from fleeing their Countries. In some Countries, non-religious people, forced to keep their beliefs hidden, have begun to use the internet as a tool to denounce their condition and openly declare their atheism. However, the use of the media has proved to be a double-edged sword: on the one hand they have enabled human rights associations to act, coordinating global responses in defence of those who are discriminated against and persecuted for religious reasons;[52] on the other hand, the blogs of free thinkers are controlled, censored, closed and the authors often persecuted, silenced, murdered. This happens frequently in Bangladesh.[53] It should be further noted that, for the purposes of international protection, "non-religious people" must include not only those who declare themselves to be non-religious, but also those who are perceived by society as non-believers

51 Humanists International, 'Freedom of Thought Report 2021'. https://humanists.international/2021/11/humanists-international-launches-2021-edition-of-the-freedom-of-thought-report/; see also Humanists International, 'The Right to Apostasy in the World'. https://humanists.international/get-involved/resources/the-right-to-apostasy-in-the-world/; A. Gilbert Nixon, 'The Case of Non-religious Asylum Seekers', *Journal for The Academic Study of Religion* 31, no. 2 (2018), 113–148; A. A. Jamal, 'The Impact of Definitional Issues on the Right to Freedom of Religion and Belief', in S. Ferrari (ed.), *Routledge Handbook of Law and Religion* (London: Routledge, 2015), pp. 93–99.

52 Among these associations there are, for example, *Atheist Refugee Relief and Humanists International*; the latter has created a specific program: *Protect Humanists at risk*: https://humanists.international/get-involved/campaigns/humanists-at-risk/.

53 Some recent examples: Avijit Roy was the founder of the blog 'Mukto-Mona' (meaning 'free mind') in Bangladesh. Through this blog, he promoted freedom of expression and his atheist and rationalist views together with other intellectuals and activists in Southeast Asia. He was assassinated in 2015. Two years earlier, Ahmed Rajib Haider had been murdered for the same reasons. Another recent example of persecution against humanists is the case of Mubarak Bala, President of the Humanist Association of Nigeria. He publicly declared himself as an atheist, a former Muslim, and for this reason, he was interned in a psychiatric hospital in 2014; since 2020 he has been detained for publishing a Facebook post deemed blasphemous. Procedural irregularities, such as the denial of the right to legal aid, did not allow Bala the right to a fair trial. On 5 April 2022, the Kano State High Court sentenced Bala to 24 years' imprisonment for causing public disorder under Sections 210 and 114 of the Kano State Penal Code.

but who in fact are not: according to Article 10 of Directive 2011/95, when assessing whether a claimant has a well-founded fear of being persecuted, it is irrelevant whether he/she actually possesses the characteristic of race, religion, nationality, membership of a particular social group or political opinion which gave rise to the persecution, since this characteristic is attributed to him/her by the author of persecution.

Cases of asylum seeking by non-religious people

Legal literature about non-religious asylum cases is currently poor. This demonstrates the need to encourage research in this area.

Despite formal recognition and protection granted at international levels,[54] and despite the fact that the UN refugee agency and the European Union have issued guidelines to help state authorities, the situation of non-religious asylum seekers is still very precarious in many countries, including EU states.[55] One of the most important reasons is related to the obstacles encountered during the asylum procedure. Immigration authorities are often unaware of the specific situation of asylum seekers, particularly the risks they face in their Countries of origin. The questionnaires used are also often inadequate to assess the credibility of applicants. One of the issues concerns the application of inappropriate criteria to non-religious people, because they are specifically modelled on the characteristics of religious people.[56] It is necessary to prove both a well-founded fear of religiously motivated persecution and the relationship that binds the asylum seeker to the doctrines that are qualified as oppressed. And the burden of proof, although mitigated by the legal provisions

54 For more see S. O. Osman, 'Il diritto d'asilo: i sistemi di protezione dei richiedenti asilo e dei rifugiati, I Dossier del Centro Diritti Umani (2009–2018)'. https://unipd-centrodirittiumani.it/it/dossier/Il-diritto-dasilo-i-sistemi-di-protezione dei richiedenti-asilo-e-dei-rifugiati/26.

55 This is what emerged from the reports and the discussion during the event held in Brussels on 20 June 2019 on non-believers seeking asylum in Europe. This event was organised by the European Humanist Federation (FHE) in collaboration with the European Parliament Intergroup on freedom of religion or belief; see https://humanistfederation.eu/join-us-for-are-you-a-true-humanist-our-event-on-non-believers-seeking-asylum-in-europe-20-june/. The FHE also exposed the critical situation of asylum-seeking non-believers in a Declaration delivered on 10 March 2020, at the 43rd session of the United Nations Human Rights Council (Point 4: Human rights situations requiring the attention of the Council). The European Humanist Federation has called on the Human Rights Council to monitor this issue and to urge States to take all appropriate measures to protect the fundamental rights of persons seeking asylum due to persecution on the grounds of atheistic, humanistic or rationalist philosophical beliefs, see https://humanistfederation.eu/hrc-43rd-session-oral-statement-on-the-situation-of-non-believer-asylum-seekers/.

56 Uwe Berlit, Harald Doerig and Hugo Storey, 'Credibility Assessment in Claims based on Persecution for Reasons of Religious Conversion and Homosexuality: A Practitioners Approach', *International Journal of Refugee Law* 27, no. 4 (2015), 649–66; E. S. Hurd, *Beyond Religious Freedom: The New Global Politics of Religion* (Princeton, NJ: Princeton University Press, 2015); W. F. Sullivan, *The Impossibility of Religious Freedom*, New edn (Princeton: Princeton University Press, [2005] 2018).

themselves (it is possible, for example, to involve experts; it is compulsory to provide adequate interpreters, no theological expertise is required, etc.), is objectively aggravated when it comes to proving non-religious convictions.

Some concrete cases will provide a better understanding.

In 2017, Pakistani Hamza bin Walayat, who had been living in the UK since 2011, applied for asylum as a non-religious person, claiming that he would be persecuted in his home country for his beliefs. Because of his apostasy, he already had received death threats from some of his family and community members in Pakistan.[57] His application for asylum in the UK was refused because he was unable to correctly answer questions about the ancient Greek philosophers. The Ministry of the Interior, under the pretext of poor answers to questions on philosophy, claimed that Walayat's knowledge of humanism was "rudimentary" and low-level, therefore his beliefs could not be qualified as sincere.[58] The fact that he joined Humanists UK shortly after submitting his application was used against him to reinforce the lack of sincerity in the profession of his matured convictions. A first clear element in the Home Office's decision is the absence of in-depth knowledge of Humanism, but as the Humanist International's website states, Humanism is not a system of doctrines, dogmas and codes of conduct to be learned and followed by adherents. The Humanist is also someone who simply rejects all religious beliefs and holds a positive conception of human values. Over 120 leading philosophers have signed a letter asking the Home Secretary to reconsider the case: "knowledge of Plato and Aristotle is not a reliable test for whether someone is a humanist".[59]

Another difficulty arises in demonstrating one's atheist conviction, especially when in the country of origin atheism is punished with severe penalties or the death penalty. Here, atheism is lived in secrecy, non-religious people cannot meet in associations, cannot found organisations or associations and cannot follow secular rites or practices. Moreover, in some countries, non-religious

57 The example is given in A. G. Nixon, 'The Case of Non-Religious Asylum Seekers', *Journal for The Academic Study of Religion*, op. cit., pp. 128, 129.

58 H. Sherwood, 'Philosophers Urge Rethink of Pakistani Humanist's Asylum', 2018. www.theguardian.com/uk-news/2018/jan/26/philosophers-urgerethink-of-pakistani-humanist-hamza-bin-walayat-asylum.

59 The letter was published by The Guardian: 'You Don't Need to Know Plato and Aristotle to Be a Humanist', 2018. www.theguardian.com/world/2018/jan/26/you-dont-need-toknow-plato-and-aristotle-to-be-a-humanist: «There is no scholarly basis to think that Plato or Aristotle were humanist thinkers, which is defined by Humanists UK as atheists or agnostics who believe in leading a good life on the basis of reason and our common humanity. Both hold that there is a divine realm and stress its philosophical importance. Plato presents arguments for the existence of a divine creator, the immortality of the soul and proposes a source of value in a supernatural domain independent of the human world (and thus does not reject religious belief). Aristotle is also complex: he believes in an objective human good, but he also believes that this good is shaped by its relation to a divine Unmoved Mover. At any rate, in general, one need not know who the humanist thinkers are to be a humanist; similarly, one need not know who the Christian thinkers are to be a Christian (by this definition there would be few genuine Christians in the UK)».

people are excluded from official population statistics on religion. An example is offered by the Report of the human rights organisation "Waging Peace". The report mentions the case of a Sudanese woman, who claimed asylum on the basis of her atheism, but her application was refused due to "insufficient information" or evidence. In particular, the UK authorities told her that "as there was no evidence about atheism in Sudan, it could be concluded that there are no atheists in the Country and that therefore she could not possibly have been persecuted for this reason".[60] Another reason for the refusal was the possibility, according to the authorities, to cover up her convictions and refrain from expressing them in public. In conversations and during questions with the Home Office and other authorities, they repeatedly argued that faith or beliefs are something one chooses and can be kept private.

Another significant case occurred in Sweden in 2017 when an Afghan atheist asylum seeker's application was rejected for failing to prove that his non-religious conviction was deep. However, during the procedure, he had also been denied an oral interview; the asylum seeker's identity had become known through the media and a letter was sent to the Afghan embassy in Sweden in which his identity and profession of atheistic views were made known. This constituted a further risk for the asylum seeker if he was returned to Afghanistan. In 2020, the Human Rights Committee considered that the removal of the asylum seeker to Afghanistan, if implemented, would constitute a violation by Sweden of his rights under Articles 6 (right to life) and 7 (prohibition of cruel, inhuman or degrading treatment) of the *International Covenant on Civil and Political Rights*.[61]

Emblematic in Norway was the case of Joseph Moradi, whose resolution in 2021 facilitated a change of perspective in Norwegian practice concerning asylum applications from non-religious people. Such applications in fact often failed: since 2010, the UNE (Immigration Appeals Board) has examined about 30 cases involving Afghan atheist asylum seekers and granted protection in only three cases.[62]

The asylum application of Moradi, an Afghan atheist and humanist, was initially rejected because, according to the Norwegian authorities, what is punished in Afghanistan is not the absence of religious faith, but only the active manifestation of atheism through acts that offend Islam.[63] Moradi could therefore have simply refrained from such acts, keeping his convictions to himself.

60 Seehttps://wagingpeace.info/wp-content/uploads/pdfs/Parliamentary_Inquiry_submission_on_persecution_for_faith_or_belief.pdf, 2017.

61 See https://processadvokat.se/2020/02/13/fn-kritiserar-sverige-pa-grund-av-beslut-att-utvisa-en-ateist-till-afghanistan/.

62 www.une.no/en/see-more-news/archive/2021/converts-and-atheists-and-the-right-to-asylum/.

63 Cfr. Human-Etisk Forbund, 'Asyl for afghansk humanist: Josef Moradi'. www.human.no/kampanjer/asyl-for-afghansk-humanist-josef-moradi e https://humanists.international/blog/meet-josef-moradi-the-afghan-atheist-who-fled-to-norway-to-find-freedom/.

But, as the Office of the United Nations High Commissioner for Refugees (UNHCR) noted: "One's religious belief, identity or way of life can be seen as so fundamental to human identity that one should not be compelled to hide, change or renounce this in order to avoid persecution . . . . In fact, being compelled to forsake or conceal one's religious belief, identity or way of life where this is instigated or condoned by the State may itself constitute persecution or be part of a pattern of measures that cumulatively amount to persecution in an individual case. Further, 'persecution does not cease to be persecution because those persecuted eliminate the harm (or threat thereof) by taking avoiding action' . . . . This reasoning also applies to applicants who are compelled to hide, change, or renounce the holding of atheist beliefs or refuse to observe a religion in order to avoid persecution. . . . Requesting applicants to conceal their beliefs (or absence thereof) and to conform to prevalent religious beliefs and traditions in order to avoid persecution is at variance with the 1951 Convention".[64]

The question is therefore not whether the applicant, being discreet, can live in that country without consequences. Having lived out one's convictions in a discreet manner in the past in the country of origin is also irrelevant: this behaviour could be motivated by the applicant's fear of persecution and could even demonstrate a risk of persecution. In support of its arguments, the UNHR also refers to the case law of the CJEU, which in *Y. and Z.* stated: "where it is established that, upon his return to his country of origin, the person concerned will follow a religious practice which will expose him to a real risk of persecution, he should be granted refugee status, in accordance with Article 13 of the Directive. The fact that he could avoid that risk by abstaining from certain religious practices is, in principle, irrelevant".[65]

Following the rejection of his application, Moradi began a six-year legal proceeding that ended with the granting of asylum. This case allowed attention to be focused on the issue of the difference in treatment between religious and non-religious asylum seekers and concrete steps to be taken to improve the procedure: the Norvegian Human-Ethical Association, in fact, assisted Norwegian immigration authorities in developing new interview guides for atheist asylum seekers. In 2020, Landinfo – an independent body within Norway's Ministry of Justice and Social Welfare that collects and analyses information on the countries of origin of asylum seekers that is useful for final decision-making – created a report examining the situation of atheists, non-believers, and people accused of blasphemy in Afghanistan.[66]

64 Submission by the Office of the United Nations High Commissioner for Refugees in case numbers 202005668/1/V2 and 202102293/1/V2 before the Council of State, op. cit., § 4.2.

65 *Ibid.*, § 4.4.

66 Available in Norwegian in https://landinfo.no/wp-content/uploads/2021/02/Temanotat-Ateisme-apostasi-og-blasfemi-LIJ-nov2020-korrigert-2021.pdf. The report takes broad account of the Humanists International report, 'The Freedom of Thought Report 2019.

2014 saw the first case of asylum recognition for an atheist in the United Kingdom. The applicant, who fled conflict in Afghanistan, had been living in the UK since 2007 and had developed atheistic beliefs during his stay in the UK. The case was referred to the Home Office under the 1951 Refugee Convention: if he returned to Afghanistan, he would face persecution on religious grounds because of his atheism. The case was followed by the Kent Law Clinic, a pro bono service provided by students and supervised by qualified practicing attorneys from the University of Kent Law School.[67]

Conclusions

The subject of these brief reflections has only been gaining visibility in international legal literature in recent years. It is still a little-explored topic, on which new lines of research must be traced. The examination reveals the complexity of an issue that needs to be framed in a broader perspective, as a piece of a puzzle still under construction. Indeed, the difficulties highlighted in the examined asylum-seeking cases fit within a legal status of non-believers that is not always fully equated with that of believers, even in some countries where religious freedom formally and peacefully includes the freedom not to profess any religion or to profess nontheistic beliefs.

Although, as highlighted in the first part of this contribution, international normative and jurisprudential developments have progressively included nontheistic and atheistic conceptions in the concept of "religion", there is some resistance to considering nontheism as an integral part of the religious phenomenon,[68] especially in its associated dimension.[69] Refugee Law, however, does not allow for differences in treatment between the religious and

Afghanistan, London'. https://fot.humanists.international/countries/asia-southern-asia/afghanistan/.

67 See University of Kent, 'Kent Law Clinic Secures Refugee Status for Atheist on Religious Grounds'. https://blogs.kent.ac.uk/development/2014/01/14/kent-law-clinic-secures-refugee-status-for-atheist-on-religious-grounds/.

68 See R. Mazzola, A. Angelucci and S. Baldassarre (eds.), *The Complex World of Philosophical and Non-Religious Beliefs. Legal and Social Aspects* (Granada: Comares Editorial), currently being published.

69 There are few national legal systems that have moved towards full recognition and equalisation of the demands coming from secular-humanist associations: one of these is Germany, where the legal status of denominational associations and philosophical associations is equalised (Art 137 GG); they can be recognised as corporations under public law (KdÖR); the Länder can conclude agreements with atheistic associations, regulating the right, for example, to establish classes in schools, to tax their members, to receive public subsidies, see on this point S. Coglievina, 'Il trattamento giuridico dell'ateismo nell'Unione Europea', *Quaderni di Diritto e Politica ecclesiastica* 1 (2011), 82 ss.; R. Bottoni, 'Germany's Cooperation with Religious and Belief Groups: Bilateral Agreements and Exemption', in C. Piciocchi, D. Strazzari and R. Toniatti (eds.), *State and Religion. Agreements, Conventions and Statutes* (Napoli: Editoriale Scientifica, 2021), pp. 125–190.

In Belgium, *sécularisme organisé* is equal to cults (Art 181 Const.) and benefits from public funds for its services, including moral assistance in hospitals and compulsory facilities and the

the non-religious: as noted earlier, the 2004 *Guidelines* point out that religion covers acts of failing or refusing to observe a religion or to hold any particular religious belief. The absence of inter-state harmony in asylum procedures risks thwarting equality of treatment, as the state decision-making process of granting applications could be conditioned by the legal position of subordination of non-believers. The recent and new character of asylum claims from atheists and non-religious people should be further noted. Indeed, the non-theist phenomenon, thanks also to globalisation, is becoming increasingly visible today. In this perspective, the number of non-religious asylum seekers can be assumed to grow in the short term because, as the European Parliament reported in 2022: "non-religious, secular and humanist organisations are facing growing persecution, including unprecedented waves of incitement to hatred and killings, in a number of countries worldwide; . . . countless individuals and civil society organisations are under assault for peacefully questioning, criticising or satirising religious beliefs; stresses that this ongoing violation of freedom of thought and expression is occurring across geographic and cultural borders, including within EU Member States".[70]

teaching of secular ethics in schools. In the Netherlands, the new Constitution of 1983 equalised religious and non-religious beliefs.

Some States, on the other hand, expressly exclude that theism and non-theism can be legally regulated in the same way. In Italy, for example, this happened with the denial of the Agreement pursuant to article 8.3 of the Constitution with the Union of Atheists and Agnostics Rationalists (UAAR).

70 European Parliament resolution of 3 May 2022 on the persecution of minorities on the grounds of belief or religion, § 8. www.europarl.europa.eu/doceo/document/TA-9-2022-0137_EN.html.

10 Greek Catholic Church in Ukraine

The Russian Orthodox Church and Catholic Proselytism

Marianna Napolitano

Introduction

According to the American sociologist Jose Casanova, Ukraine can be considered the most diverse religious market in Eastern Europe. Casanova wrote that "depending on the region, Ukraine is dominated by three Orthodox, two Catholic, and three Protestant Churches along with new religious movements."[1] According to a survey conducted by the Pew Research Centre from June 2015-July 2016, both in Russia and in Ukraine, the percentage of adults who identify themselves as Orthodox Christians has risen substantially since the end of the Soviet Union. It rose from 37% (1991) to 71% (2015) in Russia and from 39% (1991) to 78% (2015) in Ukraine. At same time, the survey revealed a strong association between religion and national identity: in Russia, 57% considered belonging to Orthodoxy very or somewhat important to being truly national Russians (in Ukraine the percentage was 51%).[2] By 2015–2016, the Pew survey showed that nearly eight in ten adults (78%) reported being Orthodox (compared with 71% in Russia). With roughly 35 million Orthodox Christians, Ukraine at that moment had the third-largest Orthodox population in the world, after Russia and Ethiopia. This finding was confirmed in an October 2018 study by the Rating Sociological Group (RSG).[3] The RSG study reported data from 2013, in which 70.6% of the population claimed to be Orthodox. By late 2018, the RSG showed

1 José Casanova, 'Incipient Religious Denominationalism in Ukraine and Its Effect on Ukrainian Russian Relations', *Harriman Review* 40 (1996), 9, and Bohdan Hud, 'Ukrainian Greek Catholic Church in Galicia (Halychyna): The Creation, the Ban, and the Resurrection, General Overview', *Proceedings of History Faculty of Lviv University* 17 (2016), 273–293.

2 Michael Lipka and Neha Sahgal, '9 Findings about Religion and Politics in Central and Eastern Europe', *Pew Research Center*, 10 May 2017. www.pewresearch.org/short-reads/2017/05/10/9-key-findings-about-religion-and-politics-in-central-and-eastern-europe.

3 'В какие церкви ходят украинцы: Как менялись религиозные предпочтения населения за последние пять лет' [Where do Ukrainians Go to Church? How Have the Religious Preferences of the Population Changed Over the Past Five Years?], *Slovo I Dilo*, 23 October 2018. ru.slovoidilo.ua/2018/10/23/infografika/obshhestvo/kakie-cerkvi-xodyat-ukraincy-kak-menyalis-religioznye-predpochteniya-naseleniya-poslednie-pyat-let accessed 12 September 2023. The survey gives data from 2013 and 2018, separated across the various religious affiliations, with

DOI: 10.4324/9781003502845-10

that the percentage had fallen to 67.3%. This was in contrast to an increase in the number of Ukrainian Greek Catholics,[4] which had risen from 5.7% in 2013 to 9.4% in 2018. The number of Latin Rite Roman Catholics had decreased from 1.3% (2013) to 0.8% (2018). Protestants increased from 0.8% to 2.2%. As far as other religions are concerned, Judaism increased slightly from 0.3% (2013) to 0.4% (2018), Muslims decreased from 0.7% (2013) to 0.2% (2017); the percentage of other religions remained stable from 2013 to 2018: Buddhists (about 0.1%), Hindus (0.1%), Pagans (0.1%), and others (0.1%). The non-affiliated or atheists had little variation: 11.3% (2005), 16.3% (2015), 11% (2018).

These percentages should help us gain a clear idea about the context of the subject of this chapter, which deals with the relation between Ukraine and Russia insofar as it relates to relations between churches, particularly between the Russian Orthodox Church and the Roman Catholic Church. While I have given sociological data up to 2018 as a reference, my analysis is limited to the years up to 2014, immediately after the beginning of the protests of Euromaidan;[5] the main sources are the official documents. While it consists of just under 10% of the population, the Greek Catholic Church (UGCC) has nonetheless had a significant impact on Russian Orthodox Church (ROC)-Roman Catholic Church relations – and the problem of proselytism. More broadly, it complicates the issue of just which Christians uphold the legacy of the Baptism of Rus' under Grand Prince Vladimir in 988 and the conception of the Byzantine tradition as a whole.[6]

---

some variations (Muslim numbers are given for 2017 instead of 2018, and atheist numbers are given for 2005, 2015, and 2018). About 1% did not indicate a choice.

4 The Ukrainian Greek Catholic Church traces its origins to the Union of Brest in 1595–1596 in which a body of Ruthenian Orthodox eparchies (dioceses) in the Polish-Lithuanian Commonwealth entered into communion with the Roman Catholic Church, placing themselves under the jurisdiction of the pope and thus breaking off relations with the Orthodox churches. They are considered fully Roman Catholic and are distinguished from the broader Catholic body chiefly by their liturgy and canon law. They retain the Byzantine Rite in their liturgies and, along with other eastern communions who have entered into union with Rome, have a distinct code of canon law. The larger Catholic church uses the Latin Rite. The term 'uniate' has been used for these Eastern Rite Catholics, especially those of Slavic or Greek origin. While this term was often used neutrally in the early years, in the past hundred years it has taken on a generally negative tone and is usually only used today by those Orthodox who are troubled by their presence.

5 Also known as the Revolution of Dignity, it was the third revolution in Ukraine since the fall of the Berlin Wall and the dissolution of the Soviet Union. It started as a protest against the unexpected decision by the government of President Viktor Yanukovich on November 21, 2013, not to sign an Association Agreement between Ukraine and the European Union.

6 I treated the topic in my dissertation *The History and Policy of the Department for External Church Relations of the Moscow Patriarchate: The Case of Ukraine (1989–2009)* (Leiden: Brill, forthcoming). There I discuss the issue in an interview with Roman Nebozhuk, priest of the parish of the Patriarchal Cathedral of the Resurrection of Christ of the UGCC in Kyiv, on March 13, 2020.

With the beginning of *Perestroika*, the Ukrainian Greek Catholic Church (UGCC) and the Ukrainian Autocephalous Orthodox Church (UAOC), previously banned, received legal status. The UGCC quickly began to restore its presence in areas where it had been strong, specifically western Ukraine. Dioceses (eparchies) were re-established, including Metropolis of Kyiv-Halych, which has its origins in the 12th century.[7] Also in 1991, the headquarters of the UGCC was moved from Rome to Lviv. Many of its priests returned from exile and started to serve in churches and in theological administration. In 2002, the UGCC again moved its headquarters, this time to Kyiv, and changed the title of its leading bishop to the Major Archbishop of Kyiv and Halych. With these actions, it asserted its claims to Ukraine's religious legacy.[8] This, of course, could not but create friction with the Orthodox communities, who were also emerging from Soviet domination. The ancient rivalry between Rome and Constantinople began to play itself out again, with the question of whether Ukrainian Christianity was more aligned with Rome, with Russia, or had a certain independence due to its bonds with the Ecumenical Patriarchate in Istanbul (Constantinople). The problem was only exacerbated as the establishment of an independent Ukraine became a reality.[9]

The rebirth of the Greek Catholic Church, which Soviet authorities had incorporated into the Moscow Patriarchate in 1946, caused deep tensions between the Roman Catholic Church and the Moscow Patriarchate. These tensions developed in the wake of the already existing problems connected with proselytism and became more serious because Christians in the regions of Lviv, Ivano-Frankovsk, and Ternopol largely belonged to the UGCC and had reclaimed buildings that had once belonged to their church. The claim of the UGCC to be heirs of the Baptism of Rus' was testified to by their official celebration of the 1020th anniversary of Russian Christianity. This gesture was not insignificant, considering the proposal of the Bishops' Council of the Russian Orthodox Church to include this holiday among the national public celebrations, along with the day of Slavic Literature and Culture celebrated on the feasts of Saints Cyril and Methodius, Equals of the Apostles.

At the same time, it is important to keep in mind the Moscow Patriarchate's irritation regarding the plan to move the seat of the UGCC from Lviv to Kyiv, along with the idea of establishing a Greek Catholic patriarchate to strengthen

7 Tetiana Havryliuk and Maryna Lukashenko, 'Roman Catholicism in Ukraine: The Contemporary Situation, Social Acceptance, and Social Service', *Occasional Papers on Religion in Eastern Europe* 40, no. 3 (2020), 34–51.

8 Thomas Bremer, 'Religion in Ukraine: Historical Background and the Present Situation', in Andrii Krawchuk and Thomas Bremer (eds.), *Churches in the Ukrainian Crisis* (New York: Palgrave Macmillan, 2016), pp. 3–19.

9 This shows the close relation between politics and religion, which is a characteristic feature of Ukraine. See, for example, Simona Merlo, *All'ombra delle cupole d'oro: La chiesa di Kiev da Nicola II a Stalin (1905–1939)* (Milan: Guerini e Associati, 2005); Nicholas E. Denysenko, *The Orthodox Church in Ukraine: A Century of Separation* (DeKalb, IL: Northern Illinois University Press, 2018); and the previously cited Bremer, 'Religion in Ukraine'.

the status of Ukrainian Catholicism and promote an increase in the number of believers. A representative of the UGCC, Roman Nebozhuk, commenting on the issue of the legacy of the Baptism of Rus', pointed out that Kyiv is one, the heritage is one, but – as declared by Pope John Paul II during his visit to Ukraine in 2001 – Kyiv's heritage draws from both Byzantium and from the West. Byzantine influence extends beyond Kyiv, up to the North, to the East, and all the way to Vladivostok. This means that, from the papal perspective, the baptism of the people of Kyiv is not limited to the present-day Orthodox. Regarding the Greek Catholic Church in this respect, Nebozhuk referred to the message of then-Major Archbishop Liubomyr Huzar, who stated that naturally Kyiv had a special role, but its church could always enter into relationship with other historical entities, that is, with the Third Rome (Moscow), the Second Rome (Constantinople/Istanbul), as well as with the First Rome (Rome itself).[10] This path involves removing the geopolitical issues in order to focus only on confessional affiliations. According to the UGCC's members, this was an urgent problem from the perspective of the Moscow Patriarchate, which saw its relationship with Kyiv through the lens of religious exclusiveness, following the principle that "the whole of Kyiv belongs to only one church. It began in Kyiv and continues in Moscow, the Third Rome. No one else, therefore, can claim this as their legacy or have different approaches and positions in its regard."[11]

This same Husar also wrote a letter to Metropolitan Volodymir Sabodan, head of the Ukrainian Orthodox Church-Moscow Patriarchate, as well as a previous letter to Patriarch Filarete (Denysenko), head of the Ukrainian Orthodox Church-Kyiv Patriarchate,[12] on April 26, 2008, and February 14, 2006, respectively, explaining the fundamental conditions for the unification of the churches of the "Kyivan tradition" that he thought had to be considered:

> (a) The future, united church will recognize the churches of Constantinople, Rome, and Moscow as sister churches; (b) the latter churches will recognize the Ukrainian church as their sister church; (c) all of them will confess the faith of the first seven Ecumenical Councils and recognize the validity of the sacraments in each of the churches. The "Kyivan

10 See Peter J. S. Duncan, *Russian Messianism: Third Rome, Revolution, Communism and After* (London and New York: Routledge, 2000).

11 From the interview with Roman Nebozhuk, 13 March 2020, in Kyiv (McDonalds), min. 11.34–11.35.

12 Since this chapter concerns Russian Orthodox-Roman Catholic relations, I have not yet mentioned, nor will treat in any detail, the Ukrainian Orthodox Church-Kyiv Patriarchate. The Moscow Patriarchate sees it, as well as the Ukrainian Autocephalous Orthodox Church, as schismatic. The two churches united to form the Orthodox Church of Ukraine on December 15, 2018.

Church" should be represented by a patriarch, who would be elected by Ukrainian churches of the various jurisdictions.[13]

These efforts would have also meant an enactment of the idea of the one nation of Ukraine.[14] The rivalry between Orthodox and Greek Catholics in western Ukraine during the 1990s has been largely resolved by the restoration of confiscated church properties to the UGCC and the construction of new buildings by the Orthodox church. From 1992–1999, the proportion of Orthodox parishes in the area decreased from 51.5% to 35.4%. In fact, from 2002–2008, 93% to 95% of the Greek Catholic communities in Ukraine were located in this western part of the country, mainly in the Lviv, Ivano-Frankivsk, and Ternopil oblasts.[15]

Mission, proselytism, and canonical territory

The problem of proselytism lies at the heart of the amendments to the *Law on freedom of Conscience and Religious Associations* approved in Russia in 1990.[16] The issue was connected to the role of new religious movements or sects, the danger they represented for the history and morality of the Russian Orthodox Church, and therefore the urgency of guaranteeing the image of Russia as an Orthodox country.[17] Indeed, in 1990 there were 6650 registered religious

13 Natalia Kochan, "'Oh, East is East, and West is West . . . ': The Character of Orthodox-Greek Catholic Discourse in Ukraine and Its Regional Dimensions", in A. Krawchuck and T. Bremer (eds.), (*Eastern Orthodox Encounters of Identity and Otherness*, Palgrave Macmillan, New York, 2014), p. 131.

14 To understand the UGCC's standing in Ukraine, it is important to keep in mind that the union of the Kyivan church with Rome at Brest in 1576 mentioned earlier was driven not by religious but by political aspirations. See also Sophia Senyk, 'Storia religiosa dell'Ucraina: Linee fondamentali', in Adriano Roccucci (ed.), *Chiese e culture dell'est europeo: Prospettive e dialogo* (Milan: Paoline, 2007), pp. 379–393.

15 Havryliuk and Lukashenko (n 7), pp. 34–39.

16 Consultant Plus, *Закон СССР от 01.10.1990 N 1689-1 (ред. от 04.06.1991) 'О свободе совести и религиозных организациях'* [USSR Law 1689-1 of 1 October 1990 (4 June 1991, ed.) 'On the Freedom of Conscience and Religious Organizations'], 15 January 2021. www.consultant.ru/cons/cgi/online.cgi?req=doc&base=ESU&n=3671#7ftjGoSkBSDy4tCy) accessed 7 December 2022.

17 The 1997 law introduced a division of believers into two groups: traditional faiths and other faiths. As the historical religion of Russia, Orthodoxy was declared to be the dominant religion, defining the national identity of the country. Then came Islam and Buddhism – partly included in the country's identity through the concept of Eurasianism – and Judaism, although many in the public debate were against considering Judaism as a traditional faith. The term 'Christianity' was used to refer to denominations in the western portion of the country but is ambiguous because it meant the non-Orthodox. This is confirmed by Article 27 and Article 7 of the new law that introduced distinctions between religious associations and religious groups and established very strict criteria to prevent the liquidation of religious groups. Moreover Article 1 of the 1997 law refers only to religious associations: 'This federal law regulates the legal relationships in the area of the rights of persons and citizens to freedom of conscience and freedom of creed as well as the legal status of religious associations' (Art 1.1). Chapter three of the law (Art 15–Art 24) regulates only 'rights and conditions for the

associations; five years later there were 21,664. In the period 1990–1995 the number of religious organizations in the Russian Orthodox Church more than doubled. Over the next six years, the growth was approximately 150%, but subsequently fell to an average of 1.7% per year. While in 1990 the number of Russian Orthodox Church registered religious associations was 3442, in 2001 it grew to 10,912 and in 2004 was 11,525. The number of registered Catholic organizations in 1990 was 32; in 1994, it was 248. Religious organizations enjoyed a five-fold increase in the period 1990–1995, then continuous growth through 2001, followed by decline. Between 1995 and 2001, there was an important increase in the number of registered Protestant associations (+185% per year). This dynamic became more moderate in the following period (+109% per year). The same happened with Buddhist organizations, whose numbers increased six times from 1990 to 1995 and then declined. Conversely, the number of Muslim religious organizations was constant (914 in 1990; 3537 in 2004).[18]

Proselytism was highlighted in the document *Basic Principles of the Attitude of the Russian Orthodox Church toward Non-Orthodoxy: Main Principles of the Relations of the ROC with Inoslavie, Foreign Policy through Interchurch Relations and Beyond*,[19] adopted at the Jubilee Bishops' Council in 2000. Sections four, five, and six present an overview of the relations with the non-Orthodox World and of the relations with non-Orthodox people in the Russian Orthodox Church's canonical territory. Section VI.2 states that, from the perspective of Russian Orthodox Church, "the mission of the traditional confessions is possible only if it is carried out without proselytism and does not attempt to steal the faithful, especially with the aid of material benefits."[20] Indeed, proselytism conducted in the territory of the Russian Federation by Protestant Evangelicals from America, by Jehovah's Witnesses, and by some representatives of the Roman Catholic Church were among the main reasons

activity of religious organizations'. It is clear that, by shifting the basis of legal equality from religions to associations, it became constitutionally possible to differentiate among faiths, as the 1997 law clearly did. See: 'О свободе совести и о религиозных объединениях' [On Freedom of Conscience and Religious Associations], 26 September 1997, N125 F 3.

www.consultant.ru/document/cons_doc_LAW_16218 accessed 12 September 2023. The text referred to here does not consider the amendments and additions of March 26, 2000, March 21, 2002, July 25, 2002, December 8, 2003, June 29, 2004, July 6, 2006, February 28, 2008, and July 23, 2008. A final modification was introduced with law 407 FZ (Dec. 2, 2019).

18 V. S. Nikol'skiy, *Osnovy religiovedeniya [Fundamentals of Religious Studies]* (Moscow: Federalnoye agentstvo po obrazivaniyu moskovskiy gosudarstvenny industrualnyy institute distantionnovo obrazovanya, 2015).

19 *Основные принципы отношения Русской Православной Церкви к инославию*, official site of the Moscow Patriarchate, 7 June 2008. www.patriarchia.ru/db/text/418840.html accessed 12 September 2023; the text in English can be found at orthodoxeurope.org, Department for External Church Relations of the Moscow Patriarchate, 'Basic Principles of the Attitude of the Russian Orthodox Church Toward the Other Christian Confessions'. orthodoxeurope.org/page/7/5/1.aspx accessed 12 September 2023.

20 *Ibid.*, VI.2.

that led to the document's adoption and to the "cooling" in the Russian Orthodox Church's participation in the ecumenical movement.

As in the case of Protestants, relations with the Roman Catholic Church were strained not only by ecclesiastical and doctrinal issues but also by political ones. That ROC Jubilee Council of 2000 expressed worries about the absence of real progress in the dialogue with the Roman Catholic Church, with difficulties primarily connected to the interconfessional situation in Ukraine where, through acts of violence perpetrated by Greek Catholics, Orthodox churches had been seized. In addition, the council expressed worries regarding the proselytizing activities of some Catholic structures in the canonical territory of the Moscow Patriarchate. Indeed, it directly called on the Roman Catholic Church to do everything it could to improve the situation. Another problem the council raised was the disagreement regarding the problem of the UGCC, which also came up during the meeting of the Joint International Commission for Theological Dialogue Between the Roman Catholic Church and the Orthodox Church in Baltimore from July 9 to 19, 2000. The Jubilee Council expressed the urgent need of a clarification of the issue through both consultations with other Orthodox churches, as well as through bilateral dialogues due to the participation of the Orthodox Church of Ukraine of the Moscow Patriarchate in the dialogue.[21]

In his statement delivered to the Jubilee Council, while presenting the new draft of the *Statute of the Russian Orthodox Church*, Metropolitan Kirill declared: "after the political changes in the early 1990s, the ROC found itself in radically different legal conditions than before: it gained freedom, and, at the same time, because of the collapse of the USSR, its canonical territory found itself within the confines of several states."[22] The statement made it clear that in speaking of *canonical territory*, the Russian Orthodox Church was referring to territories that were now spread over several new nations, as confirmed in its statute.[23] The concept of *canonical territory* was considered flexible, a reflection of the changing borders of the former Russian Empire and Soviet Union. It is now usually simply identified with those lands, with the exception of Georgia and Armenia, both of which were independent countries that by then had their own patriarchs (Georgia's was granted in 1917).[24] The new edition

21 Nicolas Lossky, 'L'église orthodoxe et le mouvement œcuménique: Les difficultés', *Recherches de Science Religieuse* 89 (2001), 225–245.

22 Russian Orthodox Church, *Архиерейский юбилейный Собор Русской Православной Церкви 2000 г.* [Jubilee Bishops' Council of the Russian Orthodox Church of the Year 2000], official site of the Moscow Patriarchate, 9 June 2008. www.patriarchia.ru/db/text/418767.html accessed 13 September 2023.

23 Russian Orthodox Church, *Устав Русской Православной Церкви* [Statute of the Russian Orthodox Church], official site of the Moscow Patriarchate, 2 December 2017. www.patriarchia.ru/db/document/133114/page2.html accessed 29 August 2023.

24 Kommersant, '*Армянская церковь традиционно дорожит связями с русским православием*': *Интервью патриарха Московского и всея Руси* ['The Armenian Church Values its Traditional Ties with Russian Orthodoxy': Interview with the Patriarch of Moscow and All

of the statute adopted by the bishops' council that took place in Moscow on February 2–5, 2013 included China and Japan in the areas of canonical territory. The bishops' council of February 2–3, 2016 also added Mongolia to the list of countries under the jurisdiction of the Moscow Patriarchate.[25]

The concept of canonical territory assumes here a particular significance. This is not only because it refers to the territories in which the ROC had traditionally exercised its influence but also because it maintained the church's status as having the largest number of believers in the entire Orthodox world, a status which is linked to the ROC's role as the promoter of a civilizational mission in the Orthodox world. Within its canonical territory, the countries that constituted the historical Holy Rus' – Russia, Ukraine, Belarus[26] – hold a special value and therefore constitute the core of the Slavic identity. Connected with Russian civilization is the concept of *Russkiy Mir*, a world united by a common religion, culture, and language. *Russkiy Mir* is an instrument of cultural expansion. Russia's soft power depends greatly on its ability to maintain its post-Soviet influence in the territories constituting a *Russian world*. An important factor to be considered is that, in trying to maintain its advantage over other religious institutions in Ukraine, the Moscow Patriarchate seeks not only the protection of its canonical territory but also of its status as the church with the largest number of believers in the universal Orthodox church. Indeed, should a strong Ukrainian national church be established, the ROC would lose its leading position to Constantinople along with its image as the spiritual leader of the Slavic-Orthodox civilization. In fact, although the Ecumenical Patriarchate is *primus inter pares* in the Orthodox world, the Moscow Patriarchate had over 180 million parishioners, while the Patriarchate of Constantinople had only 5 million.[27] It is significant that one-third of all ROC parishes are in Ukraine.[28] The withdrawal of the Ukrainian Orthodox Church

Russia], *Kommersant* 175, 26 September 2001. www.kommersant.ru/doc/284383 accessed 13 September 2023; 'Le métropolite Kirill à Berlin', *Europaica Bulletin* 59 (1 March 2005). orthodoxeurope.org/page/14/59.aspx#2 accessed 13 September 2023.

25 Russian Orthodox Church, *Митрополит Волоколамский Иларион: Церковь не сращивается с властью, а устанавливает партнерские отношения* [Metropolitan Hilarion of Volokolamsk: The Church Does Not Merge with the Authorities, but Establishes Partnerships], official site of the Moscow Patriarchate, 10 December 2013. www.patriarchia.ru/db/text/3429203.html accessed 13 September 2023.

26 Russian Orthodox Church, *Митрополит Кирилл: 'Торжества по случаю 1020-летия Киевской Руси явили торжество Православия'* [Metropolitan Kirill: 'Celebrations on the Occasion of the 1020th Anniversary of Kievan Rus' Revealed the triumph of Orthodoxy'], official site of the Moscow Patriarchate, 30 July 2008. www.patriarchia.ru/db/text/443064.html accessed 13 September 2023.

27 *Динамика Отношения Населения Украины К России И Населения России К Украине, Каких Отношений С Россией Хотели Бы Украинцы* [Dynamics of the Attitude of the Population of Ukraine towards Russia and the Population of Russia towards Ukraine, What Kind of Relations with Russia would Ukrainians Like?]. www.kiis.com.ua/?cat=reports&id=236&lang=rus accessed 13 September 2023.

28 *Ibid.*

from the jurisdiction of the Moscow Patriarchate would significantly reduce the territory under its control and would amount to the establishment of a rival to Moscow in Eastern Europe.[29]

Proselytism is also treated in *The Concept of the Rebirth of Missionaries' Activities of the ROC*,[30] issued in 1995. The document pointed out that missionary activities have always been a specific duty of the Christian church, and it formulated the forms and methods of the ROC's missionary activities in response to the challenges faced by contemporary society. The document also outlined informational, apologetic, educational, and external missions. The informational mission referred to the Orthodox witness to a large segment of people that had not yet received it, and which was to be conducted through the mass media and special publications. The apologetic mission was to provide a comparison of Orthodoxy with the doctrines of non-Orthodox denominations, which the ROC considered inauthentic, in order to counter the proselytism of non-Orthodox organizations. The educational mission was focused on providing a basic knowledge of Orthodoxy to those who were preparing for baptism, and for those who were nominally Orthodox (because already baptized) but unfamiliar with Orthodox practice, so that they could become full participants in the church. Finally, the external mission encompassed the Orthodox mission to non-Christian peoples, mostly migrants living within the ROC's canonical territory.[31] At a meeting on March 27, 2007, the Holy Synod of the Russian Orthodox Church adopted a document called *The Concept of Missionary Activity of the Russian Orthodox Church*,[32] developed by the Missionary Department of the Moscow Patriarchate. The document's preamble pointed out that the "concept of the revival of the missionary activity of the Russian Orthodox Church,"[33] adopted in 1995, had largely fulfilled its purpose. The new document considered the experience accumulated in the years following 1995, as well as the new state of Orthodox missions.

29 Morozov Ilya, 'Автокефалия Украинской православной церкви как инструмент обострения российско-украинского территориально-политического конфликта' [Autocephaly of the Ukrainian Orthodox Church as an Instrument of Aggravation of the Russian-Ukrainian Territorial-Political Conflict], *Society: Politics, Economics, Law* 2 (2019), 31–35.

30 Missionary Department of the Novosibirsk Diocese, 'Концепция возрождения миссионерской деятельности Русской Православной Церкви'. ansobor.ru/library.php?book=66 accessed 13 September 2023.

31 Olga Kazmina, 'The Russian Orthodox Church in a New Situation in Russia', in Thomas Bremer and Andrii Krawchuck (eds.), *Eastern Orthodox Encounters of Identity and Otherness: Values, Self-Reflection, Dialogue* (New York: Palgrave Macmillan, 2014), pp. 219–231.

32 Russian Orthodox Church, *Концепция миссионерской деятельности Русской Православной Церкви* [The Concept of the Missionary Activities of the Russian Orthodox Church], official site of the Moscow Patriarchate, 27 March 2007. www.patriarchia.ru/db/text/220922.html accessed 13 September 2023.

33 *Ibid.*; and Missionary Department of the Novosibirsk Diocese, *Концепция возрождения миссионерской деятельности Русской Православной Церкви* [The Concept of the Rebirth of the Missionary Activities of the ROC], 6 October 1995. ansobor.ru/library.php?book=66 accessed 13 September 2023.

The 2007 document was based on documents and materials of the local council that had been held back in 1917–1918,[34] of the bishops' councils held in 1994, 1997, 2000, and 2004,[35] on recommendations of the reports presented by Patriarch Aleksii, on the document entitled *The Bases of the Social Concept of the Russian Orthodox Church*,[36] and on the resolutions and final documents of the All Church Missionary Congresses held before 1917[37] and from 1996 to 2002. The new concept of mission formulated general principles, goals, and objectives for the ROC's missionary service, which would take local conditions and opportunities into account. One example is the more detailed explanation of the concept of proselytism that places it not only in relation to the apologetic mission – as in the version of 1995 – but also specifies important preventative measures that would prevent the emergence of "sects and schisms." Moreover, "development of all acceptable forms of anti-sectarian activity (which neither contradicts Orthodox morality nor violates secular legislation) and development of targeted missionary programs to neutralize proselytism and religious extremism" were listed among the most promising areas of modern missionary service in the church.[38]

A further relevant change introduced in the document is the definition of proselytism provided at note 5 that mentions both direct and indirect attempts to influence a person's religiosity, again leaving enough possibilities open for the church to decide what actions might be classified as "proselytism" as opposed to missionary work. In 2008, Metropolitan Hilarion noted that the concept of canonical territory was not applicable to Orthodox-Protestant relations, "but it is applicable to Orthodox-Catholic relations, since we have *de facto* mutual recognition of hierarchies and sacraments."[39] He confirmed the

34 Aleksandr Mramornov, 'Discernere il tempo presente: Il Concilio di Mosca del 1917–1918', in Lisa Cremaschi and Adalberto Mainardi (eds.), *Discernimento e vita cristiana: Atti del 26. Convegno ecumenico internazionale di spiritualità ortodossa: Bose, 5–8 settembre 2018* (Magnano: Qiqajon, 2019), pp. 269–290; Hyacinthe Destivelle, *La chiesa del concilio di Mosca: (1917–1918)* (Magnano: Qiqajon, 2003).

35 Russian Orthodox Church, *Документы* [Documents], official site of the Moscow Patriarchate. www.patriarchia.ru/db/document/100048 accessed 13 September 2023.

36 *Основы Социальной Концепции Русской Православной Церкви*, in *Ibid.*

37 Russian Orthodox Church, *Святейший Патриарх Кирилл возглавил открытие V Всецерковного съезда епархиальных миссионеров* [His Holiness Patriarch Kirill Presides Over the Opening of the 5th All-Church Congress of Diocesan Missionaries], official site of the Moscow Patriarchate, 23 November 2014. www.patriarchia.ru/db/text/3851703.html accessed 13 September 2023.

38 Russian Orthodox Church (n 32).

39 Russian Orthodox Church, *Епископ Венский Иларион призывает Ватикан обсудить вопрос о статусе католических епархий в России* [Bishop Hilarion of Vienna Calls on the Vatican to Discuss the Status of Catholic Dioceses in Russia], official site of the Moscow Patriarchate, 2 February 2008. www.patriarchia.ru/db/text/370447.html accessed 13 September 2023. This is reflected in: Russian Orthodox Church, *Епископ Венский Иларион призывает Ватикан обсудить вопрос* [Basic Principles of the Attitude of the Russian Orthodox Church to Non-Orthodoxy], cited earlier.

need to further develop a "code of conduct for Catholics in countries with a predominantly Orthodox population and for Orthodox in countries with a predominantly Catholic population. Such a code was created by the Catholic commission Pro Russia in the early 1990s, although Catholics did not always follow the recommendations of this document."[40] Nevertheless, optimism was expressed regarding the possibility of developing fraternal bilateral relations, overcoming places where proselytism had been happening. Indeed, Metropolitan Hilarion recalled a conversation about proselytism that he had had with Cardinal Kasper in 1990. The cardinal asserted that the Catholic Church's mission was to the unchurched portions of the Russian population (35% of Russians are regular churchgoers, a small percentage belong to other religions, and 20% are atheist, which means that 60–70% are unchurched, if one includes the atheists). The outreach of the Roman Catholic Church, in his eyes, could not be considered proselytism because it was not trying to get people to switch churches.

The core of the issue, as highlighted by Hilarion, lies precisely in this characterization. In the eyes of the Moscow Patriarchate, that 60–70% of the population, even though they do not go to church, would identify themselves with the Russian Orthodox Church. It falls, therefore, to the ROC to bring them closer to the Orthodox church.[41] This is because these people have Russian Orthodox roots: their parents and grandparents were Orthodox, and their children should continue in that tradition. The ROC's task is precisely to educate them in the Orthodox spirit because they are the ROC's potential flock.[42] Igor Vyzhanov, secretary for inter-Christian relations at the Department for External Church Relations (DECR), declared in 2005 that, by "proselytism," the Moscow Patriarchate meant "the actions of representatives of the Roman Catholic Church aimed at involving Russians in liturgical and other church practices who do not have a historical connection with this church, but belong to the [Russian] Orthodox tradition by baptism and cultural roots."[43] The issue concerns not only the position of the Roman Catholic Church in the canonical territory of the Moscow Patriarchate but also activities of the Greek Catholic Church in Ukraine, which was trying to extend its influence to the south and east of the – predominantly Orthodox – country.

40 *Ibid.*

41 It is important to consider here the so-called phenomenon of 'belonging without believing'. Some people do not consider themselves believers but still associate with a religious denomination because they recognize a sense of connection in that affiliation – a sense of belonging to a historical and cultural tradition, which offers a sense of identity.

42 Russian Orthodox Church, *Православно-католические отношения на современном этапе* [Orthodox-Catholic Relations at the Present Stage], official site of the Moscow Patriarchate, 15 November 2010. www.patriarchia.ru/db/text/1319482.html accessed 13 September 2023.

43 Ria Novosti, *Основная проблема в отношениях РПЦ и Ватикана католический прозелитизм* [The Main Problem in Relations between the Russian Orthodox Church and the Vatican is Catholic Proselytism], 2 April 2005. ria.ru/20050402/39607028.html accessed 13 September 2023.

The issue of uniatism and the role of the Eastern Catholic Churches

In considering these topics it is important to reflect on the results of the Theological Commission of the Holy Synod of the Russian Church that gathered in 1997,[44] presided over by Metropolitan Philarete of Minsk and Slutsk, Patriarchal Exarch of All Belarus. The document it created was a reaction to the one adopted by the Catholic-Orthodox joint commission in Balamand in 1993,[45] which treated the issue of uniatism and used the expressions "sister churches." The theological commission, in a statement issued in 1997, stated that

> Vatican II called the Orthodox Church a sister Church, thus recognising the blessed nature of the Orthodox Church and the salvific nature of her sacraments. The Orthodox Church, in her turn, always recognized the validity of the sacraments of the Catholic Church . . . . The Balamand document adds nothing fundamentally new but follows in the manner of the traditional Orthodox attitude to Catholicism. At the same time, the Synodal Theological Commission of the Russian Orthodox Church finds it important to clarify a number of the Document's affirmations, including the use of the term "sister Churches" in the text, which was motivated by emotions rather than by dogmatic considerations.[46]

Indeed, although in the official document published in 1992 the Vatican asserted that it did not intend to conduct missionary activity, much less proselytize in the area of the former Soviet Union, the Russian Orthodox Church accused the Catholic Church of "carrying out an extremely unfavourable policy towards Orthodoxy in Russia and other Post-Soviet countries."[47] The most controversial cases in this regard were the visits of John Paul II to former Soviet Republics: Georgia (November 8–9, 1999), Ukraine (June 23–27, 2001), Kazakhstan (September 22–25, 2001), Armenia (September 25–27, 2001), and Azerbaijan (May 22–23, 2002). I will here focus on the visit to Ukraine, not only for reasons of coherence with this chapter's main topic, but also because – in the view of the Russian Orthodox Church – this was the clearest demonstration of the Vatican's proselytizing intentions.

44 See Lossky, 'L'église orthodoxe et le mouvement œcuménique', as well as Russian Orthodox Church, official website of the Department for External Church Relations, Session of the Holy Synod on July 17, 1997, and July 28, 1997. old.mospat.ru/archive/en/1997/07/se170771/ accessed 7 December 2022.

45 Uniatism, *Method of Union of the Past and the Present Search for Full Communion, Balamand (Lebanon)*, 23 June 1993. www.christianunity.va/content/unitacristiani/en/dialoghi/sezione-orientale/chiese-ortodosse-di-tradizione-bizantina/commissione-mista-internazionale-per-il-dialogo-teologico-tra-la/documenti-di-dialogo/testo-in-lingua-inglese.html accessed 13 September 2023.

46 Cited in: Vladimir Kharlamov, 'Vatican II on Ecumenism, and the Eastern Orthodox Church', *Journal of Ecumenical Studies* 38 (2001), 186.

47 *Ibid.*

During his visit to Ukraine, Pope John Paul II met with President Leonid Kuchma. This was considered a violation of the principle of canonical territory and an attempt to strengthen the position of the Greek Catholic Church inside the country. The Russian Orthodox Church's assessment of the visit was staunchly negative. As Alicja Curanovic wrote: "given the equality of sister churches, it is not possible for representatives of one of them to enter the residence of another church without the owner's permission, especially with aims that are contradictory to the interests of the master of the house."[48] The official response to this statement can be found in a document entitled *Catholic Proselytism among the Orthodox Population in Russia* (June 25, 2002), which presented in detail the problems of proselytism, canonical territory, and missionary activity by the Roman Catholic Church.[49] The document's final section says that "the Vatican's policy towards Russia is perceived by the majority of our fellow-citizens as capable of inflicting serious damage on the spiritual life of the Russian people."[50]

At the time, in a letter to the pope dated January 22, 2001, His Beatitude Vladimir, Metropolitan of Kyiv and All-Ukraine, requested postponing the papal visit because of the unsettled relations between Greek Catholics and Orthodox Christians in western Ukraine and because of the uncertainty of the Roman Catholic Church's position in relation to the so-called schismatic groups[51] existing in Ukraine. Another controversial issue was the Roman Catholic Church's decision in 2002 to establish two Latin Rite dioceses in the traditionally Orthodox lands of south and east Ukraine: Odessa-Simferopol and Kharkiv-Zaporizhie. The attempts of the Roman Catholic Church to extend its influence over this area, where historically there had never been a union with Rome, were cause for deep concern. In July 2003, the pope approved the formation of the Greek Catholic exarchate of Donetsk-Kharykovsky and of Odessa-Crimea. The Russian Orthodox Church saw this as continued evidence of what it understood to be numerous cases of the infringement of the rights of believers of the canonical Russian Orthodox Church by the local authorities in western Ukraine spurred on by the Greek Catholics.

In fact, the UGCC, being historically part of these territories, had always claimed the status of a Ukrainian national church – therefore claiming a share in the inheritance of Vladimir's baptism. After all, it was widely known that the desire of the UGCC leadership was to transfer their main center from Lviv to Kyiv and to obtain the recognition of the status of patriarchate. The only obstacle to the implementation of these intentions was the lack of approval

48 Alicja Curanovic, *The Religious Factor in Russian Foreign Policy* (New York: Routledge, 2012), p. 229.

49 *Catholic Proselytism Among the Orthodox Population in Russia*, 25 June 2002. www.katolsk.no/nyheter/2002/07/08-0001 accessed 13 September 2023.

50 *Ibid.*

51 That is, the Ukrainian Orthodox Church-Kyiv Patriarchate and the Ukrainian Autocephalous Orthodox Church. See Note 11.

from the Vatican. Such a possibility was discussed at a meeting between official delegations of the Russian Orthodox Church and the Pontifical Council for Promoting Christian Unity, which took place in March 2003 in Geneva. That same month, as part of the discussion, the Department for External Church Relations received a memorandum from Cardinal Walter Kasper, president of that pontifical council, entitled *A Review of the History of the Patriarchates and their Theological Legitimacy*. The document contained a number of assessments of the history and current status of the Orthodox patriarchates that were considered unacceptable to the ROC. Since the question raised concerned the interests of Global Orthodoxy, Patriarch Aleksii II decided to send letters to the primates of all local Orthodox churches, inviting them to send in comments on the memorandum to the Russian Orthodox Church regarding the possibility of the establishment of a Greek Catholic patriarchate in Ukraine.

The responses were received in the following year. They demonstrated complete solidarity with the position of the Russian Orthodox Church. These answers were also sent to the Vatican. Additionally, in order to strengthen his relationship with the Russian Orthodox Church, Patriarch Bartholemew sent a personal message to the pope, in which he sharply condemned the aforementioned memorandum. In February 2004, Cardinal Kasper paid a visit to Moscow offering assurances that, for the near future, the Roman Catholic Church would completely respect the opinion expressed by all the Orthodox churches concerning the Greek Catholic patriarchate. Indeed, on June 3, 2004, while stating his support for the Greek Catholic church being granted their own patriarchate, the pope turned down the request of the Permanent Synod of the UGCC, concluding that it was impossible without some assessment from other Christian churches.

Although the ROC acknowledged such developments, other issues remained on the table. First of all was the issue of proselytism, since Catholics continued to take a very different perspective on the issue. Only during his visit to Moscow did Cardinal Kasper admit the existence of isolated cases of misconduct by the Roman Catholic clergy. He also stressed that the evangelization of Orthodox Christians was not a political strategy of the Vatican. During the talks, the Russian Orthodox and Roman Catholics decided to create a joint working group to discuss problems between their two churches. The group included representatives of the Department for External Church Relations of the Moscow Patriarchate, the Pontifical Council for Promoting Christian Unity, and other bodies of the two churches. On May 5–6, 2004, the first meeting of this Joint Working Group took place in Moscow.

During the meeting, the Orthodox side raised specific problems related to the proselytizing activities of Roman Catholic missionary monastics and clergy in the territory of the Russian Federation and other countries in the Commonwealth of Independent States (CIS). Particular activities condemned by the Russian Orthodox Church were: the Roman Catholic mission towards people belonging traditionally to Orthodoxy by baptism, faith, and national culture; cases of pastoral activity and catechising outreach to Orthodox children, adolescents, and young people, especially in orphanages, boarding schools, and other institutions that were barely accessible to Orthodox clergy; the preaching of Catholicism through the media, and religious education and catechesis either without explicitly stating that these were Catholic in orientation or that offered the false impression that these actions were approved by the Orthodox church. At the end of the meeting, the representatives of the Roman Catholic Church also pointed to actions that could be interpreted as a manifestation of Orthodox proselytism.

In addition to complaints, the Russian Orthodox Church also made concrete proposals, like the idea of developing a kind of code of conduct for Catholic structures in Russia and CIS countries, an idea supported by Catholics as well. However, the Russian Orthodox Church asserted that such a code already existed, specifically the *General Principles and Practical Norms for the Coordination of Evangelical Activities and the Ecumenical Commitment of the Catholic Church and Other CIS Countries* published in 1992 by the Pontifical Commission Pro Russia following the meeting of the delegations of the Moscow Patriarchate and the Vatican on March 1–2, 1992, in Geneva.[52] It urged the Roman Catholic clergy to avoid excessive zeal in their pastoral activities in these countries and to try to coordinate their activities with the Russian Orthodox Church. However, in the years following its publication, subsequent actions by Catholics did not necessarily demonstrate their intention to go along with the document.

Metropolitan Kirill pointed out that, after the Geneva meeting, the Russian Orthodox Church had made several gestures that demonstrated its readiness to comply with the document. He stated, as an example, the fact that the letters of Archbishop Tadeusz Kondrusiewicz, head of the Catholic Church in Russia, requesting meetings with the diocesan bishops of the Russian Orthodox Church, were forwarded to the Department for External Church Relations. There were also examples of positive actions on the side of the Roman Catholic Church, one example being the transfer of the Kazan Icon of the Mother of God to His Holiness Patriarch Aleksii on August 28, 2004.

Between 2000 and 2005, the work of the Joint International Commission for Theological Dialogue (the Russian Orthodox Church had entered into bilateral dialogue with the Roman Catholic Church in 1967) was interrupted precisely because of the issue of uniatism. Local Orthodox churches saw neither the sense nor the possibility of continuing discussions of theological issues before resolving issues related to the role of Eastern Catholic Churches in Eastern Europe and the practice of Catholic proselytism in traditionally Orthodox territories. It is important to reflect on the fact that one of the last plenary sessions of the Joint Commission in Balamand in 1993 – at the

52 Novosti (n 43).

insistence of the Orthodox participants – was entirely devoted to this problem.[53] The case of Poland was an important factor that influenced these relations. The election of Cardinal Joseph Ratzinger to the papacy in 2005 saw relations with the Russian Orthodox Church improve. In June 2005, Cardinal Kasper visited Moscow. In October of that year, Archbishop Giovanni Lajolo visited Metropolitan Kirill in Russia. After that visit, the archbishop acknowledged that the "ecumenical ice age" between Orthodoxy and Catholicism had ended and announced the Vatican's wish to establish full diplomatic relations with the Moscow Patriarchate.[54]

An important result of the new diplomatic measures was the meeting held between Metropolitan Kirill and the new Pope Benedict XVI at the Vatican in May 2006, which was followed by the decision to build a Russian Orthodox Church, the church of Saint Catherine, in Rome. What was crucial in this exchange was Pope Benedict XVI's decision to reduce the role of Polish hierarchs in Russia in October 2007 by replacing Archbishop Kondrusiewicz with the Italian Paolo Pezzi. Another important attempt to improve relations with the Russian Orthodox Church was the joint conference *A Soul for Europe* held at the beginning of May 2006, at which representatives of Catholic and Orthodox believers spoke of the need to oppose secularism in Europe.[55] This dialogue also helped both sides recognize that the problem of uniatism cannot be solved in isolation from the theological problems of papal primacy and its function. Orthodox participants agreed to resume the discussion of theological issues and, after a six-year hiatus, the Joint Theological Commission met again for a plenary session in Belgrade from September 18 to 25, 2006. The topic covered was *Ecclesiological and Canonical Consequences of the Sacramental Nature of the Church: Power and Conciliarity in the Church.* The plenary session's final document was adopted at a meeting in Ravenna in October 2007.

In December of the following year, the Russian Orthodox Church, represented by Metropolitan Hilarion, took part in the first European forum concerning the question of protecting the family. In the light of disputes between the Moscow Patriarchate and the Vatican, Russian authorities sided with the ROC hierarchs on the matter. While the forum's president tried to be an intermediary, encouraging dialogue between the churches, the Russian Foreign Affairs Ministry used harsh words concerning the Vatican's policies in Russia. During the visit of President Putin to Pope John Paul II in 2003 (this was his second visit, the first having taken place in 2002), Putin unambiguously

53 Department for the External Church Relations of the Moscow Patriarchate, *Современное состояние отношений между Русской Православной и Римско-Католической Церквами: Официальный взгляд, Алексей Дикарев* [The Current State of Relations between the Russian Orthodox and Roman Catholic Churches: An Official View, Alekei Dikarev], mospat.ru. https://mospat.ru/ru/news/other/57705 accessed 13 September 2023.

54 Curanovic (n 48).

55 *Ibid.*

supported dialogue between the two churches and announced the Russian authorities' commitment to bring the Vatican and the Russian Orthodox Church closer. However, the possibility of inviting the pope to Moscow remained contingent on approval by the patriarchate. It should be noted that Putin did not attend the funeral of John Paul II or the inauguration of Benedict XVI. He did, however, meet with the new pope in March 2007, when the two discussed the transfer of an Orthodox church in Bari, Italy, to the care of the ROC.

The issue of state involvement is connected to a country's secular identity and the politicization of religion. The document *On the Relationship of the Church with the State and Secular Society in the Canonical Territory of the Moscow Patriarchate at the Present Time*, issued by the ROC's bishops' council in 1994,[56] analyzed the Moscow Patriarchate's interaction with central and local governmental bodies operating in the CIS countries and in the Baltic states, as well as with individual leaders, particularly during election campaigns. The document confirmed the "impossibility for the church to support any political parties, movements, unions, blocs, or similar organizations operating in the CIS and Baltic countries, as well as their individual leaders, primarily during election campaigns,"[57] and instructed the clergy to refrain from participating in the elections for the Federal Assembly of the Russian Federation, specifically as candidates for deputy positions (determined at the expanded meeting of the Holy Synod on October 8, 1993). The document stated that the

> future participation of the clergy of the Russian Orthodox Church in the elections of any bodies of representative power of the CIS and Baltic countries, at either the national or local levels, was undesirable. It was also extremely undesirable for clerics to be members of political parties, movements, unions, blocs, and other similar organizations, primarily those leading the election campaign.[58]

The document already manifested deep concerns regarding relations with the Catholic Church, especially regarding the situation in Ukraine. Indeed, the council noted that, despite repeated assurance from the leadership of the Roman Catholic Church and the Ukrainian Greek Catholic Church regarding the improvement of Orthodox-Catholic relations, Orthodox Christians located in western Ukraine continued to be victims of gross violations of human rights as a result of the actions of local authorities under the direction of Greek Catholics. Deep concerns were expressed about the problems

56 Russian Orthodox Church, *О взаимоотношениях Церкви с государством и светским обществом на канонической территории Московского Патриархата в настоящее время*, official site of the Moscow Patriarchate, 18 January 2009. www.patriarchia.ru/db/text/530460.html accessed 13 September 2023.

57 *Ibid.*

58 *Ibid.*

existing in Ukrainian church-state relations because of state authorities who had not protected the rights of the Ukrainian Orthodox Church's members. The council pointed out that "the citizens of Ukraine suffer because they belong to the only canonical Orthodox Church in Ukraine – the Ukrainian Orthodox Church."[59]

Conclusions

Commenting on the work of the 13th plenary session of the Joint Commission for Theological Dialogue held in Amman, Jordan, on September 16, 2014, Metropolitan Hilarion reflected that the Joint Commission was established in 1979 as a platform for discussing important theological issues for the two churches. The commission, which included an equal number of representatives from the Orthodox churches and the Roman Catholic Church, began its work in 1980. During its more than 30 years of work, the commission adopted a number of joint documents – *The Mystery of the Church and of the Eucharist in the Light of the Mystery of the Holy Trinity*; *Faith, Sacraments, and the Unity of the Church*; and *The Sacrament of the Order in the Sacramental Structure of the Church* – which revealed many common points in the teaching of the two churches on the sacraments.

Hilarion recalled the value of the document signed in Balamand in 1993, *Uniatism, Method of Union of the Past, and the Present Search for Full Communion*, in which Roman Catholics for the first time officially agreed that uniatism – which the Orthodox saw as a policy of subjugating the communities of Orthodox Christians – not only did not contribute to rapprochement between the Orthodox and Catholics, but on the contrary, further alienated them from one another. In that document, Roman Catholic proselytism towards Orthodox believers was expressly condemned. Unfortunately, this document, successful from a theoretical point of view, could not solve the problems existing in the relations between Orthodox and Greek Catholics that arose as a result of the revival of the structures of the churches in western Ukraine, Romania, and other countries in the late 1980s and early 1990s. The worsening of Orthodox-Catholic relations that occurred against this background, as we have seen, interrupted the work of the Joint Commission for some time.

The issue of proselytism was, however, not felt to be as urgent in later years as it was in 1990. This was because of the results of the Joint Commission established in 2004 devoted to the study of problems in the relations between the Russian Orthodox Church and the Roman Catholic Church.[60]

59 *Ibid.*

60 Russian Orthodox Church, *Интервью Святейшего Патриарха Кирилла сербской газете 'Вечерние новости'* [Interview of His Holiness Patriarch Kirill to the Serbian Newspaper 'Evening News'], official site of the Moscow Patriarchate, 29 January 2012. www.patriarchia.ru/db/text/1986268.html accessed 13 September 2023.

Besides the issue of primacy in the church, which has been the subject of many disagreements between Catholics and Orthodox, the issue of uniatism has been the most difficult, and has been taken up again in the joint dialogue.

In late 2013, on the eve of the Euromaidan revolution, the main problem in the relations between Orthodox and Greek Catholics remained the situation in western Ukraine, in particular the seizure of churches. Metropolitan Hilarion recalled that in Western Ukraine there were places where Russian Orthodox were still deprived of worship space and stated how important it was for the Moscow Patriarchate that other churches not conduct proselytizing activities on its canonical territory.[61] From his perspective, the events in Ukraine and the loud politicized statements of the UGCC leaders in those days confirmed that uniatism continued to be a bleeding wound in the body of world Christianity.[62] Metropolitan Hilarion also confirmed that events in Ukraine set the Russian Orthodox Church back significantly. Greek Catholics continued to be perceived by the Roman Catholic Church as a "bridge" between East and West. The Russian Orthodox Church instead continued to perceive them as a serious obstacle to dialogue.

In Hilarion's opinion, uniatism had always been and still remains a special project of the Roman Catholic Church, aimed at converting the Orthodox to Catholicism. He asserted that, with the help of secular powers, the uniates have for many centuries acted to the detriment of the Orthodox Church, seizing churches and monasteries, converting the common people to Catholicism, and oppressing the Orthodox clergy in every possible way. This was the case in the Polish-Lithuanian principality after the Union of Brest in 1596, as well as at the turn of the 1980–1990s in western Ukraine. In fact, he noted that during the Maidan protests, Greek Catholics immediately took the position of one of the political parties and entered into active interaction with those he saw as schismatics. The head of the UGCC, together with the head of the so-called Kyiv Patriarchate, visited the offices of the US State Department, urging the American authorities to intervene in the situation and restore order in Ukraine. The Russian Orthodox Church saw all these initiatives as another crusade against Orthodoxy. It did not help that the Vatican, while asserting the autonomy of the Greek Catholics and its inability to control them, still did not disavow the actions. This made it even more difficult to consider a meeting between the pope and the patriarch of Moscow in the near future.[63]

61 Russian Orthodox Church (n 25).

62 Russian Orthodox Church, *Митрополит Волоколамский Иларион: События на Украине обострили проблему унии перед христианским сообществом* [Metropolitan Hilarion of Volokolamsk: Events in Ukraine Have Exacerbated the Problem of Union in the Christian Community], official site of the Moscow Patriarchate, 18 September 2014. www.patriarchia.ru/db/text/3748925.html accessed 13 September 2023.

63 Russian Orthodox Church, *Митрополит Волоколамский Иларион: 'Уния была и остается спецпроектом Римско-Католической Церкви, направленным на обращение православных в католичество'* [Metropolitan Hilarion of Volokolamsk: 'The Uniates Were and Remain a Special Project of the Roman Catholic Church Aimed at Converting the Orthodox to

In one of his addresses, Patriarch Kirill declared that with the outbreak of hostilities following the protests in Maidan, those he called uniates and schismatics received weapons and began carrying out direct aggression against the clergy of the canonical Ukrainian Orthodox Church in the east of the country under the guise of an anti-terrorist operation. In Kirill's eyes, the Ukrainian Orthodox Church, unlike the Greek Catholics and schismatics, remained outside any political engagement, and continued to provide spiritual guidance to its large flock, which included people who found themselves on opposite sides of the conflict, and tried to call for dialogue.[64] The patriarch condemned the actions that, as can be seen from these pages, represented historical problems between Greek Catholics and Russian Orthodox in Ukraine and therefore in relations between Catholics and Orthodox. He indicated that Greek Catholics (and schismatic churches as well) at Maidan preached hatred for the Orthodox Church, calling for the seizure of its churches and its eradication from the territory of Ukraine, and he listed several acts of violence conducted by Greek Catholics against the Ukrainian Orthodox Church of the Moscow Patriarchate. This confirmed that the existence of the UGCC in Ukraine remains a significant problem in ecumenical dialogue between Catholics and Orthodox. Besides the issue of uniatism itself, therefore, the fact that UGCC activity and the activity of so called "schismatic churches" were often seen as the same thing confirms that the main problem lies with the issue of canonical territory and the role of the Moscow Patriarchate in Ukraine.

Catholicism'], official site of the Moscow Patriarchate, 4 April 2014. www.patriarchia.ru/db/text/3618371.html accessed 13 September 2023.

64 Russian Orthodox Church, *Обращение Святейшего Патриарха Кирилла к Предстоятелям Поместных Православных Церквей в связи с ситуацией на Украине* [Address of His Holiness Patriarch Kirill to the Primates of the Kocal Orthodox Churches in Connection with the Situation in Ukraine], official site of the Moscow Patriarchate, 14 August 2015. www.patriarchia.ru/db/text/3704024.html accessed 13 September 2023.

Index

For Product Safety Concerns and Information please contact our EU
representative GPSR@taylorandfrancis.com
Taylor & Francis Verlag GmbH, Kaufingerstraße 24, 80331 München, Germany

www.ingramcontent.com/pod-product-compliance
Ingram Content Group UK Ltd.
Pitfield, Milton Keynes, MK11 3LW, UK
UKHW020003200926
475702UK00015B/2453
* 9 7 8 1 0 3 2 8 2 0 7 7 4 *